holy beautiful table

Holy Beautiful Table

Written by Jennifer Howard and the Holy Beautiful Team • www.HolyBeautifulLife.com

Published by Exodus Christian Book Publishing • www.exoduschristianbookpublishing.com

Edited by Richard Cotterman, Exodus Christian Publishing

Book Cover Design and Interior Layout by Kristine Cotterman, Exodus Design Studios, www.exodusdesign.com

ISBN: 978-1-950960-56-9

contents

dedication

This book is dedicated to all the holy and beautiful women who invited me to the table of Christ.

Bonnie, Sherry, Amanda, Megan, Patty, and Pat,
may the Lord continue to bless you and
keep you all the days of your life.

And to my holy and beautiful ministry team who continue to show me how to feast at His banquet.

Amen

We are glad you’re here!

introduction

The Holy Beautiful Ministry sees the beauty in the power of all women, from all over the world, all walks of life, all different cultures and communities coming together at one table and sharing their stories. This book, Holy Beautiful Table, allows us to break bread with our sisters in Christ and join hands at the most beautiful banquet, the Lord's table. Here we not only feast on His Word but allow it to enter and move through us, transforming us into His likeness.

They set the table, they spread out the cloth, they eat, they drink; "Rise up, captains, oil the shields!" (Isaiah 21:5 NASB)

The Holy Beautiful Table calls you to come, dine and to feast on who Jesus Christ is and learn more about Him through His Word and the stories of His daughters.

The Holy Beautiful Ministry encourages you to share your stories with others at your own tables because they are the tapestry of what God is doing in our lives. Don't ever underestimate the power of one invitation to His table.

Amen

Jesus at the Table

Jesus loved to use meals to engage with people and to teach important lessons about life. Today, He continues to call us to His table to feast on His Holy and Beautiful Word.

His example represents for us today how we too are called to invite everyone to the table and tell our stories of God's love, salvation, and redemptive nature.

When the hour had come, He sat down, and the twelve apostles with Him. Then He said to them, "With fervent desire I have desired to eat this Passover with you before I suffer;" (Luke 22:14-15 NKJV)

When we join hands at the table of Christ, we become open to the great truths about His nature. The table then becomes a place of gratitude, provision, beauty, forgiveness, abundance, holiness, and celebration.

So they took away the stone. Then Jesus looked up and said, "Father, I thank you that you have heard me. I knew that you always hear me, but I said this for the benefit of the people standing here, that they may believe that you sent me."

(John 11:41-42)

The Table is a Place of Gratitude

Jesus lived in thankfulness to God. He expressed His thanks to His Father publicly for the benefit of others that they too might learn to be grateful to God (see John 11:41-42).

Jesus appreciated God as His Father, who watched over all His beautiful creation. (see Matthew 6:26-30). He thanked Him for providing food (see Luke 24:30), for listening to Him (see John 11:41), and for the opportunity to minister to others (see Matthew 14:19, 15:36). He was grateful for all things. Jesus constantly displayed a heart of gratitude as an example to others. We, as women then need to replace any comparison or envy at our tables with this same kind of appreciation and gratitude.

Jesus, as an example, began and ended His prayers with words of thanks and praise to God our Father. With the Lord's Prayer, He taught His followers to do the same (Matthew 6:9-13).

The Lord's Prayer

Our Father, which art in heaven,
Hallowed be thy Name.
Thy Kingdom come.
Thy will be done on earth,
As it is in heaven.
Give us this day our daily bread.
And forgive us our trespasses
As we forgive them that trespass against us.
And lead us not into temptation,
But deliver us from evil.
For thine is the kingdom,
The power, and the glory,
Forever and ever.

Amen

(Taken from *The Anglican Book of Common Prayer*, 1662)

The Table is a Place of Provision

Jesus has made us worthy through His blood on the Cross. It was not by any accomplishment of our own. The full worth of the provision of the Lord's Table is not only for the forgiveness of sins but also for every matter in our lives as women. His cup represents the testimony of how He paid the ultimate price for everything we need. We now can sit at His table and rest that in our faith He has given us a meal that is our ultimate provision.

"Jesus then said to them, "Truly, truly, I say to you, it is not Moses who has given you the bread out of heaven, but it is My Father who gives you the true bread out of heaven. For the bread of God is that which comes down out of heaven, and gives life to the world." Then they said to Him, "Lord, always give us this bread." Jesus said to them, "I am the bread of life; he who comes to Me will not hunger, and he who believes in Me will never thirst" (John 6:32-35 NASB).

The Table is a Place of Beauty

One of my favorite stories comes from Matthew 9. Jesus called a tax collector named Matthew to follow Him and be one His disciples. Matthew was not really living a life that was an example of beauty and holiness. However, everything Jesus does and teaches gives us unique and valuable insight into the heart of the Father. This story reveals in very concrete ways how the new Kingdom of Heaven should look and how we as His daughters are invited to the celebration feast at His table.

From all the crowds of Pharisees and religious experts who were following and listening, Jesus singled out a tax collector. He invited him to the table. He made him a welcomed guest in the new Kingdom. A Kingdom that everyone is welcome to dine and feast at if they would only open their heart to receive it.

Then, Jesus even goes to dinner at Matthew's house, where all of Matthew's friends are invited. Naturally, some are shocked that Jesus would choose to spend time with, share community, and break bread with those who are so obviously against what God says is beautiful. These people were actively sinful. None of them were on the verge of repentance. They weren't even ashamed of their ungodly behavior. It was a table full of people who were greedy, who had cheated people, who had turned their back on the holy and beautiful life that God calls His people to live. But there was Jesus, inviting them, and sharing His stories with them. Everyone sat at the same table.

Jesus said, "It is not the healthy who need a doctor, but the sick. But go and learn what this means: 'I desire mercy, not sacrifice." For I have not come to call the righteous, but sinners" (Matthew 9:12-13 NIV).

The Table is a Place of Forgiveness

"Some men came, bringing to him a paralytic, carried by four of them. Since they could not get him to Jesus because of the crowd, they made an opening in the roof above Jesus and, after digging through it, lowered the mat that the paralyzed man was lying on. When Jesus saw their faith, He said to the paralytic, "Son, your sins are forgiven." Now some teachers of the law were sitting there, thinking to themselves, "Why does this fellow talk like that? He's blaspheming! Who can forgive sins but God alone?" Immediately Jesus knew in His spirit that this was what they were thinking in their hearts, and He said to them, "Why are you thinking these things? Which is easier: to say to the paralytic, 'Your sins are forgiven,' or to say, 'Get up, take your mat and walk'? But that you may know that the Son of Man has authority on earth to forgive sins...' He said to the paralytic, "I tell you, get up, take your mat and go home." He got up, took his mat, and walked out in full view of them all. This amazed everyone and they praised God, saying, "We have never seen anything like this!"

The challenge at the table is the same today as it was then.

Jesus has clearly shown us what the Kingdom of Heaven is about. We as His daughters must let go of any empty traditions, own up to our own deficiencies and beg God to take away all the things that separate us from participating in His banquet. Jesus offers an ongoing ministry of forgiveness and reconciliation (see 2 Corinthians 5). We as women need to stop standing in judgment over the table, graciously take a seat, and share a meal with Christ and others.

The Table is a Place of Abundance

The Abundant Table is a place of heavenly abundance. It never includes anything from an earthly perspective. When we as His daughters rely on Jesus, we have no need to worry about material things. If we seek first the kingdom of God, all these things will be given to us (see Matthew 6:33).

Furthermore, we are promised that, "my God will supply every need of yours according to His riches in glory in Christ Jesus" (Philippians 4:19). If our hearts and minds are focused on our relationship with God, He will meet us at the table with all of our needs. Sometimes this will include an earthly treasure, and we should Praise His Holy Name. Sometimes, it does not, and we should still praise His Holy Name.

From a heavenly perspective, eternal life is knowing God the Father and Jesus, His Son. Thus, since abundant life is eternal life, it is knowing God. 1st John 5:12 says, "Whoever has the Son has life," so as Christian women, we have this eternal life from the moment of our salvation. That is an abundance to celebrate at His table.

"So Jesus said to them again, "Truly, truly, I say to you, I am the door of the sheep. All who came before Me are thieves and robbers, but the sheep did not hear them. I am the door; if anyone enters through Me, he will be saved, and will go in and out and find pasture. The thief comes only to steal and kill and destroy; I came that they may have life, and have it abundantly. "I am the good shepherd; the good shepherd lays down His life for the sheep" (John 10:7-11 NASB).

The Table is a Place of Holiness

"Holy, holy, holy, Lord God Almighty." A. W. Tozer in his beautiful book called, *The Knowledge of the Holy,* he wrote about God's holiness:

"Holy is the way God is. To be holy, He does not conform to a standard. He is that standard. He is absolutely holy with an infinite, incomprehensible fullness of purity that is incapable of being other than it is. Because He is holy, His attributes are holy. That is, whatever we think of as belonging to God must be thought of as holy."

Psalm 99:1-2 it says, "The LORD is great in Zion; He is high above all the peoples. Let them praise Your great and awesome name- He is holy." This is referring to His unique person. The person of Jesus Christ. It is revealing His exalted position at the right hand of the Father.

In Isaiah 57:15, it says, "For thus says the High and Lofty One Who inhabits eternity, Whose name is Holy." God is unique and separate in a divinely, holy, and beautiful way. He now dwells in Spirit within His believers. In other words, if He is therefore holy and His holiness resides in us.

When we, His daughters, invite people to join us at the table of Christ, it is the most beautiful invitation anyone can ever receive. Nothing can surpass this request. It is the most exquisite banquet and feast beyond human imagination. This feast never ends and only gets more magnificent the longer we stay.

We all need this kind of invitation to the table of holiness. In our commitment to serve God and worship Him, we need to seek to be holy.

"Be Holy for I am Holy" (1 Peter 1:16 NKJV).

The Table is a Place of Celebration

We have eternal life at the table of Christ.

We, as His daughters, can sit and hold hands and celebrate the eternal resting place of our souls in Christ Jesus forever.

"All that the Father gives Me shall come to Me, and the one who comes to Me, I will certainly not cast out. For I have come down from heaven, not to do My own will, but the will of Him who sent Me. And this is the will of Him who sent Me, that of all that He has given Me I lose nothing, but raise it up on the last day. For this is the will of My Father, that everyone who beholds the Son and believes in Him, may have eternal life; and I Myself will raise him up on the last day" (John 6:37-40 NASB).

The Apostle Paul continually expressed beautiful certainty about our lives beyond this realm as believers in Christ Jesus. “And we know that all things work together for good to those who love God, to those who are called according to His purpose” (Romans 8:28 NKJV). When our tired and exhausted bodies take a seat at the table of Christ, we can always celebrate. Through any trial or tribulation that this world hands out, His table rebukes it and calls us home. “For we know that if our earthly home is destroyed, we have a building from God, a house not made with hands, eternal in the heavens” (2 Corinthians 5:1 ESV).

At this moment, sisters, you can bow your head at the table and say, “God, be merciful to me a sinner!” (Luke 18:13 ESV) Jesus will hear that simple prayer and the Spirit of God will come into your heart. Amen

"This is the testimony, that God gave us eternal life,
and this life is in His Son. Whoever has the Son has life;
whoever does not have the Son of God
does not have life."

(1 John 5: 11-13 ESV)

The Holy Beautiful Table

The Holy Beautiful Table is a place where the holiness of the Gospel is on full display. Understand that the table of Christ is an invitation that no matter who you are or what you have done, you are welcome to attend. This table represents all the aspects of Christ's attributes and puts them out for everyone on full display. Any guest can drink and feast to their heart's content and will never go hungry or thirsty or be asked to leave.

Again, we are glad that you are here.

the cross and the eucharist

Jesus' table calls all to come and dine, to feast on who He is and learn more about Him through fellowship, prayer, and His Holy and Beautiful Word.

Christ's example of table ministry provides us with an opportunity to invite friends, outcasts, and even our enemies to know God's holy and beautiful story of love, forgiveness, reconciliation, and salvation.

There are millions in this world who have yet to receive Jesus' invitation to the table. Please pray and continue to invite those who have not been given the opportunity to know Him. Let's let our tables become our churches.

Amen

When the hour had come,
He sat down, and the twelve apostles with Him.
Then He said to them, "With fervent desire I have desired to eat
this Passover with you before I suffer..."

(Luke 22:14-15)

The Cross

In the account of the multiplication of the five loaves and two fish, we read that Jesus first looked up to heaven, and blessed, and broke and gave the loaves to the disciples who then gave them to the crowds. We are told they all ate and were satisfied leaving twelve baskets full of the broken pieces. We further read that those who ate were about five thousand men, besides women and children (see Matthew 14:19-21). This story is now an intimate link between the Last Supper where Jesus broke bread and shared it with His disciples and then died for us on the cross.

The meaning of Eucharist is Thanksgiving. However, it is also representing Jesus' saving, sacrificial death, and makes that death present and more personal for us as His daughters. "For as often as you eat this bread and drink the cup, you proclaim the Lord's death until He comes" (1 Corinthians 11:26 ESV). Jesus' death on the cross was offered to the Father to atone for our sins by making compensation for them that satisfied divine justice in the eyes of the Father. "And He Himself is the propitiation for our sins, and not for ours only but also for the whole world" (1 John 2:2 NKJV). Dear sisters, this is because any sin is so serious that it could only take the death of God's Son on the cross to atone for them. There is no such thing as a small sin.

Because of this death on the cross, we who believe in Him, repent, confess our sins, and ask for forgiveness will receive mercy. God offers mercy to us because of His Sons death. When we believe in Him and truly repent of our sins, He is faithful. Our faith, which includes repentance, is a requirement to obtain mercy. "And when Jesus saw their faith, He said to the paralytic, 'My Son, your sins are forgiven'" (Mark 2:5 NKJV). To the sinful woman, whose sins Jesus forgave, He said, "Your faith has saved you; go in peace" (Luke 7:50). Therefore, it is the sacrifice of Christ on the cross that saves us, and this sacrifice is made present to us in the Eucharist, which Jesus' feeding of the multitudes foretells. The is the holy and beautiful relationship between the Cross and the Eucharist.

Christ offered Himself once for all on the Cross. He said, "It is finished!" (John 19:30)

The Eucharist does not repeat this sacrifice but re-presents it to the Father." It is finished. It is holy, beautiful, and perfect.

"In the Eucharist Christ gives us the very body which He gave up for us on the Cross, the very blood which He 'poured out for many for the forgiveness of sins' " (Matthew 26:28; CCC 1365). We know this is true because Christ said so:

"This is My body which is given for you," and "This cup which is poured out for you is the new covenant in My blood" (Luke 22:19-20).

The Eucharist

In the Eucharistic sacrifice, Christ offers to His beloved bride, the Church, the possibility to be associated with Him in offering to the Eternal Father a perfect sacrifice of love and beauty for the sins of humanity. He has taken on our nature. Jesus associates us with Himself in this holy and beautiful mystery. In Himself, He summarizes and, in a sense, takes with Him all humanity to the Father at His table.

In the Eucharist, Jesus gives us a gift of eternal life. He guarantees it. "This is the bread which comes down from heaven, so that a person may eat it and not die. I am the living bread which has come down from heaven. Anyone who eats this bread will live forever, and the bread that I shall give is My flesh for the life of the world" (John 6:50-51).

Another aspect of the Holy Eucharist is that Jesus associates with Himself not only all humanity but also all of creation and offers all to His Eternal Father in the unity of the Holy Spirit.

The Son of God became man "that He would gather together in one the children of God who were scattered abroad" (John 11:52 NKJV). By His death and resurrection, He redeemed humanity.

The work of His redemption goes beyond human beings in its effects and involves all of His creation. Original sin had turned many created things against man. And man was not always honoring God with them, as he should. The whole creation has been awaiting its own redemption, "groaning in labor pains," as St. Paul puts it in Romans 8:22. "The whole creation is waiting with eagerness for the children of God to be revealed" (Romans 8:19).

Therefore, when we partake in the Holy Eucharist, it should make us want to promote justice and peace for all people and honor the entire created world. There should be no competition between God's people. As God's daughters when we leave the table of the Eucharist, we need to examine our hearts and what we can do for the poor and the needy in the world and where we need to make our own changes within ourselves to be more like Christ. This transformation at the Eucharistic table is essential to living a holy and beautiful life filled with grace and purpose.

As you read the testimonies in this book, my prayer is that you adore and thank our Lord Jesus Christ for saving us and praise Him. He has given all of us the honor and the possibility of being associated with His holy and beautiful sacrifice, which allows us to sit at His table for eternity.

The Holy Eucharist also calls on us as His daughters to be the voice of creation in offering everything to God. This includes our families, work, culture, politics, media, and everything else we can possibly think of. It should all be offered to Him. For all of our creation is redeemed by Christ. It should, therefore, be offered to God for what He did for us hanging on the cross. This is the essence of living a holy and beautiful life.

The Collect

Almighty God,

Unto whom all hearts be open, all desires known, and from whom no secrets are hidden: Cleanse the thoughts of our hearts by the inspiration of thy Holy Spirit, that we may perfectly love thee, and worthily magnify thy holy Name; through Christ our Lord.

Amen

Table Testimonies & Recipes

Lord Jesus

You alone are the joy in our hearts.

Thank you for inviting us to Your banquet.

You are the living bread.

We long to feast upon Your Word and drink from Your fountain.

Our restless spirits have longed to rest at Your feast.

We give thanks to You with every breath.

For You are our deepest delight.

Nothing is sweeter to us.

All that You have created sits firmly in place at Your celebration.

We, Your daughters, are raising our glasses to You.

For You are our Savior.

Drench our souls with life as we dine in Your presence.

Thank you for letting us share our stories with each other. We hope they bring more people to know who you are.

We could not imagine wanting to be any other table than Your Holy and Beautiful table.

Amen

"One person esteems one day as better than another,
while another esteems all days alike. Each one should be fully
convinced in his own mind. The one who observes the day,
observes it in honor of the Lord. The one who eats, eats in honor of
the Lord, since he gives thanks to God, while the one who abstains,
abstains in honor of the Lord and gives thanks to God."

(Romans 14:5–6)

The Cross of Betrayal

By Jennifer Howard

In one of his letters to Timothy, the apostle Paul describes a time when life and ministry got really hard. **He had been slandered, and no one came to his defense or supported him.** Instead, they deserted him and left him all alone.

Yet in the midst of feeling hurt by others and abandoned by friends, Paul tells Timothy that God stood with him and gave him the strength to keep standing in the place where God had called him.

My personal ministry Holy Beautiful actually began under these same kinds of circumstances.

I had been leading and running a very large women's ministry in Texas before moving to Virginia. To say running this ministry gave me joy is an understatement. I absolutely loved it. It was where my heart was.

I was working with women who were my dearest and closest sister-friends, and one of them particularly was like a mother to me. I adored her, treasured her, and she truly nurtured my faith. I relied on these women and felt so close to them. We did everything together in church and outside of church. God's hand was upon our ministry for women and young girls, and it was flourishing. It was a joyous time for our church, and everyone involved.

Circumstances arose where the son of the woman who was like a mother to me was soon to be released from prison. After his release, he started attending our church with his mom. Another woman who was one of my best friends and an integral part of our women's ministry started dating him. I, like so many others in our church, was very concerned about the relationship. It was fast, furious, and got very serious. He began living at her home. Being that he was on parole, he was not supposed to be anywhere but his mother's house. Someone called and reported him to his parole officer. As you could imagine, blame started to be put everywhere. Bitterness and slander took its root. Deceit, selfishness, gossip, and lies took hold of our once beautiful ministry, and no matter how hard I tried to resolve the situations the devil took hold and slowly and strategically destroyed everything that we had built together. I felt utterly helpless to stop it, and at each turn, the cross of betrayal got heavier and heavier to carry until I broke under its weight and resigned altogether.

At this same time, I was being betrayed by others that were in my close and personal circle. I begged and cried out to God to take the pain and burden off me and to restore the truth, love, and beauty that once existed within these relationships.

I felt so alone and distant from everyone, including God. My pain deepened, and I entered into the dark night of my soul. Depression took its ugly hold on me, and I felt like a shell of the once strong and passionate leader I was.

Then one-night almost a year later, with tears streaming down my sleepless and broken face God spoke the words Holy Beautiful to me. It was so soft it was but a whisper.

Somehow, in that sacred, holy, and beautiful space of brokenness, the Holy Spirit reminded me of Jesus. He had been misunderstood and misrepresented by people He loved too. People had hurt Him, betrayed Him, and abandoned Him, yet He still stayed.

He stayed on the path God put Him — in our messy world, in broken relationships, in hard and dark places. But most of all, He stayed on the cross so we would never have to stand alone. He reminded me that night that He had not left me. He reminded me who I was in Him, and He reminded me that He had a holy and beautiful purpose for my life.

The next day, I prayed. I prayed harder than I had ever in my life. I ate His Word. I became so in awe of who He was; I wanted to know everything about Him. I decided to go to seminary. I wanted to be equipped for whatever journey He had for me. Within two weeks, I applied to go to Liberty University Seminary in Lynchburg, Virginia.

I also knew God was trying to tell me to do something. I now just had to figure out what it was. So, I started writing, thinking, and planning.

Fast forward seven years and I have now graduated from Liberty University Seminary, written my first book and the Holy Beautiful Ministry for Women reaches thousands of women each day with the message of redemption, reconciliation, and forgiveness that only a relationship with Christ Jesus can provide.

So, ladies don't ever doubt the call that God has for your life. The road is never going to be easy, and you will carry a cross to get there. The burdens will be heavy, and the work will be hard. You will go through periods of darkness, but the light of Christ will always shine your way if you look for it.

As you continue to read the testimonies from women all over the world, my personal prayer for you is that you see your own story and you see that He is writing it. It cannot ever end up being anything but holy and beautiful because these are the attributes of Christ Himself, and He is holding the pen.

Always remember...
"He has made everything beautiful in its time" (Ecclesiastes 3:11).
In love, grace, mercy, and kindness,

Jennifer Howard

Recipes from the Kitchen of

Jennifer Howard

Mexican Fettuccini with Chicken

Serves 6 • Cook Time: 30 min

Ingredients:

1 bag wide noodles or any package noodles you want
1 package of 12 chicken breast strips
1 onion sliced
1 red bell pepper sliced
1 orange bell pepper sliced
2 containers 16-ounce heavy cream
2 sticks of salted butter
2 Tbsp. olive oil
1 Tbsp. cumin
1 Tbsp. thyme
1 Tbsp. paprika
Salt and pepper to taste
2 cloves garlic chopped
1 cup shredded Mexican cheese blend

Directions:

- Cook noodles in boiling salted water to package directions and drain and set aside.
- In a deep-dish fry pan put 1 stick butter, sliced veggies, garlic, all the spices and cook down while stirring. (about 8 min).
- Then add the heavy cream and bring to a boil. When it starts to thicken, add the cheese and stir. Turn off the heat, so the sauce does not burn.
- In separate fry pan place, olive oil, 1 stick of butter and bring to a medium-high heat. Add chicken and brown on both sides until fully cooked, turning as needed.
- Serve noodles with chicken and cover with creamy cheese sauce.
- Serve with bread and a side salad.
- My kids ask me to make this once a week.

Super Easy Peach Cobbler

Serves 8 • Cook time: 45 min

Ingredients:

1 stick of butter
1 cup all-purpose flour
1 cup sugar
1 cup milk
1 Tbsp. baking powder
Pinch of salt
1 can of peaches drained
1 Tbsp. sugar and cinnamon mix

Directions:

- Heat oven to 425°
- Place stick of butter in 9 by 13 glass pan and place in the oven to melt
- In a bowl, combine all dry ingredients and then add the milk and stir.
- Once butter is melted and starting to bubble, and brown add the batter to the pan. Place peaches on top and arrange in pan. Sprinkle with sugar and cinnamon mix. Bake for about 30 min until brown on top. Remove from oven and let cool. Serve alone or with ice-cream.

"Be not conformed to this world but be transformed by the renewing of your mind in Christ Jesus."

(Romans 12:2)

Never Alone

By Patricia "Patty" Diana Jager

My first clear memories of just knowing that I was not alone in this world were when I was about 11 years old. It was at this age of awareness that I realized that my home life was not "normal." As an adult, I now know that what I experienced was abuse, but as an innocent, trusting child, it was confusing, and I didn't feel safe enough to confide in anyone. So, I pushed it deep inside and pretended it wasn't happening until I had the courage to stand up to it and protect myself. But I was about to meet the most loving and awesome guardian.

"You will seek me and find me when you seek me with all your heart" (Jeremiah 29:13 NIV).

When my father retired from the military, our family moved into a house in a rural neighborhood just down the street from a little Baptist Church. On the school bus, my new best friend, who lived a few houses away, invited me to a youth revival at the little church. I asked my younger sister to go with me after the first few evenings, and that is when we heard the pastor telling us about this wonderful savior, Jesus. How Jesus loved us as His own children. This Jesus would protect us, and we could call on Him for peace and courage. My sister and I walked down that aisle. At first, our parents feared that we had been brainwashed, but they agreed to allow us to be baptized.

In the '60s, when I was coming into my teens, so much was happening in our country. Pres. Kennedy was assassinated, Rev. Martin Luther King, Jr. was shot, the Civil Rights Movement took hold, and the Viet Nam War was dragging on with more and more young Americans, some in my neighborhood and even my own family, returning home wounded or in coffins. Protests and violence broke out across the nation. In the midst of all this, Woodstock and drug use ushered in a new generation of free love and peace-loving free thinkers. And I was so drawn to it all. I longed to be in San Francisco on the corner of Haight and Ashbury. But God was there and about to snatch me up and out of this mire of social rebellion.

"For the Lord will never walk away from His cherished ones, nor would He forsake His chosen ones who belong to Him" (Psalm 95:14 TPT).

Soon, I was getting married barefoot in the park with flowers in my long hair reciting vows borrowed from a Bob Dylan song. Thankfully, over time, I settled down, and God blessed me with the birth of a baby girl to love and nurture. I knew that I had strayed from God and frankly never expected redemption, but I still felt a gentle nudging to return to church. I wanted to raise my child in the church. I never wanted her to feel dirty or unloved. But her father never went to church with us and didn't even attend her baptism. When she was 14 yrs. old, we divorced.

It was 10 years later that I experienced God's all-consuming love. I had remarried and was living in Hawaii. I became quite ill, and after tests, six physicians came into my room, semi-circled at the foot of my bed to let me know that one of my lungs was completely collapsed and trapped and my aorta was dissected. My chance of surviving the necessary surgery on the island to repair the tear was 40 percent. One year later, we were in N. California when I awoke in the night with a stabbing pain. When I was told that it was time for the aortic repair, I rather expected that I would be terrified. Instead, I experienced the most amazing peace. It was as though Jesus was sitting next to me and assuring me that He loved me dearly, and I was never alone through all the wrong turns, bad decisions, and sin. The next day, when my daughter flew to California for the surgery, I found out what Joy was all about. I heard the word thrown about by Christians, but I just thought they meant happiness. I know that it sounds ludicrous to find Joy on the eve of a surgery I might not survive. But nonetheless, there it was, Joy. I had my husband and daughter at my side, and I had Jesus holding my other hand.

"When my worry is great within me, Your comfort brings joy to my soul" (Psalm 94:19 NLV).

Fast forward nine years later. My husband and I had moved back to NW Louisiana. And my daughter was expecting her first child. And she had just gone through a divorce. She stayed with us the latter part of her pregnancy because she had some medical problems. One night, my husband was awakened to my daughter banging about downstairs. He realized she was in distress, so wakened me. She was having great difficulty breathing. We did not know it at the time, but her lungs were filled with fluid. She almost died in my arms, but God sent the most wonderful First Responders to our door. My daughter was rushed by ambulance to the hospital, where she had an emergency C-Section. By this time, she had suffered heart damage and her precious baby boy, Matthew had suffered severe oxygen deprivation.

I fell in love with my grandson immediately. My daughter's health improved, so we decided that she would return to work teaching, and I would be Baby Matthew's primary caregiver. My daughter loved her little man, and he was the center of her world. As Matthew grew, he had developmental problems, unable to sit up on his own or walk, and eventually, he had a feeding tube. But I know that Matthew knew he was loved. On Christmas Eve morning, I was awakened by the answering machine downstairs. It was my daughter screaming hysterically that her Matthew had died in the night. She had just moved next door to us one week earlier. I ran barefoot across the rocks in a dream state, not accepting this traumatic news. She had called an ambulance, and the First Responders arrived as we were hopelessly trying to revive him. But it was too late. At the tender age of 22 months, God called precious Baby Matthew home.

You may ask, "Where was God in all of this?" I will not lie. It was the most agonizing time of our lives. My daughter was traumatized and, though we went to counseling with a wonderful organization that ministered to those who had experienced the death of a child, the pain of Baby Matthew's death was almost too much to bear. At this, the darkest and most painful time of our lives, God reached in and carried us. He gave us the strength to live through another day and then another.

"Blessed are they who mourn, for they will be comforted" (Matthew 5:4 NIV).

One Sunday, months later, as my daughter and I were leaving the church and waiting for my husband on the steps this sweet woman came over to talk to us. She was so full of life and just exuded joy. She introduced herself, and warmly invited us to a lady's luncheon meeting. When we gathered at that table, we were embraced by the most amazing group of women, many who are still dear friends. It just gives me chills to think of how God placed this precious woman, Jennifer Howard, in our path that morning. She has been such a blessing in my life, and it is so inspiring to see her faithfully follow Jesus and spread His message, despite the battles she has fought. An invitation to gather around a table and share our journey with Jesus can fill up a gaping hole in another's heart.

Sometimes, I can hardly believe how God works in our lives. My daughter decided to return to work as a Paralegal. She interviewed with a very kind man, and after he hired her, she found that his wife had a son who drowned in his teens. She was a counselor and later became the co-founder of the same organization that had helped us after Matthew's death.

It has been nine years since Matthew's death. My daughter has remarried and become the step-mother to three beautiful girls, one married and two teens in school. We have the most caring and compassionate son-in-law. About two years following her marriage, the girls' mother died from cancer. My daughter knew that kind of pain personally and was able to pour out her love on the girls when they wanted to talk, needed some space, or needed a hug.

Now let me tell you about the church they attend. It turns out that the rector was formerly a counselor. When I visited my daughter recently, she quietly pointed out the parishioners before church service, who each had a child who died. It was the majority of those in the pews. God knew exactly where she needed to be, and she is now surrounded by loving, caring people.

And I am now a grandmother to these beautiful girls. I know, without a shadow of a doubt, that God loves me, and He is always with me. And I know that I will hold Matthew in my arms again. God has never left my side. By His grace, I am alive to share this story. Don't EVER think that God has abandoned you.

I know that God is with me, every breath I take. I falter, fall down, make mistakes, but I get back up because I know God has placed me here and now for His purpose.

"Let joy be your continual feast. Make your life a prayer. And in the midst of everything be always giving thanks, for this is God's perfect plan for you in Christ Jesus" (1 Thessalonians 5:16-18 TPT).

Recipes from the Kitchen of

Patty Jager

Bolognese Sauce

Serves 6 • Cook time: 45 min • Prep time: 30 min

Ingredients:

1- 2 lbs. mild or sweet ground italian sausage
1 (6 oz.) can unsalted tomato paste
1 small onion, finely chopped
2 carrot, shredded or finely chopped
2 ribs celery, finely chopped
3 cloves garlic, minced
1/8 cup olive oil
1/2 stick (4 Tbsp.) butter
3/4 cup red wine (you can substitute broth)
1 cup beef broth
3/4-1 cup shredded parmesan cheese

Directions:

- Melt olive oil and butter in a large skillet. Gently sauté chopped veggies until softened and a golden hue.
- Add Italian Sausage and cook until meat is almost done. Let the liquid evaporate, stirring frequently.
- Add wine (or substitute) and cook on medium heat until the liquid starts to evaporate.
- Slowly add the beef broth and tomato paste. Allow time for the sauce to cook down to a good consistency
- Add the parmesan cheese. Ladle over your favorite pasta when the cheese begins to melt.
- Serve with a nice green salad, garlic bread and a glass of Cabernet Sauvignon.

Strawberry Pie

Serves 8 • Cook time: 30 min • Prep time: 45 min

Ingredients:

1 cup (8 oz.) heavy whipping cream*
1/4 cup confectioner's sugar

* For stabilized Whipped Cream: Dissolve 1 tsp. unflavored gelatin in 4 tsp. cold water. Cook over low heat until dissolved. Remove from heat and allow to cool, but not set up. Slowly pour into whipped cream, beating well.

Directions:

- Bake the pie crust according to package directions and let cool on a wire rack.
- Rinse strawberries and remove stems and hulls. Divide the strawberries equally into two bowls. Slice 1 lb. of the strawberries into quarters. Set aside. Mash the remaining pound of strawberries. Place mashed berries, along with 1 cup sugar, in a medium saucepan. Heat on med-high heat until it boils, stirring frequently.
- Whisk together the cornstarch and cold water in a small bowl until smooth. Add 1 tablespoon of the hot berry mixture to the cornstarch and stir quickly with a fork. Slowly incorporate the cornstarch mixture into the boiling strawberry mixture. Reduce the heat and stir until it thickens, about 8 minutes. Remove from heat and allow to cool.
- Spread the sliced, quartered strawberries in the bottom of the cooled pie crust shell. Poor the cooked strawberry mixture in the shell, spreading to cover. Let cool on wire rack 1 hour. Then, refrigerate at least 3 hours (you do not want to put whipped cream on warm filling).
- Prepare whipped cream topping. In a large bowl, beat the heavy whipped cream, adding the confectioners' sugar gradually. Continue beating until stiff. *If serving later, prepare stabilized whipped cream. Spread the whipped cream evenly over the cooled pie and serve or refrigerate. You can sprinkle finely sifted confectioner's sugar on top if you wish.

"So now I live with the confidence
that there is nothing in the universe with the power
to separate us from God's love.
I'm convinced that His love will triumph over death,
life's troubles, fallen angels, or dark rulers in the heavens.
There is nothing in our present or future circumstances
that can weaken His love."

(Romans 8:38 TPT)

Good Isn't Good Enough

By Connie Barngrover

I have been a believer in Jesus Christ as my Lord and Savior since 1977. I was raised Catholic all my life attending Catholic school from K-12th grade. I came from a close-knit family with 3 brothers and 1 sister and many aunts and uncles and tons of cousins. We had picnicked every Sunday, Christmas Eve with all of them at grandma and grandpa's on the farm every year, 4th of July reunions and Christmas Day pot luck dinners at a rented hall because there were too many of us to fit in anyone's home. There were enough of us to have two teams for baseball after our Sunday fried chicken picnic lunch. We lived in Iowa where our family had come cross country in covered wagons and settled there as farmers back in the 1800s.

I was a pretty obedient child following all the rules, mostly out of fear of not getting into heaven. I never drank, did drugs, never stole, did my best never to lie, shared whatever I had with others, was respectful to my elders, loved my parents and followed all the church do's and don'ts. We were pretty much a "*Little House on the Prairie*" family. I lived a pretty sheltered life filled with love and laughter and fun.

I married my high school sweetheart who I had been dating since I was 15. We will have been married for 48 years this December 26. We lived a life of service to our country in the Navy for 23 years. We raised two children, and have 7 grandchildren and 1 beautiful great-granddaughter. I guess you could say I pretty much lived a fairytale life. Don't get me wrong, we had our trying times, but we never experienced a tragedy as many families have.

I had a good life, but as time passed and I drew close to my 26th birthday, I began feeling like there was something missing. I couldn't put my finger on it. I just felt like there was an empty hole in my heart, but I had no clue what fit there. I wasn't even sure where to look for whatever it was. All I knew was that I was getting lonelier as time went by. Nothing had changed on the outside, so I figured it was an inside job.

Being Catholic, I never knew about needing a personal relationship with Jesus. I knew He was the Son of God and He died on the cross for us, but that's as far as it went. I was taught

He was holy in fact too holy to even talk to, so we had to go to Him via Mary or the many saints that were in heaven. I never imagined Him being my personal anything. Then one day, I found myself at a Catholic charismatic prayer meeting. The only prayers I knew to say was the rosary, so going to a prayer meeting seemed a little scary. The only reason I went was that it had the word "Catholic" in it.

I went by myself, slipped in, and sat in the back row in case I needed to make a quick get-away. I remember listening to all the sad stories of the people who were giving their testimonies and wondering how they could still be smiling and praising God. They even raised their hands as they prayed and swayed to the guitar music. First of all, what was with the guitar music? Where were the organ and the choir robes and the sad faces? I was sure glad I sat in the back row because this was already getting too weird for this Catholic girl.

These people were going through some terrible stuff like cancer, loved ones who had recently passed on, bills they couldn't pay, family members who had treated them like dirt and a myriad of big, big problems but they were singing and smiling and clapping and kept saying things like, "Praise the Lord and thank You, Jesus!" I was confused and nervous and kept telling myself to get out of there, but as hard as I tried, I couldn't get out of my chair. It was like something was holding me down, so I had to sit through the whole meeting.

Then I heard someone say something about receiving Jesus as your Lord and Savior. I didn't even know what that meant, but because of the joy and peace these people were experiencing, I knew I wanted, no, needed what they had. My only consolation was that they were all Catholic so it must be ok, and I dove in not sure what to expect. People gathered around me and prayed for me and then led me in what they called the sinner's prayer. I said what they told me to say and then they all hugged me. I don't know what I expected, maybe a lightning bolt or raising my hands like they all seemed to be doing, but I felt nothing. To be honest, I felt a little letdown or like maybe I didn't do it right. Anyway, I made my way to the door and was stopped by someone who asked me if I just got "Born Again" I said I didn't know (I didn't even know what that meant). The person said that I must have because my face was glowing. I just said ok and went home not sure what all had taken place.

My husband was on deployment and was going to be gone for several months, so I had plenty of time to figure it all out before he got home. As the days went by, I found myself wanting to read the Bible nonstop and find more prayer meetings. Without realizing it, I was growing more and more in love with Jesus every day. I remember writing letters to my husband that sounded pretty odd to him. I was excited about Jesus and wanted him to know that I was changing. Oh, believe me, he knew because in one letter I got back from him he said that he was not going to be married to a Jesus freak. It must have all been pretty scary to him. Well needless to say we are still together still in love and my favorite part we are still holding hands. Thank You, Jesus!

The years marched on, and I grew deeply in love with my Jesus and went to many more prayer meetings. Then one night as I was listening to someone's testimony of how the Lord delivered them from a life of drugs and drinking and sexual issues setting them free and turning their life completely around, I found myself feeling a little letdown. I began to talk to the Lord about my conversion. I told Him that He didn't have to deliver me from anything horrendous, and I know this sounds crazy, but I was kind of jealous of the wonderful miracles He did in their lives. I told Him that I didn't have a powerful testimony to share as they did so how could I be an effective witness of His life-transforming deliverance?

The Lord, being who He is, was very gentle in His reply to my ridiculous comment. He spoke to my heart with such love and tenderness that I was ashamed of even saying what I had said to Him. I felt His presence cradle me as He began to show me that I too had a wonderful and very effective testimony of His saving grace. He told me that I was proof that being good isn't good enough to get anyone into a relationship with Him and have eternal life. He told me they were innumerable people who believe that all you had to do to get to heaven was to do all the right things. Living by the all the "golden rules" was not enough to get anyone into heaven. He said that people who count on themselves to work their way to heaven by being good were the hardest to get to realize they need a Savior. People whose lives are a wreck were easier to reach because they are the ones who are crying out for help knowing they can't fix themselves. As He revealed more of this truth to me, I began to understand the Scripture that says, "All have sinned and fallen short of the glory of God" (Romans 3:23).

My whole outlook changed about my testimony as I came to see that I too have lives to speak into, lives that might otherwise be lost forever because they thought being good was good enough. God has covered all bases in this game of life. He has seen to it that no one need be left behind that everyone needs His gift of Love, Jesus, to be saved. He loves us all too much to leave the work up to us to get to heaven. He did it all in Jesus because being "Good isn't good enough."

Recipes from the Kitchen of

Connie Barngrover

Corn Casserole Spoonbread

Serves 8 • Cook time: about 30 min

Ingredients:

1 stick of butter, plus about 1 tablespoon to grease the dish.
1 can corn, drained
1 cup sour cream
2 large eggs
2 Tbsp. sugar
1/2 tsp. salt
1 box Jiffy corn mix

Directions:

- Heat oven to 350°
- Grease the sides and bottom with butter of casserole dish
- Melt butter and pour into a large bowl
- Add corn, sour cream, eggs, sugar and salt.
- Stir well
- Add the cornbread mix and combine
- Put into greased dish.
- Cook until center is done and slightly browned on top.
- Cool before serving.

"The Lord, your God, is in your midst,
a mighty One who will save.
He will rejoice over you with gladness,
He will renew you with His love,
He will rejoice over you with singing."
(Zephaniah 3:17 MEV)

His Grace is Sufficient

By Mechthild Roth

It was in 1990, and I needed to choose a Bible verse for my prayer card since I was preparing to leave for Chad, Africa, as a missionary with the goal to help the women leaders in the national church in their ministry. My support was insufficient, my French feeble, and my English close to non-existent. Then 2 Corinthians 12:9 struck me. If one translates it from the German translation by Martin Luther, it sounds like this: "Let My grace be sufficient for you, for My power is mighty in those who are weak." What an encouragement!

Four months before leaving for Chad, an ophthalmologist told me that I was getting blind (Some years later another ophthalmologist stated that that prognosis had been wrong.). After arriving in the south of Chad, I soon discovered that it is impossible to teach women leaders how to do a Bible study if those leaders did not know how to read or write. So, I started to teach it to them without having any training myself and while still learning their local language, Lele. Talk about weakness. Later on, I worked on the revision of their songbook and catechism, once again without training.

In 1999 I was asked to take responsibility for the course materials of the "Bible Schools in Local Languages" that train pastoral couples for the Evangelical Church of Chad. This ministry has grown from using five local languages in seven schools and about 170 couples in training to six local languages used in fifteen schools and about 390 couples in training in a four-year program. Today I have two main responsibilities. 1) Writing the course materials – and I am not a trained teacher – that nationals translate before I do the typesetting and layout to have it printed in the local print shop and which other nationals teach in these schools, and 2) having an annual retreat with the Bible school directors to review the curriculum (they are using all the same one, no matter which language), review the running of the schools, prepare the next Bible school year, train them in andragogy or other relevant topics, distribute the resources for the schools, …

My ministry is not easy, especially working as a single woman exclusively with men in a male-dominated society. But there are also other obstacles: electricity is limited, internet access is difficult and expensive, there is no local library, and the only Christian bookstore is about 500 kilometers away. As a result, access to research materials for developing new course materials is challenging. In the last years, I have also developed sleeping issues that result in chronic fatigue.

When the project was started, the idea was that it would be finished in ten years. Now, after two decades, we are still far from reaching the goal of providing course materials for every topic taught in the four-year program in every language used for teaching. I am comforted by the knowledge that God carried me through and that I can let His grace be sufficient for me, for His power is mighty in my weakness.

Recipes from the Kitchen of
Mechthild Roth

Curried Lentils with Rice - Chadian Style

Serves 6 • Cook time: 20 min

Ingredients:

1 cup lentils
2 1/2 cups water
2 beef bouillon cubes
1 tsp. salt
1/4 cup margarine
1 large onion chopped
1 clove garlic, minced
1 tsp. salt
1/2 Tbsp. curry powder
2 Tbsp. lemon juice
chopped parsley
1 1/2 cups rice
1/2 tsp. salt
yogurt
chopped pineapple or mango
chopped bananas or apples
roasted peanuts
coconut (shredded)
Chadian piment
mango chutney or coriander chutney

Directions:

- Bring lentils with water, bouillon cubes, and salt to a boil and simmer for 20 minutes.
- Sauté margarine, onion, and garlic. Add salt and curry powder. Fry briefly. Add to cooked lentils with lemon juice and parsley.
- Prepare the rice as basic steamed rice.
- Put yogurt, chopped fruit, raisins, peanuts, coconut, chutney into bowls. Chadian Piment can be replaced with Heinz Hot Pepper Chilli Sauce.
- Place rice and lentils surrounded by the other ingredients on the table (in Chad all bowls are placed on a big round serving platter). The secret to this dish is the combination and balance of sweet and savory. Bon Appetit!

Slice 'n' Bake Currant Cookies

Bake time: 12 min • Prep time: 60 min

Ingredients:

1 cup butter or margarine
1 1/2 cup sugar
1 egg
2 tsp. vanilla
2 1/4 cup flour
1/2 cup baking soda
1 cup currants (can be replaced by raisins, small cut dates or coconut)

Directions:

- Combine butter, sugar, egg, and vanilla; beat until light and fluffy.
- Combine flour and baking soda. Stir into butter mixture, mix well. Stir in currants.
- Shape into a 12-inch roll. Cover, chill until firm.
- Slice into 1/4-inch slices, place on ungreased cookie sheets.
- Bake at 360°F (175°C) for 10-12 minutes.
- Cool on wire racks. Makes 4 dozen cookies.

"My grace is sufficient for you,
for My power is made perfect in weakness."

(2 Corinthians 12:9)

A Freedom Story

By Saralyn Hamilton

I have distinct memories of going to church as a family when I was a little girl. The smell of the pews. The checkered hallways, the smell of nursery books and toys. It felt so safe.

Growing up in an Episcopal church, we were often there on Sundays and even participated in church plays and functions.

After my parents divorced when I was six years old, I no longer attended church. Through middle and high school, I was still not involved. However, during high school, I did connect with my basketball team. They were my saving grace. It's important that I mention this sense of community simply because not only did I get an idea of what true community was, but I also got glimpses into other friends' lives who did attend church regularly.

I was always curious.

I knew people who attended the Fellowship of Christian Athletes or Young Life. To be honest, I thought they were kind of a nerdy crowd. See, at the time in high school, I was already into a heavy social life that included unhealthy relationships with boyfriends, drinking, and throwing parties when my mom was out of town.

I also came from a family cursed with unhealthy habits and addiction. I could not wait to get my older sister's ID so I could use it to buy alcohol. That was the cool thing to do back then, right?

Going back to my basketball team, I often look back on those days because it is such a big part of my story. Not just because we were so successful, but because this was my extended family. We were together every weekend and during practices year-round. There I learned about teamwork, honesty, discipline, hard work, and what it took to be at the top of my game. This will come into play later…

I wanted to continue playing basketball even after our team won the state championship. I played for two years in college until I was ready to live a "normal life" without being tied down to that discipline.

During my time in college, my faith was nonexistent, and not something I pursued at all. I was involved in my sorority and partying. I was a great host and was the life of every party!

My husband, Stephen, and I met in college and got married in 2007. My husband grew up in church and had heard the stories from the Bible throughout his entire life. When I first attended church with him and his parents one Easter Sunday, I was so uncomfortable, but...I felt safe.

Once we started having children, we decided that we needed to find a church. In May 2017, we finally landed at a church where we felt challenged and where we could grow.

I will never forget the feeling when I walked into the sanctuary for the first time. It was a similar feeling to when I tried on my wedding dress at the store. I knew it was the ONE!

I was cautious, yet I felt safe.

It was here where I met the Lord. Words were spoken to me that I have never heard before. The people speaking were incredibly transparent and open. They were all sinners, just like me. Before, I was used to the church culture that emphasized, "follow the rules" and "show up on Sunday."

Here it was different. I felt safe.

That October, I felt led to join a women's Bible study. This intimidated me so much. I think I owned a Bible, but I didn't know how even to look up verses or individual books. I didn't know where even to start. I somehow trusted and walked in. It was awkward, but I felt ready.

It felt safe.

The book of Mark cracked me wide open. It showed me so much, and I love how the older ladies fed off of my "newborn" belief. It was energizing for us both and especially life-changing for me.

At the beginning of my walk, I had two small children, a husband, a job, and a busy social calendar. I imagined that once I left college, adulthood would just carry into more adult-type things. You buy a house, host parties, go to fancier parties, travel, etc. That was us…always on the go and doing what we wanted.

Over time, the Holy Spirit started working within me. He so sweetly showed me things. A big thing that He showed me was that my drinking had become very unhealthy. He began to reveal some of the reasons why I drank alcohol, too—busyness, demands of family and work, mixed with other people's expectations and my own insecurities.

I considered my situation "gray area" drinking. I did not consider myself addicted; no one got hurt; there were no DUIs or job losses. However, alcohol was a way for me to manage my anxiety and numb things that I did not want to feel in my life. I don't know that I ever really had a pattern per se, but it would go something like this.

I loved chardonnay.

Cold.

Oaky.

California chardonnay.

I usually had a glass of wine while the kids were getting settled from school. Not all, but many nights that one glass turned into a second one while I was bathing them. Then I'd rush to tuck them in so I could finally "relax" and get another glass. And sometimes, I went ahead and emptied the bottle since it was almost gone. Why waste it, right?

Then there were some nights where I didn't drink or those weeks where "I was taking the week off." Usually, by Tuesday, I had a glass again.

Either way, it always took up headspace.

Did I have any wine at home?

Was it cold?

Did I have enough to get through the weekend?

And on and on. I would even get irritated with my husband if we didn't have any in the house like it was his responsibility to help me with my habit!

One night in January 2018, we had the kids and went to another family friend's house. It was one of those nights where we started drinking red wine at 5 pm, and we ate way too late. Once we were finally ready to go home, I was less than helpful getting the kids into the car. When we got home, I got the children into the bath. They were tired and not cooperating. They were just little babies, so how could you blame them? I remember yelling at them in a way I will never forget. It breaks my heart each time I think about this part. But it's important that I leave it in because this is where the healing happens. This is where my love story with the Lord begins.

Get ready…

After the children were down, I walked into our master bedroom. I stood in front of the mirror, crying. I asked the Lord to take this pain from me. I remember feeling so weird, even crying out to Him. Like I was not even sure what I was really doing if that makes sense? I was just sad and in so much pain. I told Him how I had no idea what I was doing and that I didn't know how to do this on my own. He met me right where I was.

I felt safe.

The next day, I told Stephen that I wasn't sure if alcohol was good for me anymore. Of course, I was nervous about this because so much of our relationship had been having a good time in college and entertaining as a married couple. He was and continues to be extremely supportive of my decision.

We were leading into Lent, which was a practice I had participated in many times in the past. Monday, February 12, 2018, was two days before the Lent season began. On that day, I decided to fast from alcohol.

I was nervous and scared but trusting in what the Lord had for me during the next 40 days.

Over that time, it was incredible what He showed me. He never left my side.

When the Sunday before Easter came up, I began to feel a bit nervous. Was I going to go back to drinking? I prayed about it during the entire Easter service. When we came home, I had a conversation with my husband, and I told him that I was going to take it one day at a time from here on out.

In the first 30 days, I cried the hardest I'd ever cried, and I laughed the hardest I'd ever laughed. I was no longer numbing the hard feelings or the good feelings. The next months were full of pruning that the Lord was doing for me. At times this can be very painful, especially when you are getting outside of your comfort zone. I no longer had that crutch, but I was now so much closer to Him. He gave me more energy to do His work. I was reading more and consuming His Word. I've been able to recognize and to be present in meaningful relationships in my life. I've also found my identity in Him, and to me, that has been so incredibly freeing.

Since my decision to take on an alcohol-free life, it has been one of the biggest blessings in my life. I'm often still shocked at how faithful the Lord has been with me throughout this time. It makes me smile so big! My relationships have shifted and will continue to as the Lord is pruning me of my old life. I often reference Galatians 2:20: *"I have been crucified with Christ and I no longer live, but Christ lives in me; and the life which I now live in the flesh I live by faith in the Son of God who loved me and gave Himself for me."*

I have empathy for those who mourn the loss of the Saralyn they used to know.

The Lord is the only reason that giving up alcohol has been possible for me. Through Him and His strength, I know that I am here for a greater purpose.

Sharing my testimony about my relationship with Jesus, and the gray area of drinking has been one of the wildest things. He has turned it into a small ministry. Almost every time I share something about my story, a woman comes out of the darkness, reaches out to me, and asks that I connect more deeply with her about how to do this too. It's sometimes unbelievable how faithful the Lord has been

I'm grateful to be able to share my testimony even if it helps just one more person feel like they are not alone.

If it helps one family break the cycle of addiction…

If it helps one parent be a better parent…

To show them, there is another way. And that way is through a relationship with Jesus.

Lord, I knew you were always there, I just thought you were too big for me. Now I am all yours. I am all in. Thank you for always loving me.

And for keeping me safe.

Recipes from the Kitchen of
Saralyn Hamilton

Rosemary Blueberry Smash

Serves 4 • Cook time: 10 min

Ingredients:

7-8 blueberries
1 rosemary sprig, stripped
1 oz. honey syrup
1 oz. fresh lemon juice, strained
4 oz. sparkling mineral water
Ice

Directions:

- Gently muddle blueberries, rosemary leaves, and honey syrup in the bottom of a cocktail shaker.
- Add lemon juice and shake, covered, with ice vigorously for 10 seconds.
- Strain through a mesh strainer into a tall glass of fresh ice.
- Top with sparkling water and stir to incorporate.

"Be on guard, stand firm in the faith,
be courageous, be strong and
do everything in love."

(1 Corinthians 16: 13-14)

Healing Through the Pain

By Deborah Persons

I was raised in the South with grits and cornbread and sweet iced tea. I'm a Georgia Peach by birth, and I spent my childhood in the middle of the Bible belt. My first memories of Jesus are of my mother singing "Jesus Loves Me" as a lullaby. My first memories of going to Sunday school and church are with my paternal grandmother and my mother. My parents divorced when I was not yet 4 years old, so of course, my mother wanted to move back to her hometown. We went to church occasionally with my dad's mom on Sunday mornings, and I remember learning of Jesus in Sunday school and hearing my Granny sing the old Gospel hymns in the service. My parents were remarried right before my 6th birthday. Job requirements moved us away out-of-state for a little while, but as soon as my father could transfer back to Georgia, we made our home in a rural community near Atlanta.

I hadn't been to church for a very long time, but as soon as we were settled, my mother began taking my baby brother and me to Sunday school and church in the local Baptist congregation. I was learning so much about the Lord and His Son. I received a beautiful New Testament from my Sunday school teacher, and I treasured it!! (I still have it now, safely tucked away.) On a rare occasion, my father joined us.

These periodic moves were all stepping stones for my father to get back to central Georgia for his work with the government, so near the end of third grade, we moved back to the base where my father had originally begun because it was much closer to their home towns. One day a lady, who had known my father from working with him years before, wanted to know if she could take me to church with her. I absolutely loved it!!! She took me to every function on Sunday morning, Sunday evening, and Wednesday evening. I learned about John 3:16 and what that meant for me. When I first heard it, I thought, "Oh no! I'll never be able to memorize that long verse!!" I was gaining in my head knowledge and growing with my heart knowledge. I sat and listened attentively to our preacher.

One day when I was 9 years old, I went up and told the preacher that I was ready to be baptized. At this point, I'm pretty sure I was more terrified of dying and going straight to hell, but I believed that Jesus Christ IS the Son of the Living God, that He died for the remission of my sins and rose again, and that He loved me and wanted me to be His child. My parents went to watch my baptism. Occasionally, they might go to church. My father usually just dropped me off at the door and returned at the right time to take me home. At Christmas, my granny gave me my first Bible, a King James Version, with my name on the front. I was so proud of that gift!! I began to read it daily because now I was a good reader, so my knowledge of facts grew steadily.

Fast forward a few years. My freshman year in high school, we made yet another move because my father was promised a promotion. This time we ended up in the Florida panhandle. This wasn't an easy move for me, but I had been picked on mercilessly and bullied by so many kids for so long that I didn't really care. I didn't have many true friends in junior high in Georgia, and I just wanted to start from scratch with high school where NO ONE knew anything about me or my family. I slowly began to make a few friends. I went to a church a few times where a friend's father preached. As always, I went alone.

My home was not a safe haven for me. My father became a functioning but raging, alcoholic, and a bad day for him, of course, meant a really bad day for the rest of us. He had been drinking for so many, many years anyway, but it became so much worse when we made this move. Nothing was ever right, everything was always wrong, and no one was ever good enough. He could be such a mean and cruel man. I would have done anything NOT to have to be at home. My mother and my brother received the bulk of his anger and fits of rage. Occasionally, he would get on his soapbox and yell and swear and say the same thing to me over and over and over, like I couldn't hear him or comprehend. It was very mean and very immature on his part, but I didn't dare to speak because it would either be the wrong thing to say or it would be in the wrong tone, etc. It was so difficult to be at home. I often thought of running away, but I had no idea what to do, where to go, or how to get there. I was a total chicken!

Halfway through my sophomore year, I met a young man. He was handsome, sweet, and a really nice guy. We began to date in the spring. (Now I have to say at this point in my life, I've never had a real "Sex Talk" with anyone. My mother just simply said to "never do this or that," and "always do this or that" with no explanation of WHY!!! I never had a Sex Education class. I was never told that God didn't approve of sex outside of marriage!)

Right about the time I met my boyfriend, Dad was drinking extremely heavily, and I felt totally hopeless. My boyfriend could do nothing to help. We were only 16 and 15. I loved him so very much, and six months in we entered into a sexual relationship. I so desperately needed that attention and affection which I received from him. I also began attending church with him. (Never did I once hear from the preacher or Bible teacher how God expected us to behave if we were in a dating relationship.) We just wanted to be close. Nothing was wrong with that, right? Uh-huh. For nearly two years, we were together pretty much every single week. We lied and hid and sneaked around. We graduated from high school together. We had talked forever about getting married someday down the road. And then…after graduation, we had a huge fight and broke up. When we decided to get back together a few weeks later (ALMOST the worst mistake of my life, even though I really loved him), of course, we had to make up. I found out that I was pregnant less than 6 weeks before I was supposed to leave for college. I was scared to death, and all that I could think was, "what am I going to do?" and "how's it going to happen?" I knew better than to go to either one of my parents. He was scared to death to tell his parents.

So we drove to the clinic together 40 miles away, and he went shopping at the next-door mall, while I was inside getting an abortion. I wondered exactly what I should be feeling and thinking as we made our way back home. I did not allow myself to dwell on it. It was over, and I couldn't change my mind. No tears. They wouldn't help anyway. We returned to our "normal" lives as though nothing in the world out of the ordinary had occurred. We never had complete closure in our relationship. I couldn't wait to leave for college in another state, where no one knew me or anything about me. The slate was clean to begin a "new" life. Hmmmmm. I buried all of this messiness away in the back of my mind and heart. No one knew except for my boyfriend and me (oh, and God, of course!). I could walk away as if nothing had ever happened. I began classes at a Christian college (how's that for irony?) just a few weeks after the abortion, so happy to just be somewhere besides where I'd been!! No one knew me or anything about me, and I intended to keep it that way.

Fast forward a few decades…I had met a wonderful man at this college and married when I graduated. After his graduation, we moved to his home state of Vermont. We attended the congregation in which my husband was born and raised. We had two beautiful baby boys. I began to suffer from PAS (Post-Abortion Syndrome), unsure of what to do to help myself. As my sons grew up and were interested in dating, I was very open and upfront with my past, assuring them that IF anything similar happened with them that they could always come to us for help and love and guidance. I didn't want them ever to experience what I had gone through. I never sought counseling because that was a taboo word. I even contacted my local pregnancy center for help, but it turned out that someone that I knew worked there, and I just couldn't go.

Through the years, I was always plagued with grief and what-ifs throughout January,

Sanctity of Life month. I wouldn't even attend church on days when I thought the preacher might be speaking about abortion. Fast forward to 2011—my elderly mother moved in with my family because it wasn't safe for her to be alone anymore. Somewhere down the road—I do NOT know what happened to me—but I began to have a terrible time with PAS. I locked myself away, doing Bible studies, reading everything I could get my hands on about recovery, and trying to move on with my life. I fought hard to get to that place of freedom and forgiveness!! It was the most horrible time in my life. But God…brought me through it. I didn't die, and I didn't just give up!!

My mama knew that something was wrong, but I never could bring myself to tell her about the horrible thing that I had done. When my mama needed more care than I could provide for her, she went to a nearby nursing home. It was right after she was settled that I heard our local pregnancy center was looking for volunteers, so I eased into Care Net. A few months later, the job of Client Advocate was offered to me. I did the Bible study, *Forgiven and Set Free*. I have always wanted to be able to help other mothers in some way, any way!!! Jesus touched the broken places in me and healed them. He washed me clean and forgave me. His grace and mercy flowed through me and has empowered me to reach out to others.

Now I meet and greet, counsel, teach, and love on these beautiful women!! I was even able to share my testimony with a woman who had many children already and was seriously considering abortion. I shared my story with her, and when she left, she and her father were totally for carrying to term. (She delivered a baby girl!!) I felt like I had come full circle!!! God is so faithful!! There are still days that I struggle. There are still times I wonder what it would have been like if I hadn't made that choice. But I know God is in control of it all. I know there is more to the story when I get to the other side, and someday I will hold that child as Father God holds me. I have named my child "Hope" because that is what God has given to me, in spite of me!! And my greatest joy someday will be, other than my Jesus, holding my child in my arms some sweet day!!!

Recipes from the Kitchen of

Deborah Persons

Spinach Dip

Serves 6 • Cook time: 10 min

Ingredients:

24-oz. sour cream
1 8-oz. can water chestnuts, chopped
1 Envelope dried vegetable soup mix
Cloves of garlic, to taste
10-oz. box frozen chopped spinach, thawed and squeezed dry

Directions:

- Blend well the first four ingredients. Stir in spinach with a fork until well blended. Chill thoroughly and stir before serving.
- Use either crackers or fresh vegetables for dipping.

Creamy Chicken and Broccoli Casserole

Serves 4-6 • Cook time: 30 min

Ingredients:

2 6 oz.-pkg. stuffing mix
1 large can French fried onion rings
1 fresh broccoli crown or 1 bag of frozen and thawed broccoli florets
1 can cheddar cheese soup
4-oz. of sour cream
2 cups shredded cooked chicken

Directions:

- Prepare stuffing mix according to package directions.
- Place in a greased 9x13 dish.
- Heat the cheddar cheese soup.
- Blend the cheddar cheese soup and sour cream together.
- Add the shredded chicken and stir.
- Pour on top of the stuffing.
- Place the broccoli florets into the cheese/chicken mixture, stem down.
- Bake covered at 350° for 30 minutes.
- Remove cover and spread the onion rings on top, return to the oven for 5 min.

Chocolate Cake with Peanut Butter Buttercream Frosting

Serves: 9x13 pan • Cook time: 35 min

Cake Ingredients:

2 cups sugar
1 cup of milk
2 cups flour
1 1/2 cups hot coffee
3/4 cup cocoa
1/2 cup olive oil
1/2 tsp. salt
2 eggs
2 tsp. baking soda
1 Tbsp. vanilla
1 Tbsp. baking powder

Directions:

- Mix all dry ingredients well.
- Add wet ingredients.
- Mix until well blended.
- Pour into a greased 9x13 pan.
- Bake at 350° for 35 minutes.

Frosting Ingredients:

6 oz. white chocolate chips, melted
1 cup butter, room temperature
2 cups confectioner's sugar
4 Tbsp. milk
Peanut butter to taste (I usually use 2-3 heaping tablespoons)

Directions:

- Mix all ingredients thoroughly.
- Spread evenly over cooled cake.
- I leave in pan and pile on the frosting.
- When completely cooled, there is a nice thick layer of yumminess on top.

"For God alone, O my soul, wait in silence,
for my hope is from Him."

(Psalm 62:5 ESV)

Journey with Jesus

By Bethany Douglas

If you are curious, I wanted to give you the amazing story of my journey with Jesus. It's amazing not because of me in particular, in fact, I'm pretty much the least interesting part of it. Rather it is amazing because of what Christ has done in my life.

I grew up in a middle America home with a loving and Christian family. My parents were (and still are!) wonderful, God-fearing and God-following people. I was raised in strong churches and with overall great relationships with friends and family. On paper, I was the poster child of obedience, smarts, drive, morality, and spirituality. I was every parent's dream- until I got married. And all that church, even my somewhat strong personal relationship with God, wasn't enough to protect me from evil, both inside and outside of myself.

I got lazy in my faith; I got flaky in my relationship with God, I was hurt, I had baggage and, like us all…a LOT of fleshly nature. I was (am!) a sinner- plain and simple. Holy moly have I got a corner on the market on sinning! I'm (unfortunately) extremely good at it, and I've (also, unfortunately) had a ton of practice at it. I'm an adulteress (twice over! The first time with a woman and the second time with a married man), I've dabbled in drugs, considered stripping for a while to make money, I went through a time of pathological lying, of demonic warfare, of being within 2 days of divorce proceedings with my husband. During the really rough stuff, I was diagnosed with multiple personalities (which was, in my opinion, some for-reals demonic oppression). I was sexually abused by my uncle for many years as a child, I spend years of my high school and college years, and even my early marriage just "kind of" seeking God. I was so lost and had so much baggage. So many hurts haunted me wherever I went- both thrust upon me, but many that I inflicted on myself.

I was so utterly lost.

But God has changed me!

The minute my husband, Gabe, served me with divorce papers in 2003, I had a major decision to make. To finally and fully commit myself to God, or shake the dice and continue to do life by my own rules. I was knee-deep in the middle of a lesbian relationship at the time. Gabe and I had been separated for many months at this point. I was a shell of the person I could be- lonely, defiant, stressed, depressed, prideful, angry, hurt, you name it. I was a mess.

I made the decision to seek God mostly out of fear of losing my marriage…but it was made with anger and insolence. I was not happy with life! I was so angry- I remember telling God, "*You'd better make this decision worth it because I know what I'm giving up* (what I thought was the love of my life) *and I'm not sure You can beat it!"* (Looking back, I'm so glad that fire and brimstone didn't rain down on me that very second! I certainly would've deserved it five times over!)

I went into intensive counseling with an amazing older gentleman and someone who came to be a father-figure, mentor, and friend to Gabe and me both. It was years in the process. During this time, I started remembering abuse I'd had in the past, issues that I had with trust in men, and overall the utter brokenness that was so manifest in my life. I had been a Christian all my life; I'd given Jesus my heart at an early age, and yet my life had slowly slithered down into the abyss. Through the guidance of my counselor, a lot of love and support from my husband and family, I slowly trudged out of the gates of Hell.

And what a journey it was! The demonic warfare that raged around me was intense! The devil wasn't giving me up without a fight…but I had the Overcomer in my corner and ultimately rode in victory to the healthy, happy, and whole woman that I am today! Praise God for His everlasting and far-reaching mercies and grace!

But the story doesn't end there back in those days. Even coming out of the affair and fixing my marriage, I faced a lot of judgment and black-balling from the church, from people who *should* have been praying and encouraging me. Gabe got much support; I, however, did not. He was embraced; I was not. It was an unexpected development during those hard times. I was surprised and deeply wounded by those who I turned to in my need. Our church failed me big time. I was hurt perhaps more by the judgment and hypocrisy of the Body of Christ during that time than maybe anything else. It wounded Gabe deeply too. Both Gabe and I spent several years healing from the wounds inflicted on us during that season.

As if that wasn't enough, as if I hadn't learned the lesson fully (which clearly by my behavior I had not), in 2007 I had another affair, this time with a married man. I knew it was wrong, and thank God it was not as 'physical' as my previous one. However, it exposed much additional healing that I obviously needed- both in myself and in my marriage. The affair ended on its own without Gabe finding out about it. I had never planned on telling him, figuring he would leave me for good this time, until one fateful afternoon many many years later, during a time that we were actually thriving in our relationship, in our personal lives, with a great church, and with God.

One sunny afternoon in 2012, Gabe had a confession *for me*, he had hidden a porn addiction from me–for literally our entire marriage. I was stunned. He had lied to me about it dozens and dozens of times, and I had believed him. I felt my world turn upside down; I felt betrayed, humiliated, a fool. It was an impossible pill to swallow. And yet I had to because I was convicted that afternoon to tell him about my second affair finally. Whew, you can just imagine how that conversation went–on both our sides! There was a lot of crying, confession, repentance, forgiveness, and renewal. It took time for both of us, but God (once again) walked us through it.

God is so good! He is the great physician, the great healer, the great Prince of Peace. And He has brought real peace, real truth, real confession, real repentance, and real transformation to our house! Without Him, I would be lost (still and forever!)

Today I want to encourage you, dear one- as I can personally attest, there is NOTHING that you've done or gone through that God cannot fix completely. In fact, I'll go a step further and proclaim that what your issues are, God will not only fix, *He will make it better*! That unholy vow I told Him during my first affair He has answered me in spades. I work at it, I practice walking with my Savior, I have to commit to being intentional and on guard in this journey called life. I refuse to let those years of hard work not be proclaimed from the mountain tops- because, in my weaknesses, God is made great! He is the ultimate savior and redeemer! My life now is more blessed, more fulfilling, more peaceful, more complete than anything I could have possibly imagined. It is not perfect, and I am still a sinner (I always will be, though I try not to!) BUT (and that's a BIG BUT!) I am a living, breathing testament of what the blood of Jesus can do in a life. Please do not ever think that you are beyond redemption! I believe that Christ literally descended into the bowels of Darkness to retrieve me out of its depths- He only asked me to take the steps with Him. And if I can do that, you can too!

If those steps need to be taken today, I beg you to take them. Walk with Him, step by step, He'll carry you, if needed, for a while (He definitely did that for me), but you have to LET HIM. Please let Him today!

Recipes from the Kitchen of
Bethany Douglas

Brown Sugar Green Beans

Serves 6 • Cook time: 30 min

Ingredients:

3 cans whole cans green beans- drained
1/4 cup Crumbled bacon
1 stick butter-cubed
2 Tbsp. soy sauce
1 cup brown sugar
1/2 tsp. garlic powder

Directions:

- Melt butter then mix in brown sugar, garlic powder, and soy sauce until thoroughly mixed.
- Pour mixture over green beans in a casserole pan and mix around until beans are coated.
- Sprinkle bacon crumbles over mixture.
- Bake at 350° for 30 mins or until bubbling.

White Parmesan Chicken

Serves 8 • Cook time: 45 min

Ingredients:

6 chicken breasts
1/2 cup Parmesan cheese
1 cup Italian bread crumbs
1 cup Ranch dressing
1 cup shredded mozzarella cheese
1/4 cup butter cubed

Directions:

- Mix Parmesan cheese and Italian bread crumbs together.
- Rinse and dry chicken breasts.
- Coat chicken in ranch dressing then coat thoroughly in the bread crumb mixture.
- Place chicken in a non-stick pan with cubed butter on top of it. Bake at 350° for 40 mins or until juices run clear.
- OR chicken can be skillet-fried in butter, turning every 8 minutes on med-high heat until juices run clear (this will result in tons of yummy crunchies!)
- Put shredded mozzarella over chicken about 5 minutes before done cooking to let melt.
- May be served over rice or pasta.

Banana Chocolate Chip Bread

Serves 12 muffins or 2 loaves • Cook time: 70 min

Ingredients:

1 1/4 cup sugar
1/2 stick butter, softened
2 eggs
3-4 ripe bananas- mashed
1/2 cup milk
1 tsp. vanilla
1/8 tsp. nutmeg
2 1/2 cups flour
1 tsp. baking soda
1 tsp. salt
1/2 cup mini chocolate chips (if desired)

Directions:

- Mix sugar and butter well in a large bowl.
- Add in eggs and beat well.
- Add in rest of wet ingredients and thoroughly mix until smooth.
- In a separate bowl, mix dry ingredients.
- Add dry ingredients to wet until just mixed- don't overbeat.
- Stir in choc chips by hand.
- Half the mixture and pour into 2 well-greased bread pans.
- Loaf pans bake at 360° for approximately 55-70 mins, until a toothpick comes out clean.
- Muffins bake at 400° for 15-20 mins, until a toothpick comes out clean.

"The Lord bless thee, and keep thee. The Lord make His face shine upon thee, and be gracious unto thee. The Lord lift up His countenance upon thee, and give thee peace."

(Numbers 6: 24-26)

A Journey Through Turmoil

By Sarah Du Toit

At the beginning of January I found a small marble size lump (1cm) in my breast, my journey started on New Year's Day when I saw my GP who was working, he sent me to get the lump scanned, the ultrasound scanner who is a friend said to do something quickly, and within a month I was having surgery.

Two weeks before my surgery, I went to my church for an amazing service and training for the healing ministry for our Peninsula Tent Revival event in March. Pastor Tim called me up, knowing nothing about me and said your breast issue will be healed today, He then touched my forehead, and I awoke on the floor!

I had my surgery on Tuesday 19th as the first case, I had bought some front zipper cotton bras from Big W, and when my surgeon had finished practicing his art on my chest, I told them, he was delighted and took one so instead of bandages they put on my soft support bra. I was in recovery for a while and got to the ward by just after lunchtime. I felt God with me when I fell asleep and when I awoke — feeling calm, still, and knowing that it is Him.

I was sore and didn't venture out of bed at all that first day. I then heard that they had removed the tumour now 3 1/2cm on the right breast and the surrounding tissue, plus the same amount of tissue with the left and gave me a lift and reduction on both, praise God a silver lining Amen.

I have been sore but good at home, again alone and feeling sad and useless due to a few to many careless comments plus being unable to do many things I had before. Then came my outpatient's appointment where I was dropped off by my son's girlfriend, and where I was told my diagnosis had changed from encapsulated tumour to invasive ductal stage 3 carcinoma, I was alone again and totally unprepared. I was really upset initially and tearful until the breast nurse practitioner said that when I had my nuclear medicine test where they injected blue radioactive dye into me, the radiographer and my surgeon said they had NEVER seen just a circle of dye around the tumour. My surgeon said they thought the node or lymph was blocked, but it wasn't.

That weekend was hard, my husband angry and not coping with my pain and sadness. I was feeling very alone. I felt crushed. I had spent many hours in prayer that week, that feeling of loneliness and deep sadness inside because people I thought would support me, never did, including ladies from church. It was then that God reminded me whilst reading a Lysa TerKeurst quote where she wrote: "Lord, when life feels too hard & nothing makes sense, help us fix our eyes on You. Keep reminding us that You can bring good from even the very worst of situations. We're choosing to rely on Your unfailing love."

"And so, we know and rely on the love God has for us" (1 John 4:16a).

He also reminded me that when we end up really disappointed, Satan will use that to chip away at our focus on Him and that little by little I was starting to feel sorry for myself, He reminded me that my thinking people would reciprocate what I do for them by helping me out as I do for them isn't why I do it. "Not everyone has the same heart as you" the Lord allowing His words into my mind.

So, I have changed my feelings of sorrow to feelings of joy; I just decided that I will do what I do for others through Jesus Christ without expectation of repayment as I always have before. God sees my heart and all I do in His name and all that is done for them, and I know that He blesses me accordingly.

I decided that whilst I waited to see the surgical teams and find out the results, I would be brave and retain that belief that God knows all and is in control. I made a pact with God that no matter how this ended, I am a child of God and He is sovereign, and all I need to do is remember the healing prayer and accept that God, the I am, is doing His work, so that I can shout from the rooftops that all glory should go to my Father, the mighty healer who loves us all so much.

I saw my surgeon last week, and he was stunned! He said there was NO cancer in the tissue surrounding the fast-growing tumour, nor was there any sign of cancer in the lymph nodes outside of the breast! However, I am still going to see the oncologists and see what they want to do to make sure that everything has gone. I know that I am clear because my God is so good!!

God's Mighty Miracle in My Life

By Sarah Du Toit

I was 27, a deacon at church and with boys of 2 & 1 years old, I was so in tune with God and loving the Ministries I was leading. A youth gathering on Sundays every second week out of the service or leading worship.

I was 14 weeks the first bleed I had, 20 weeks the second, and when I started bleeding at 29 weeks into my pregnancy with my daughter, I was at a wedding. We went to the Private Hospital in Harare and were turned away, and I remember my husband driving 90km to a tiny private country hospital in Zimbabwe called Borodaille Trust.

I was taken for a scan when I awoke on Sunday, covered in monitors and when I saw her pulse so low, I knew I was to have a caesarean when the man doing the surgery had finished his church service. He was a missionary pastor.

We had left our two little boys with their Ouma and my in-laws, my husband sleeping in the back of our truck under the canopy.

I remember getting down on my knees with the monitors and gown on and reading my Bible and spent a great deal of time praying and handing my operation over to God while we waited. I went in, and I awoke to people bustling around my husband and me staring into my face looking shocked and white-faced. I was told my baby was being rushed to Harare to Intensive care, and I demanded to see her. She was beautiful with a mop of dark curly hair. I also demanded that a Pastor come and pray over her for me as I was not letting her out of my sight until that happened.

They pulled the Pastor out of a private school called Peterhouse, he left the evensong service to someone else to finish, and he came and prayed for my tiny 1.9-pound baby.

A few days later, I found out from my GP who had done the anesthetic what had happened. I had bled out due to a tiny nick in the placenta, and the missionary surgeon who didn't have fancy equipment couldn't stop the bleeding. My pulse faded to nothing, and I was to all intents and purposes dead. Apparently, the surgeon fell on his knees after a long time of pressure on the point of the bleeding and cried out to God. My GP doing the anesthetic told me it was a miracle as he was about to pronounce me dead. I woke to a feeling of the Holy Spirit surrounding me like a blanket; I was euphoric and happy. I got out of bed 2 days later despite severe anemia and demanded to go see my baby 90 km away in Harare at the hospital that had turned us away and where my specialist was a consultant. Two weeks later, I was home with my precious child, and she was feeding normally. To this day, I say if I had been anywhere else, I might not have survived, but I was where I was known and loved, and God was there with me all the time.

Recipes from the Kitchen of
Sarah Du Toit

Poor Man's Pudding

Serves 4 • Cook time: 30 min

Ingredients:

1/2 cup sugar
1 egg
1 cup flour
1 tsp. bicarbonate of sofa
1 tsp. baking powder
1 Tbsp. of apricot jam
1/2 Tbsp. white vinegar
1 cup of milk

Directions:

- Beat the egg and sugar.
- Add all the other ingredients
- Bake at 180° C (350° F)
- For 1/2 hour or until the mixture bounces back when pushed down.

Sauce Ingredients:

1 cup boiling water
1/2 cup milk
1 cup sugar
2 Tbsp. butter

Sauce Directions:

- Boil together and pour mixture over the pudding while it is still hot.

Melt in the Mouth Steak

Serves 6 • Cook time: 3 hrs

Ingredients:

750g beef – I use braising steak cut in thick sliced
Salt, pepper & cayenne pepper
70g cake flour
2 large onions
25ml oil
25ml cornflour
25ml gravy powder
750mls boiling water
1 beef stock cube
50mls Worcester sauce
50mls Tomato sauce

Directions:

- Season meat with salt pepper and cayenne pepper
- Sprinkle flour onto a working surface
- Place meat slices on to the flour and rub the flour into both sides of the meat
- Oil the bottom of a casserole dish with a lid
- Pack as follows: Place meat slices at the bottom, squeeze them in with no overlapping pieces. Place onions in a layer on top of the meat
- Mix the cornflour and the gravy powder with a little cold water, mix then add to the boiling water.
- Crumble the stock cube, the tomato sauce, and Worcester sauce into the boiling water
- Pour this mixture over the meat and onions
- Cover with a lid and bake for about 3 hours in a preheated oven at 150°C (300°F)
- Serve with rice or potatoes and vegetables. I love it with a nice creamy mash.

"So if the Son sets you free, you will be free indeed."

(John 8:36)

In Christ, I'm Alive and Free!

By Adriana Morales

My dad wanted me to become a famous concert pianist at a young age. He even dreamed about traveling together for competitions and performances over the course of my adolescence.

My Dreams were different. I wanted to help people in their distress, so I became a mental health provider and achieved my 'American Dream' over the course of three decades.

Now, my friend, there is nothing wrong about having dreams or specific goals in today's world. It is healthy to be intentional about our daily, monthly, quarterly, and yearly goals. Our Lord even recommends for all of us to be purposeful in life and maintain a clear vision; otherwise, we would perish in the long run.

"So go ahead and be intentional every day in pursuit of your American Dream." I am thankful for accomplishing my 'American dream' and so much more. I know God had the best plan for me and He even took me further than I ever imagined or expected.

Be cautious though, not to be blindfolded along the way, I know I was!

For so long, I was so proud of my career pursuits and hardly ever acknowledged God in my plans early on in my career.

When our goals become idols, "I must attain this right now" attitude, we may neglect God's will. I was disobedient and even rebellious when I was on the 'fast track.' I worked 70-80 hours a week, did not rest a day, smoked up to two packs of cigarettes a day, rushed throughout the day so I would get to the next action step, never had time for family or friends, completed three graduate schools' programs in a timely manner, and finally attained professional licensure in two different States and a worldwide Board certification at a high price and cost!

Whew!

I am quite exhausted right about now just thinking about the energy I spent all of those years striving for peak performance. Do not be impressed, my friend. I am not here to boast or impress anyone.

I'm here to share briefly with you about the damaging effects of idolatry.

I have been an overachiever since my early college years. I can now relax and enjoy my professional career! I thank God for His wisdom and discernment in the past decade; otherwise; I would have probably self-destructed. I never had an opportunity to be still and allow God to speak to my heart much less time to renew or be transformed by His Word.

If I would have known He was already there fighting on my behalf, I would have listened to all of His whispers, obeyed His commands and waited on His promises to be fulfilled in His perfect timing. His Truth reminds me today, "The LORD will fight for you; you need only to be still." (Exodus14:14).

I've got quite a few regrets today such as broken, strained, and distant relationships with family members, significant upper-respiratory health issues, and the fact I never had time to consider having children.

I was in bondage for way too long! Yes, I was indeed.

Trapped. Blind. Lost. Dead in my transgressions.

The "American Dream" blindfolded me. I was self-centered and selfish when achieving all types of goals.

Until one day…

I heard the Gospel preached at a local Church; It finally came all together. I admitted I was a sinner who was dead in my transgressions and caught up with today's cultural pursuits and success track.

God was relentless in His pursuit, and He never let me go. I finally surrendered it all and started to renew my mind with His Word; my life was transformed thereafter.

The Cross has the Final Word, sweet friend, not the "American Dream."

I am now free from the "American Dream" bondage.

I still work hard in everything I do, but my purpose is not to please man anymore. My main purpose is to maintain an eternal perspective, fear our Lord and glorify Him at the end of the day in everything I do.

In Christ, I'm alive and free.

"It is for freedom that Christ has set us free. Stand firm, then, and do not let yourselves be burdened again by a yoke of slavery" (Galatians 5:1).

How about you, my friend? Do you fear man, or do you please the Lord today?

We all have a choice.

I chose Christ.

I am alive and free today.

Recipe from the Kitchen of

Adriana Morales

Tropical Fruit Salad Dessert

Serves 8-10 • Cook time: 5-10 min • Prep time: 10 min

Ingredients:

1 can mandarin oranges
1 large can fruit cocktail
8 oz. cool whip
1 cup of sour cream
1 cup of small marshmallows
1 cup of coconut

Directions:

- Separate cherries from the can of fruit cocktail so you may add these cherries to the top of the Tropical Fruit Salad Dessert at the end,
- Add the fruit cocktail to a bowl,
- Add the mandarin oranges,
- Add the cool whip,
- Add the sour cream,
- Add the marshmallows,
- Add the coconut and save a small amount for the top at the end.
- Mix all ingredients well together in the bowl. Note, the sour cream will add a soft and creamy texture to the tropical fruit salad dessert,
- Spread extra coconut on top of the dessert,
- Add a few cherries on top and enjoy!

You are sons of light and sons of the day.
We do not belong to the night
or to the darkness.

(1 Thessalonians 5:5)

From the Darkness into the Light

By Karen Guthrie

For you were once darkness, but now you are light in the Lord. Live as children of light (for the fruit of the light consists in all goodness, righteousness, and truth) and find out what pleases the Lord. Have nothing to do with the fruitless deeds of darkness, but rather expose them. For it is shameful even to mention what the disobedient do in secret. But everything exposed by the light becomes visible for it is light that makes everything visible. This is why it is said: "Wake up, O sleeper, rise from the dead, and Christ will shine on you" *(*Ephesians 5:8-14 NIV).

Holy Spirit, be my voice and let the words I speak be yours. Hide me that only Jesus may be seen. Amen.

I gave my heart to Jesus when I was in the 4th grade, but I didn't give my life to Him until after I married and began attending church with my husband. I didn't know how to live in the light, so I spent the next 15 years in classes, Bible Study, worship, and service. I learned all I could and tried to live an obedient life. I discovered my spiritual gifts and began to use them.

I can remember revivals with a visiting preacher, special music, or concert and as I watched the people pour out the message of their hearts, I thought they looked and acted so happy – joyous – sold out to God. I remember thinking, "I want that kind of Christianity; that kind of power; that kind of relationship with Jesus!"

From the time we were dating, my husband and I planned to leave our little home town, but every time we tried to leave, our path was blocked, so we remained. Sometime in 1988, God began opening the door for us to leave. The church we attended no longer felt like home and family. It became clear God was telling us to leave.

So, in August 1989, after much prayer, we moved to Gassville, AR. We got there about two weeks before school started and began to settle in. We tried several churches asking God each time, "Is this the one?" We finally found a small church where we felt God wanted us.

The people there were warm and welcoming. We began to feel at home.

After about three years, we moved closer to Mountain Home, AR. Both of our boys attended school, had friends, and participated in sports there. We felt they were losing interest in our small church with an almost non-existent youth group and no youth leader. We found a slightly larger church and began the process of settling in again.

Eventually, after our sons graduated from high school, we moved again: first to a farm in NE Oklahoma, then to a farm in NW Arkansas, and then to a farm in SW Missouri. During this time, we didn't attend church but still prayed, read the Word, watched and listened to Christian teaching on TV, radio, and tape, and held many lively discussions about what the Bible taught about living life.

While living on the farm in SW Missouri, I first slipped into depression. I'm not sure of the cause, but I feel the combination of hormones, my age, out of control high blood sugar, isolation, and stress brought me down.

During that time, I felt overwhelmed by all my responsibilities. Both of our sons were with us again – a great help to their dad with the farm work, and we were glad to have them with us. We also had a cousin recovering from a divorce, a homeless nephew (diagnosed as schizophrenic while living with us) and a friend trying to "find himself" came to live with us. Our granddaughters, ages 5 and 7, were with their dad (and consequently with us) nearly all of the summer and any school breaks. And finally, my husband's mother became unable to live alone or with other family and came to us, too.

That was when I began to doubt my self-worth. I felt useless, of no purpose, undeserving of love. I felt sure my husband would be better off and happier without me. He could find someone better suited to him and to this lifestyle. I became so convinced of these thoughts that I began to plan my death. I called it "leaving." I wrestled with what God would do to me if I ended my life. I didn't want to bungle an accident and end up more trouble to my family – someone needing care for the rest of my life. I didn't want either of my sons to be the one to find me. I wondered who would influence my granddaughters for good. God used those thoughts and kept me from actually doing any real harm to myself.

Most of the time, I felt numb. I cried until I had no more tears. I saw a counselor. I took some medications. I prayed. I got no better.

We sold the farm, and I leveled off as my responsibilities lessened. My husband is a truck driver, and in 2006, I went on the road with him for a year. Then, because of business decisions,

I began to stay home full time to do the paperwork to run our trucking business. I knew this was a necessary thing, and I was willing to do it. It wasn't a full-time job but was just enough more than I could take care of from the road.

The summer of 2007, I began another downward spiral with each day a little worse than the one before. I prayed. I counted blessings. I wrote in my journal. I asked God to take me out of this life. My husband tried to convince me he loved me, needed me, and would be devastated without me. I didn't believe him. He made me promise not to hurt myself. In spite of this promise, the thought of "leaving" lingered in my mind. But God was there! I began to hear from Him (repeating over and over in my thoughts) that what I needed was to be among His people. I needed to find a home, a family, and a place of service.

Going to a new place, knowing no one, completely alone terrified me. I resisted. I begged. But then I surrendered, and God brought me to CBC, my home.

I will never forget how one of the elders met me at the door, introduced me to his wife, and helped me find a seat. I will be forever grateful for him as he may have saved my life. Our Pastor's Wife introduced herself after that first service and invited me to the Women's Ministry Event coming in about two weeks. I felt welcome and saw the first gleaming rays of light.

I came back, and more women reached out. I went to the Women's Event and met some others. I joined a small group for prayer and sharing. I began to help in the church library and did other small acts of service. These things helped me to remember that I am intelligent and capable. I attended Bible Study where I was reminded from *Psalm 139:14 (NIV)* that I am *"fearfully and wonderfully made"* that God has a purpose for me and a work for me to do.

"For we are God's workmanship created in Christ Jesus to do good works, which God prepared in advance for us to do" (Ephesians 2:10 NIV).

I attended worship services. I developed and maintained a gratitude list. I began to talk to people. **The shadows began to recede.**

At the 2007 Women's Fall Retreat, God showed me through the lessons, and especially during the sharing time, I needed to shift my focus from me to Him! This was a **Huge Turning Point** in my recovery. My prayers began to be full of praise, thanksgiving, and worship instead of child-like ranting, pouting, and tantrums.

I was part of another small group the next spring. The women there opened their hearts to me. They prayed with me and for me. **The Darkness Lightened.**

Day by day, God sheds His light on me. Now I have only an occasional dark thought, and I have many, many more good days than bad. God has brought me this far; to this point in my life's journey. I believe He is healing me through the women in my church family.

Please understand. This sounds like I did all of these things, and now I am better. I know that it has been God working through His people.

- It was the elder and the pastor's wife that first day
- God, in our teacher, as she led our Sunday School Class and asked those thought-provoking questions
- God in all of the women who listened and encouraged me as I read my "Names of God" Prayers
- Talks about prayer
- Meeting for coffee and listening to my rambling
- The Praise team, leading Worship through music
- The sermons taught
- Talks about hearing God
- The Church gathering around those suffering from life-threatening illnesses.
- Our oldest member always greeting me with a smile and whispering "Precious Lady" as she hugged me
- Another elder always smiling and greeting me
- Unexpected encouragement
- God has spoken to me through the Elders as they called us to prayer
- Words from a dear encourager pushed me to stretch and grow, and the way she listened when all I could do was weep
- Another's quiet wisdom
- The laughing children
- The boisterous youth

The list could go on and on as I think of each one of our church family.

That is what this church has become. My Family! Each time I think of them, each time I see them, God gives me a smile – a ray of sunshine.

These have walked in the light and have shined God's light on me. They have welcomed me with a holy love. They have loved me to wholeness, and I thank God for them. Because of Christ's love shining in them, I have come **From the Darkness into the Light**.

Recipe from the Kitchen of

Karen Guthrie

Tex-Mex "Quiche"

Serves 6 • Cook time: 30 min

Ingredients:

2 ounces nacho cheese tortilla chips, finely crushed
2 Tbsp. butter, melted
1/2 lb. ground beef
1 Tbsp. chili powder
1/4 tsp. + 1/8 tsp. black pepper
3/4 cup milk
1 small green pepper, diced in 1/2-inch pieces, about 1 cup chopped
4 ounces white mushrooms, quartered
3 scallions, about 1/3 cup
1 cup taco flavored shredded cheese
6 eggs

Directions:

- Heat oven to 350˚.
- Combine crushed chips and melted butter in a medium bowl.
- Stir until crumbs are evenly moistened.
- Press into the bottom of a 9-inch fluted quiche pan (or in a 9-inch glass or ceramic pie plate.
- Bake for 10 minutes.
- Set aside.
- Meanwhile, add ground beef to a large non-stick skillet over medium heat. Cook, stirring to break apart lumps, for 4 minutes or until pieces are no longer pink.
- Add chili powder, 1/2 tsp. salt, 1/4 tsp. black pepper and cook 1 minute.
- Add green pepper, mushrooms, and scallions. Lower heat to medium.
- Cook, occasionally stirring, 4 minutes. Remove from heat.
- Sprinkle 1/2 cup cheese over the baked crust.

- Top with the meat and vegetable mixture.
- In a medium bowl, whisk together the eggs, milk, 1/4 tsp. salt, and 1/8 tsp. black pepper.
- Pour over meat mixture in dish.
- Sprinkle top with remaining cheese.
- Bake in 350° oven 25-30 minutes.
- Let cool 5 minutes before serving.

"You are sons of light and sons of the day. We do not belong to the night or to the darkness."

(1 Thessalonians 5:5)

Preparing the Table

By Katie Marie (Blanton)

Every time I pull the china out from the cabinet, I recall the lessons my grandmother taught me about the table. “When you set out the plates, always set one or two extras. You never want someone to show up and feel as though they weren’t wanted, welcomed, or expected. It is easier to remove a setting than it is to shift the table and add one.” Friends, family, and sometimes strangers filled our table. I don’t ever remember removing a setting. Regardless of the number of settings, there was always a promise of community.

I learned how to break bread and communicate with older and younger generations at Grandma’s table. Our loud, feisty meals allowed for dreams to become a reality. In typical Italian manners, multiple people gave opinions based on their generation. The older always thought the younger ones were careless and reckless, but, in the end, we were all encouraged and supported.

As a little girl, going to Grandma’s meant walking into a house filled with the aroma of garlic and tomatoes bubbling on the stove. An Italian feast was always prepared at the hands of very strong-willed women with loud banter as the backdrop. I would plop black olives on the ends of all ten fingers as I sat on a countertop, watching grandma prepare our meal. Great Grandma would scold me for my reckless behavior.

Truly, where were my lady-like manners? Grandma would shew her away, assuring her my mis-mannered behaviors were not a big deal. Ironically, it was a very big deal. Sitting on the counter was where real-life conversations were etched into my heart. The yummy smells, olive-tipped fingers, china on the table, and a large family gathering warmed my soul.

At 18, grief stuck me hard when I lost my greatest cheerleader. Grandma suddenly passed away at the age of 58. I was devastated. Anger replaced love around the table. The table grew silent. The place where we shared love was now awkward. My heart grew cold.

Where was she? Where had she gone? I could still feel her loved wrapped around me, but she was nowhere to be found. Secretly, I searched for her everywhere. Maybe it was all a bad dream, and I would find her eating a cannoli in a deli. She couldn't really be gone, could she?

Grief consumed every ounce of my being. I knew of a God, but I did not yet know my Savior. What I did know was my friend, my confidant, my encourager was gone. She was stolen from me too soon, and I wanted her back.

Both fists shaking at God, screaming at Him to give her back, I knew I needed to find Him. I needed to know she was okay, and one day, we would be together again.

My screams of anger turned to questions with hope, "God are you real?"

God redeemed me from this place. The more I sought Him, the more I found Him. It often brings me back to Jeremiah 29:13 (NIV) "Seek me, and you will find me when you seek me with all your heart."

Months went by, and I sought God in all my spaces. I was the strange girl that would sit in the front row at college group. During closing prayer, I would sneak out the door. Then the pastor began praying in front of the door. Reluctantly, I accepted his counsel. I leaned in and fell at the foot of the cross. Every now and then, I cry when I miss the touch of my grandma's hand or the sound of her voice. These tears are accompanied by the comfort of Christ's love.

In the early morning, Grandma was found with her feet on the coffee table. Her earthly body was lifeless. Eyes appeared to be looking up at the heavens with a rosary in her hand. Peace had consumed her as she was called home. I can only imagine what her conversation with God must have been leading up to the moment Jesus came to get her. I wish I could have sat with her, held her hand, and prayed with her.

When I set the table, I remember we are commissioned to love others well. My upbringing was not one that I would call religious. We didn't talk to God, but now I can see I was taught how to gather, love, and serve. My table is a gathering place where God is always at the center.

Friends set your table with love, and God will be the host. Gather friends, family, and even a stranger and welcome them to this sacred place. Set the table with love, grace, and opportunity to shine the light of Christ. Grandma may not have "talked God" but she sure shined His love.

Recipe from the Kitchen of

Katie Marie

Grandma's Broccoli Pasta

Serves 8 • Cook time: 20 min • Prep time: 10 min

Ingredients:

Broccoli (2 heads, or 16 oz bag)
Himalayan sea salt
Olive oil 1/4 cup
Penne pasta or pasta noodle of choice 1lb
Garlic clove sliced or chopped (to taste)
Grated pecorino romano cheese 1/2 cup
optional sundried tomatoes
optional crushed red pepper
optional sliced black olives
optional mushrooms

Directions:

- Trim the broccoli and cut into bite-size pieces
- Bring 8 quarts of lightly salted water to a boil in a large pot
- Add 2 garlic cloves and broccoli to boiling water for about 5 minutes. You want the broccoli to be soft but not mushy
- Prepare a sauté pan large enough for broccoli and pasta with olive oil and sliced garlic cook over medium heat for 2 minutes
- Sieve the broccoli out of the water (do not drain water) into the sauté pan.
- Smash the boiled garlic so it has a paste-like consistency.
- Add that to the pan as well. Sauté until broccoli is very soft. About 10 minutes.
- Add penne pasta to the leftover boiling broccoli water. Do not skip this step and try to save time by boiling pasta on its own. This adds flavor to your pasta noodles. (If you are gluten-free add noodles or noodle of choice)

- When noodles are tender but not “done.” Scoop 1 cup of cooking water out and set aside. Drain noodles.
- Add noodles, water, and optional ingredients to the sauté pan. Stir frequently for about 5 minutes. (Water will absorb into noodles and broccoli)
- Sprinkle cheese, toss, and serve immediately!

"You are the salt of the earth. But if the salt loses its saltiness, how can it be made salty again? It is no longer good for anything, except to be thrown out and trampled underfoot. You are the light of the world. A town built on a hill cannot be hidden. Neither do people light a lamp and put it under a bowl. Instead they put it on its stand, and it gives light to everyone in the house. In the same way, let your light shine before others, that they may see your good deeds and glorify your Father in heaven."

(Matthew 5:13-16)

From Empty Void to Overflowing Vessel

By Lori Alderson Shafer

Growing up, I can't remember a time that "church" wasn't part of our family routine. It was a given every Sunday, and we were all involved, in some form or another, with weekly church activities. After high school, college partying took priority and, well, God took the back seat. I saw myself becoming the "black sheep" of the family and was pretty much disgusted with my family's attempts to guilt me back to church. My law school years didn't lend themselves to much in the way of church attendance either, although people were always asking me about the bumper sticker on my car at the time, "Christians aren't Perfect, Just Forgiven." (The car had been my sisters for a time) Given the life that I was living then, I'd say there was more truth to the statement than I cared to ponder.

After law school, I found myself in a new career, and although I had just achieved one of my goals, I couldn't help but feel that I was missing something. I just didn't quite know what that "something" was. I just knew that there was a "hole" in my life. My sister seemed to have it all together, so for several years I followed where she attended church, got involved in Sunday School, Bible studies and young adult activities, met a bunch of great new people in love with the Lord, but still never quite felt like I had found what I seemed to be longing for. I had become more than a "C & E"er, but I would eventually find myself falling back into old habits which, more often than not, would mean sleeping in on Sunday mornings.

I finally met and, after what must have been the longest courtship in history, married my husband. We didn't attend church regularly, although we had both grown up in Christian homes. After our children were born, I decided that it was time that we got back to church and brought our kids up in the right environment. I at least wanted my children to have the opportunity to know about God and maybe have a better relationship with Him than I had. A glossy mailer caught my attention, and the informality of a young church meeting in a school cafeteria was the perfect mix. We went, we loved it, we had found our church home. Funny thing, but I still felt like there was something missing. After hearing about a course called ALPHA and being prodded by our new-found friends at the time to sign up, we took the plunge and decided to find out what it was all about - who knew, maybe it was just what I was looking for.

It was on a stormy Saturday afternoon in 2000, standing in the sanctuary of that church, where my "sanctuary" was transformed, forever. I have never really been able to find words adequate to describe what happened to me that afternoon, but I know, without a doubt, that the Holy Spirit became real to me that day. I had a conversion experience that literally changed my life. What I had been missing had now been filled with a new-found relationship that I don't think I ever realized was possible. It was amazing to discover that I had a best friend in Jesus.

In the months and years that have followed that day, I have been able to look back at so many times in my life when I can now see the hand of God at work, especially during my "desert" years, how He had stood guard over my heart and my mind and fought to ward off the enemy on far too many occasions, but most importantly, I am amazed that He has never given up on me. I came to the realization that for so many years growing up; I had simply gone through the motions, repeating prayers and honoring customs without truly understanding their meaning or significance. And to think all I had to do was pray and ask the Holy Spirit to come into my life. Funny thing, prayer - My mother told me that she had never stopped praying for me, that one day I would find my way back to church and to the Lord. I'm grateful that my mom lived long enough to see her prayers answered. And now, I can't seem ever to leave, nor do I want to.

Recipe from the Kitchen of

Lori Alderson Shafer

Heavenly Popcorn Snack

Serves 3-4 • Prep time: 20 min

Ingredients:

1 bag microwave popcorn (plain)
1 10 oz. bag Fritos corn chips
6 cups Kellogg's Corn Pops cereal
8-10 squares white bark coating (I usually use almond bark or white chocolate)

Directions:

- Pop the popcorn according to the package directions and place in a large bowl (I use my large Tupperware bowl with a lid).
- Remove as many of the unpopped kernels as possible.
- Add Fritos and Corn Pops cereal. Stir the mixture up a bit.
- In a separate Pyrex bowl or measuring cup, melt the white bark squares in the microwave according to the package instructions (it's usually a minute, stir, another 30 seconds, stir, and repeat until completely melted - I do NOT recommend the squares that come in a heatable container as it tends to burn easily).
- Pour over popcorn mixture, coating entire mixture (I pour about 1/3 of the bark into the dry mixture, mix, pour another 1/3, mix until the dry mixture is completely coated).
- Cover the bowl and place in the refrigerator for approximately 5-10 minutes.
- Remove from the refrigerator, stir the mixture and, if necessary, place back in the refrigerator for another 5-10 minutes to allow the bark to harden. After the bark appears to have sufficiently hardened, remove from the refrigerator and store in an airtight container until ready to serve (but do NOT leave the mixture in the refrigerator after hardened).
- Please eat responsibly as this is sinfully addicting :)

Breakfast Casserole

Serves 8-10 • Cook time: 45 min • Prep time: 25 min

Ingredients:

1 lb. sausage, browned and drained
10-12 eggs, beaten
1 1/2 lb. cups shredded cheese (I like mexican blend or asiago)
2 cups milk
1 package of croutons (any flavor, but seasoned is best)
Salsa/Picante Sauce
Sour cream
sliced jalapenos

Directions:

- After browning and draining sausage, place in a large mixing bowl.
- Add beaten eggs, milk and cheese, and mix.
- Pour into a 9" x 13" baking dish (glass is best - if you use a metal pane, grease the pan first).
- Add the package of croutons to top of mixture and press into the mixture to completely coat with the mixture (I often add a little more grated cheese before covering).
- Cover with foil and place in refrigerator overnight.
- Remove from refrigerator for about 15 min. before baking.
- Bake covered at 325° for approximately 45 min., or until mixture is slightly browned and bubbling. (Sometimes I uncover the pan and continue to bake for another 5-10 min. or until knife or toothpick inserted into the center comes out clean.).
- Cut and serve with a topping of salsa/Picante sauce, sour cream and/or sliced jalapenos.

Sausage Biscuits Serves

4 dz. • Cook time: 20 min. • Prep time: 15 min

Ingredients:

1 lb. shredded sharp cheddar cheese
1 lb. Uncooked bulk port sausage (Jimmy Dean's Hot is good, or deer sausage)
3 cups dry Bisquick mix

Directions;

- Allow grated cheese (best to grate a block of cheese) and sausage to be at room temperature.
- In a large bowl, mix cheese, sausage and mix until it is well blended (easiest to use your hands - messy but helps get it thoroughly mixed).
- Form into nickel-size balls.
- Place on an ungreased cookie sheet and bake at 350° for about 20 min.
- Best served warm.
- These freeze beautifully and are best reheated in a slow oven.

"For I know the plans I have for you," declares the Lord,
"plans to prosper you and not to harm you,
plans to give you hope and a future."

(Jeremiah 29:11)

Crafting a Faithful Heart

By Michelle D Howe

It's was a Wednesday morning, and I had just finished my Holy Yoga class when I received the call from my mom. She said, "Aunt Valerie's breath has changed, and they think she is going to go today." "What," I said surprised. Hospice had just come in on Monday, and though it was towards the end, no one thought it would happen that fast. We had even planned to visit that weekend to say goodbye.

I took a breath and thought about the verse I had shared in my class that morning. I felt the tug of the Spirit to call my Uncle and read the verse over my Aunt Valerie. Oh, that was so hard and seemed impossible. I cried out, "Lord, help me through this!"

As I arrived home, I went straight back to my backyard wooden swing that overlooks the lake. I sat down, dialed the number, and my Uncle Bill answered. He was crying overcome by how quickly she spiraled. I told him my request, and he said, "Ok, I'm going to put the phone up next to her ear." I read these words to her:

"Let all that I am praise the Lord; with my whole heart, I will praise His holy name. Let all that I am praise the Lord; may I never forget the good things He done for me. He forgives all my sins and heals all my diseases. He redeems me from death and crowns me with love and tender mercies. He fills my life with good things. My youth is renewed like the eagle's!" (Psalm 103:1-5 NLT)

Uncle Bill came on the phone and said, "She heard you!" We visited for a moment more than hung up the phone. I began to sob with overwhelming sadness. My last memory of my favorite Aunt Valerie was her patting breath as I read these words over her. She was taking her last breathes here to enter into the arms of the Breath of Life.

The emotions of grief are real, and I walked through it like no other year of my life in 2018. But I didn't do it alone! God knew. He prepared the support community. He prepared my heart. He prepared the table.

This table was set long ago with a table cloth woven with a legacy of faithful women. The foundation of my faith in Jesus Christ started with generations of women on my mom's side. Even though I didn't necessarily grow up in church, God was woven into my DNA, and I'm so grateful!

I came to Christ when I was nineteen years old. At the time, a sophomore in college, I was living in a state of darkness amongst a mental and sexually abusive relationship. I didn't realize it at the time but looking back it was very unhealthy. It was God's people that drew me in – their light, their love, and grace. You see, I was invited to a church event, and this one event shifted my life.

The women in my life, my grandmother, my mom, and my aunt are all the crafters of my faith too. They prayed for me. They were my example. They loved deeply and without regard. They served well their families and communities. They created and gave back.

My grandmother passed on December 7, 2015 (my birthday) and at her funeral, I learned more about how she loved and served her community. She shared the gospel. She sang in the choir. She ran her own business and gave back. I loved my grandmother but didn't truly know her. We spent holidays with her and my grandfather but no real quality time necessarily.

My Aunt Valerie as mentioned she passed February 21, 2018. She was my favorite Aunt. Ten years younger than my Mom, she was fun-loving, creative, successful, a dreamer, and a risk-taker. Everything about my Aunt that I loved, and relate to today. I too am these things, and she was my greatest cheerleader and mentor. After retiring from the corporate world at the young age of 46, my Aunt and Uncle moved to their dream farm in the middle of Florida. Not too many years later, she started a ministry called The Faithful Crafter, where she designed beautiful stationery pieces for weddings and special events. She always adorned each piece with God's word.

My Mom is the most positive encouraging woman I've ever known. Always there throughout my life loving me no matter what. We have had some scares over the years with her health and a car accident, but through it all, my Mom remains diligent to love and give of herself without complaint. I don't think I have ever heard my Mom speak ill will to anyone. She has the eyes of Jesus to see the hurting and bring love and light into their life.

I am the legacy of these three women, and it's an honor to carry this on. The verse I live by is 1 Corinthians 6:19-20 that says, "Do you not know that your bodies are temples of the Holy Spirit, who is in you, whom you have received from God? You are not your own; you were bought at a price." In short, my daily prayer or mantra is "My Life Is Not My Own!" What this means to me is my life belongs to Christ, so use it to serve others and to bring Glory to God. Also, when I step out in faith to live out my God-given purpose, it opens up the opportunity for you to live yours. We are all crafted by the Great Designer for a purpose, and whether God is woven into your legacy or not, you can be the first to weave that thread.

The table was set for me by my family and church. Now it's up to you and me to keep inviting – our children, friends, co-workers, neighbors and whoever God places in our path to the table crafted with His acceptance, love, light, and grace. We were never meant to walk this life alone. Find your community and find the love of Christ waiting to heal the grief and the hurt.

Recipes from the Kitchens of
Michelle D. Howe's Family

"Kids-Can-Help" French Toast

Serves 4-6 • Cook time: 10 min • Prep time: 15 mins

Ingredients:

4 eggs
3 tsp. sugar
1 cup milk
1/2 tsp. of cinnamon (more if wanted)
Slices of bread (stale bread works great)

Directions:

- Break eggs into a bowl.
- Add sugar, milk, cinnamon, and beat.
- Soak bread in the egg mixture.
- If you want to add more cinnamon to mixture, it's ok.
- Put in frying pan and brown on each side.
- Serve with maple syrup or jelly.

Corn Pudding

Serves 8 • Cook time: 45 min • Prep time: 10 mins

Ingredients:

1 can of whole kernel corn (15 oz)
1 can of creamed style corn (15 oz)
8 oz sour cream
1 stick of soft margarine or butter
1 egg
2 Tbsp. of sugar
1 box of Jiffy corn muffin mix

Directions:

- Preheat oven to 400°
- In a large bowl, mix with a mixer both cans of corn then add sour cream.
- In a separate smaller bowl, mix butter, egg, and sugar.
- Add egg mixture to the corn mixture.
- Fold in into a large bowl until blended.
- Finally, add corn muffin mix in and again fold into the rest of the mixture.
- Use cooking spray to coat the casserole dish. For best results, use a glass casserole dish
- Place mixture into the casserole dish and then into the oven for 45 minutes.

Cranberry Casserole

Serves 8-10 • Cook time: 45 min • Prep time: 15 mins

Ingredients:

1 package of raw cranberries
1 cup sugar (white)
3 cups raw apple (unpeeled & chopped)
1/2 cup walnuts
1 uncooked oatmeal
1 stick of melted butter
1/2 cup brown sugar

Directions:

- Grease the bottom of a casserole dish.
- In a bowl, combine cranberries, chopped apples, walnuts, and white sugar.
- Spread out into the casserole dish.
- Now mix oatmeal, melted butter, and brown sugar in a bowl.
- Spread crumble over the top.
- Bake at 325° for 45 minutes.

"Do you not know that your bodies are temples
of the Holy Spirit, who is in you,
whom you have received from God?
You are not your own; you were bought at a price.
Therefore, honor God with your bodies."

(1 Corinthians 6:19-20)

My Jonah Moment

By Shurayah Wilkerson

Obedience isn't easy.

It goes against what our stubbornness and selfishness want to do. Just watch any child, and you'll quickly see that.

For over 10 years, I was having a "Jonah moment," as I like to call it. Clearly knowing what the Lord wanted me to do but choosing to go the other way. Let's be honest; it was more of a very long season.

Instead of listening to the gentle nudge of my savior, I was crippled by thoughts of fear and inadequacy.

It wasn't easy to leave my job of 10 years and pursue a ministry I have been trying just as long to avoid. It wasn't easy to choose to be faithful to my husband when times were tough. It wasn't easy to step into something I had to 100% rely on God to carry me through because I wasn't qualified.

It wasn't easy to obey…But it in the obedience that's where we learn to let God supply the fullness of our heart's desire for safety and wholeness.

Why do we disobey in the first place?

From fear?

Thoughts that we know better than God?

Could it be that you believe your needs won't be met?

I thought about all those things. But when I slowed down enough and took a step of faith, EVERYTHING shifted.

Just like Jonah, when I chose the right path of obedience, lives have been changed.

Marriages restored (including my own)

Faith increased

Intimacy with God rekindled

Souls came together in worship

Strangers turned into friends that become warriors on behalf of each other

Kingdom of heaven impacted

My own stubborn and stoney heart has softened

And my purpose had become clear...
I'm not here on this earth to wake, labor and rest but to make a difference.

I'd like you to sit with yourself and wait for the Lord to show you where you're turning a deaf ear to Him. Maybe it's an area you're channeling the stubbornness of Jonah and blatantly saying, "NO! I won't go there."

Pray - Where can I be humble and teach me to be quick to obey.

"For just as through the disobedience of the one man, the many were made sinners, so also through the obedience of the one man, the many will be made righteous" (Romans 5:19 NIV).

So, what did I learn from all this?

Be quick to obey. Watch as He blesses through the obedience.

"I give all to follow your revelation-light; I will not delay obeying" (Psalm 119:60 TPT).

Recipes from the Kitchens of
The Wilkerson's

Humble Pie

Serves 8 • Cook time: 35 min • Prep time: 45

Ingredients:

Crust:

1 2/3 cups unbleached all-purpose flour
1/4 tsp. salt
1/2 tsp. baking powder
1/4 cup vegetable shortening
1/4 cup butter
1 large egg
1 to 2 tsp. of water

Filling:

1 1/2 cups fresh or frozen berries
2 to 3 peaches, peeled and sliced
2/3 cup sugar
1/4 cup unbleached all-purpose flour

Garnish:

1/4 cup sparkling white sugar

Directions:

Crust:

- Whisk together the dry ingredients and cut in the vegetable shortening and butter.
- Whisk the egg and water together, then sprinkle over the flour mixture.
- Knead together, adding a bit of extra water to make the dough cohesive, if necessary.
- Form the dough into a disk, wrap it well, and refrigerate for 30 minutes.

Filling:

Toss the berries and peaches with the sugar and flour. If the berries are frozen, don't thaw them. If they're dry (like blueberries), run them under water first; this makes it easier to combine them thoroughly with the sugar mixture.

Assembly:

- Preheat oven to 425°F.
- Roll the crust into a 13" to 14" round, and transfer it to a pizza pan or baking sheet.
- Mound the sugared fruit in the center of the crust, leaving about a 3 1/2" margin of bare crust all the way around.
- Fold the crust up over the fruit, pinching or pleating as you go, leaving 5" or so of fruit exposed in the center.
- Spritz the crust with water and sprinkle with sparkling white sugar, if desired.
- Bake the pie for about 35 minutes, or until the filling is bubbling and the edges of the crust are brown.
- Remove it from the oven, and cool for 15 to 30 minutes before cutting into wedges.

"If you bow low in God's awesome presence,
He will eventually exalt you as you leave the timing in His hands.
Pour out all your worries and stress upon Him and leave them
there, for He always tenderly cares for you."

(1 Peter 5:6-7)

God's Face in a Woman

By Yasinta Nyaika-Maliro

I am a young woman whose life has not been perfect. I try every day of my life to make it better. The past week as I kept reflecting on my life's path, I came to a point where I realized that God wants my perfect imperfections to help to perfect the world. I believe He is happier when my wounded heart is healing the wounded healing.

I grew up being so close to my father until his death when I was fifteen. My father is the one who introduced me to Christ. Like many other young people, I liked singing and dancing. One Saturday afternoon when I was getting prepared to go for a dance, my father asked me to accompany him to church to pray. When we got inside the church, He said, talk to the Lord, and tell Him all that bothers you. We spent three hours in silence, and when we got out, I felt an extraordinary happiness within me. Three years later, my father passed on to be with the Lord. A week before his death, we had a lengthy discussion of how he would be proud if I were to continue to work hard in school, and my make it into the University.

My mother switched her role as a mother and became a father too. I had seen my mother struggling with her life to get herself back in pieces when she lost her husband. Despite her agonies, she tried all she could to be as close to me as possible. My father's death made me develop bitterness. I had tough times forgiving those that had wronged me. I never trusted and loved anyone. I misused alcohol and dated different men.

My mother taught me how to forgive others. I still remember how I stayed for over a year without talking to my classmate because I felt he talked to me baldly in front of my friends. One summer holiday my classmate called on over the phone to apologize and to make peace with me and refused to take his apology. When my mother listened to our conversation, talked to me of the need for forgiveness, and helped me to forgive myself too.

On several occasions, I never listened to my mother's advice. It turned out that all things never worked for me, and I still went back to let her know how destitute I was at that point.

Many times, in my tears, telling her how things never worked out for me, my mother got hurt too, and I cried with me. Each time, she hugged me and made sure to be there and told me that it would be alright with me.

Today, I sit down and look at all these occasions, and reflect on how bad I have been as a living creature. The past year of my life, I have dedicated my life to the Devine Mercy Apostolate, a grouping of people who believe in Gods infinite Mercy. My association with this grouping has deepened my love and trust in God's endless love and mercy. My past inflictions tortured my mother, but every time, she welcomed me back as her child. If my mother has this endless love for my life, how about the type of Love and Mercy that God has for me? Is God's face, a woman's face, or a mother's face?

"Bad as you are, you know how to give good things to your children. How much more, then, will your Father in heaven give good things to those who ask Him" (Matthew 7:11 NLV). If my mother, as sinful as she is, she has the ability to give her love to her children, how more would God, our Lord, Love us?

Today, I live a happy life, knowing that my life has been saved by His Love and Mercy. Even though the world may look at me with my past logs, my Lord has saved me and got my life.

In His Mercy, I live.

Yasinta

Recipe from the Kitchen of

Yasinta Nyaika-Marlilro

Conquering Devils Temptation

Serves The Whole World • Cook time: 1 hr • Prep time: 1 hr

Ingredients:

Prayer
Love
Honesty
Integrity
Proclamation

Directions:

- Set aside some time to pray every day in your room or in the holy place
- Thank the Lord for the gift of Life and all the graces He has bestowed upon your life
- Tell the Lord of all your needs and worries
- Be honest enough to pour your weaknesses unto Him
- Promise to do well because of your imperfections
- Try to live your words and promise made to God your Lord
- Believe that He will give you all your needs
- Proclaim His greatness to others
- Wait upon the Lord and see and enjoy His Love on your Life

"For God, who commanded the light to shine out of darkness, hath shined in our hearts, to give the light of the knowledge of the glory of God in the face of Jesus Christ."

(2 Corinthians 4:6)

I'll Love Him Forever

By Jamie Taylor

Inside I'm still the little blonde headed girl with the big smile who has loved Jesus for as long as I can remember. Things have become much more complicated over the years, and my faith has been tested and tried. Just last year, I found myself looking for a God I couldn't see anymore and begging Him to speak if indeed He still existed. I knew He did; I just needed to be reminded.

Mine has been a life full of adventure and sacrifice. I moved with my family to Africa when I was just seven years old, our normal routines uprooted by the unfamiliar territory of missionary life. The challenges we faced during our years on that beautiful continent were nothing compared to the meaningful moments we enjoyed. I learned a lot about myself and God during those formative years. Armed robbery, loss, and upheaval were part of my story. And yet, I would not erase the comfort of God that came with the crisis.

I've been learning lessons my whole life. I've had it good, but it hasn't been easy. Anxiety and depression became one of my biggest struggles. I felt alone and afraid many times and didn't think I could share my struggles with anyone. I begged God to deliver me from my intense fear miraculously, but He has not seen fit to remove my human tendency toward anxiety. I've worried at times that I haven't had enough faith, mostly because that message permeated my mind from different sources. Perhaps you have had a similar experience. Maybe you have felt alone and distanced from people around you. I can assure you there is still hope. I've had to walk a different path than instantaneous healing. My heavenly Father has walked beside me as I've prayed, sought counseling, and faithfully taken medication. I'm the picture of a working faith, a slow healing process. And it's okay. The miracle is still breathtakingly beautiful.

Last year when I felt like I couldn't see God's hand in my life, I knew what I had to do. I'd learned from my many trips through the Bible that others before me had struggled to believe God at times in their lives too. I also knew that they had chosen to keep walking when life was hard. They didn't quit when the bumps threatened to knock them off course. They relied on the God they couldn't see until their eyes caught up with their faith. So that's what I did too. I kept praying. I kept reading my Bible. I continued to lean on the promises of God even on the days when I felt abandoned. Months went by without much hope. But I kept walking.

So many amazing things have happened since then. He began to whisper slowly at first, and then His voice grew loud. I felt Him with me as I climbed out of that dark valley. I trusted Him before I saw Him, and He was faithful to show up. My relationship with Christ is deeper now that I've endured that test. I know it won't be the last time I will have to journey through tough trails, but I am more confident than ever that He will never leave me or forsake me. I'll love Him as long as I have breath and into eternity.

Recipe from the Kitchen of

Jamie Taylor

Gluten-Free Applesauce Muffins

Serves 12

Ingredients:

1/2 cup sugar
1/2 cup brown sugar
1/2 cup canola oil
1/2 cup applesauce
2 eggs
1 tsp. vanilla
1/2 cup sour cream
1 1/2 cups GF flour (I like Bob's Red Mill 1 to 1 blend)
1/2 tsp. soda
1/2 tsp. salt
1/2 tsp. baking powder
1 tsp. cinnamon

Directions:

- Preheat oven to 350°
- Mix sugars and oil;
- Add applesauce, eggs, vanilla, and sour cream; beat well.
- Add combined dry ingredients and mix well (at least thirty seconds).
- Pour into either a greased muffin pan or a greased loaf pan.
- For muffins: Bake at 350° for 15 minutes
- For loaf pan: Bake at 325° for 45 minutes or until center is done.

Crustless Egg Casserole (Gluten-Free)

Serves 8-10

Ingredients:

3 Tbsp. oil (divided)
2 Tbsp. butter
18 eggs, beaten
1/2 white onion, finely diced
2 cups mushrooms, chopped
6 cups spinach
3 cups cheese (your preference)
1 lb. turkey sausage (I use Jennie O)
Garlic salt, black pepper, cayenne pepper (to taste)
1/2-3/4 cup half and half

Directions:

- Preheat oven to 350°.
- Grease a 9x13 inch pan.
- Sauté onions in 2 T. oil for 2 minutes.
- Add mushrooms and sauté until tender.
- Add in spinach and season with salt and pepper. Set aside.
- Brown the turkey sausage in 1 T. oil. Add 2 Tbsp. butter at the end of cooking and stir well.
- Whisk the eggs, add half and half, 2 dashes of cayenne pepper, garlic salt, and black pepper and set aside.
- Layer the veggie mixture, 1/3 of the sausage and 1 cup of cheese. Pour 1/3 of the egg mixture over the layers.
- Repeat this process two more times.
- Bake at 350° for 45-50 minutes. Let sit for 10 minutes before serving.

Chocolate Layered Delight (Gluten-Free)

Serves: 10-12

Ingredients:

1 package GF chocolate sandwich cookies
1/3 cup butter
1 8-oz package cream cheese, softened
Large container of cool whip (not frozen)
1 cup powdered sugar
1 small package vanilla instant pudding
1 small package chocolate instant pudding
3 cups milk
1/2 cup chocolate chips, finely chopped

Directions:

- Crush the package of sandwich cookies, reserve about ¼ cup and add it to the ½ cup chopped chocolate chips.
- Combine the crushed cookies and the butter.
- Mix well and press into the bottom of a 9x13 inch pan.
- Chill for twenty minutes.
- Meanwhile, combine cream cheese and powdered sugar.
- Add 1 cup of the cool whip and mix.
- Spoon cream cheese mixture over the chilled crust. Chill again.
- While this chills, combine the pudding mixes and three cups of milk.
- Add this to the layers in the pan.
- Cover the pudding with cool whip.
- Sprinkle the chocolate chip/cookies over the top and chill for at least an hour before serving.

"Say to those with fearful hearts, 'Be strong, do not fear; your God will come, He will come with vengeance; with divine retribution He will come to save you.'"

(Isaiah 35:4)

When God Answers Prayers

By Ashley Farrar

October 6, 2002, is a day that will forever be the best day of my life. It was the day I truly realized what the scars in Jesus' hands and feet really meant and understood the verse John 3:16 and what it spoke over my life. I surrendered it all that day, knowing that from that moment on, no matter what happened in my life, I was safe. I was free. And I was a daughter of the King. There were numerous storms raging in my life at that time, and hope and peace were things I desperately prayed for. Looking back now, I can see God's hand in every storm helping me through, resulting in lessons learned and a deeper faith.

I had two wonderful Christian parents, along with the best grandmother, who all poured into me and taught me right from wrong, and to always treat everyone with respect. I thought I was the luckiest little girl on the planet. But my world was turned upside down the summer of 1996, and my life would forever be changed. My precious grandmother passed away, which meant that my best friend was suddenly ripped away from my life. I was eleven years old and didn't fully understand what losing her meant. I just knew my heart was broken, and I wasn't sure how to fix it. Over the next few months, my battle with depression would begin, and before long, I started searching for anything that would take the pain and emptiness I felt inside away. I just wanted the pain to stop. I had no way of knowing that my life was going to change once more, just a couple months later drastically.

On Labor Day in 1996, a family friend, who I adored and looked to as another father figure, began molesting me. Being eleven years old, I knew what he was doing wasn't right, but I didn't understand the seriousness of it or the lifelong effects it would have on me until many years later. I was threatened by him and told that if I spoke of what was happening, he would make sure no one believed me. I truly believed that he meant every word. I had always trusted him and had grown up thinking that he would never do anything to hurt me. I never thought he would have done anything like that to me. With the depression from my grandmother's death, the abuse added to it made it unbearable. I was terrified to tell anyone, so for 6 years; I kept this secret. In those 6 years, the emotional pain I experienced was almost more than I could bear. I had never in my life felt so alone. I was just a child, but my innocence was gone forever. My depression worsened, and I soon found myself turning to pills to numb the pain. I would take any that I could find or buy from other students at school; not even caring what they were. When the pills no longer seemed to be helping me, I started drinking. I knew that both of those were dangerous behaviors, but I had become so reckless at that time I didn't care. The only thing I cared about was taking the pain I was feeling on the inside away. It seemed that nothing I tried would work in numbing the pain for very long. It was as if I needed more and more things to control the pain and rage inside.

My attitude changed drastically, and my mom and I began fighting all the time. She just didn't understand what was going on with me. I was keeping them in the dark. As I came into my sophomore year of high school, I began cutting and burning myself. I had learned about self-injury from a TV show and prayed that it would be the thing that helped me. I was so depressed; I couldn't see or understand the severity of the destructive behaviors that I was engaging in.

Even with all these things, I was still drowning in emotional pain and became suicidal. I felt that the world would be better off without me. So, one day, I took an entire bottle of pills at bedtime and went to bed. It is by the grace of God that He let me live. I honestly feel that because of the years I had been abusing pills; my body had built up a tolerance to them. I, luckily, was just very sick for a few days. I somehow managed to keep all of this from my parents. I knew that it would have destroyed them, and I just felt that they didn't need to know what was happening to me. I had been so brainwashed by this man that I truly thought no one would believe me anyway if I confided in them.

Looking back in reflection of those years, God carried me through many dangerous situations, and He kept me here for a reason. My story wasn't, and isn't, over. I was seventeen years old when the abuse came to an end. I was so broken. And I wasn't sure where to turn. I didn't feel like I had anyone in my corner fighting for me. I remember praying for God to get me out of my situation and let me be loved for who I was. I wanted love without conditions.

God did answer my prayers; in ways I never thought possible. God sent me angels on earth to love me, unconditionally; the very love I had craved for years. I would love to say that I recognized those blessings right away, but I didn't. In fact, I spent my entire 20's running from my past, and from those God had placed in my life to help put the broken pieces back together. My answer came in the form of a very patient man and his sweet mother.

I met the other half of my heart, the piece that was missing, in the summer of 2002. I had just graduated from high school, was working as a nursing assistant, and would soon be a full-time college student. I wanted to get a good education and move far away from where I was living. I truly thought I could run from the previous seventeen years, and the deep emptiness and pain I felt, Oh, the naivety of a child.

When I first met my husband, I was severely depressed and had major trust issues. I felt as if everyone around me only liked me if I gave them something, a byproduct of the abuse, no doubt. But he remained gentle and proved that I was worthy of love and respect, even though many days I treated him horribly. The October 6, 2002 date that I mentioned above happened because of his encouragement and care for me. We had only met 3 months prior to that, but he immediately began sharing Jesus with me. I had been in church my whole life, but God used my husband to help nudge me to make the greatest decision I would ever make. I never looked back after that day. He and I share a strong marriage, and he supports my ministry. He is still patient with me when the devil tries to trip me up and send me back into that pattern of thinking that I am unlovable and a failure.

The other angel in my story is my sweet mother in law. Without her love and guidance, I wouldn't be where I am today. You probably wouldn't be reading these words. For the seventeen years thus far, I have been a part of her family, she has loved me as a daughter, even when my actions haven't been so loveable. She has refused to give up on me. She has held me while the tears have fallen freely. When I try to run from my past, or when my depression hits hard, she is right there to listen and remind me why it is important to stay focused. She corrected me by using Biblical truth when I had needed it, even when I didn't want to hear it. She was by my side for many of the most important days of my life, from my baptism, the marriage to her son, the birth of her grandchild, and the day I stood before 200 women and shared my story publicly for the first time. And she was there the day my mom went to her Heavenly home. She stood by my side, holding me, and never let go. She encourages me every day to keep pushing and to keep sharing my story and faith with others, even when I feel like I am not good at it. When I am down, God uses her to help me get back up. I put her through a lot for the first ten years of my husband and my relationship. I feared a close relationship and of trusting someone to help me through the trials of life. I thought I could do it alone and she showed me I was wrong. I thank God every day; she never gave up on me. Because of her willingness to let God work in and through her, I am a better wife, mother, daughter, and child of God. She truly is my best friend and angel on earth. For the rest of my life, I will be thankful for the impact that she has made on my life, and that she will always be a part of my story.

One of the lessons that I had to learn was that no material thing or person can ever completely fill you up. The deepest thirst of our soul can only be quenched by God. People in your life can make the trials easier to walk through, but true comfort and security will only come through and be filled by God alone.

I thank God every day for His Mercy and Grace in my life. I am truly thankful for all that I have been through. I wouldn't understand what grace is if it hadn't of been for the abuse and all it caused. And I certainly don't think I would have learned to love and be loved if it hadn't of been the trials and storms God allowed me to walk through. I wouldn't appreciate the blessings God has given me. I have always thought the saying, "If you want rainbows, you have to withstand the rain" is true. If you want to understand God's love, mercy, and grace, you must walk through the rain. In the trials and storms of life, we must remain faithful that God knows what He is doing and that He is holding us close as we journey on. Nothing that you or I will ever go through in this life is in vain. Every moment of our life has a purpose, and He will use it for His Glory. We must remain obedient, even when we don't understand.

These days, I am heavily involved in ministry. Helping people is what I am passionate about. I care deeply about their heart and their stories. I spend my days sharing Jesus with anyone who will listen. I find great joy in praying for others and walking through the journey of life with them. Life is much sweeter when lived with others. I get up every day and ask God to lead me to where I am needed the most. God promised in Romans 8:28 that He would use everything I have gone through, and will go through, for good. In Jeremiah 29:11, He tells me that He knows the plans that He has for my life and that He won't harm me, but will instead prosper me. That is my motivation to get up every day and go out into the world to be a vessel for Him. There are so many hurting souls walking around, begging for understanding, and begging for answers. Being faithful and obedient just might mean that you or I might be the answer to someone's prayer. We might be the one God uses to bring that person to Him. Be obedient, love God with your whole heart, and watch what He does for the Kingdom through you.

Recipe from the Kitchen of

Ashley G. Farrar

Fresh Apple Cake

Serves 16-24 • Cook time: 75 min • Prep time: 30 min

Ingredients:

3 cups chopped apples
3 cups plain flour
1 1/2 cups sugar
1 cup oil
3 eggs
1 tsp. salt
1 tsp. baking soda
4 Tbsp. margarine
2 tsp. cinnamon
1 tsp. nutmeg
1/2 tsp. allspice
1 cup black walnuts or pecans
2 tsp. vanilla

Directions:

- In a bowl mix apples, vanilla, nuts, and cinnamon.
- In a separate bowl sift flour, baking soda, salt, nutmeg, and allspice.
- In a separate bowl mix sugar, oil, eggs, and margarine.
- Beat until blended.
- Fold in apple mixture and stir well.
- Pour into a greased Bundt or pound cake pan.
- Bake at 325° for 1 hour and 15 minutes (or until a toothpick comes out clean).

Glaze

1 cup of confectioners' sugar
2 Tbsp. honey
3-4 Tbsp. milk
Mix well and drizzle over warm cake.

"And we know that in all things
God works for the good of those who love Him,
who have been called according to His purpose."

(Romans 8:28)

With Tables Between Us

By Sheila Taylor

As a little girl, I dreamed about a home filled with love, joy, laughter, and security. A home far different than the one I grew up in. As a child, from the outside looking in, we seemed ordinary and sometimes happy. We, the occupants, worked very hard to keep up those pretenses. From the inside, the man of the house was either absent or abusive, the marriage was a disaster, money was always scarce, and the stress level was always high. No matter how often we moved to different houses or states, the new walls didn't change our reality.

Despite the tragic circumstances of my childhood and the constant lack of money, there was a thread of peace, maybe even hope, that wound its way through my mother's kitchen to those who ate her food. My good memories are mostly tied to her kitchen and the delicious dishes my Mom managed to create with a few simple ingredients and all the love in her heart. On a fairly regular basis, we tidied up the house and our lives long enough to feed people around our table.

As my husband and I have shared twenty-eight years and three children together, our home has been a place of love, grace, peace, and safety. It's also been a place of learning and growing through hardships and living forgiven and healed. It is our family's purpose that from within the ordinary walls of our home and with ordinary tables between us, the redeeming love of an extraordinary God is served up in heaps, right along with bowls of delicious food.

Recipes from the Kitchen of

Sheila Taylor

Sheila's Potato Salad

Serves 15-20

Ingredients:

8-10 large Russet Idaho Potatoes
5-6 hard-boiled eggs
1/2 onion, sautéed
1 package bacon, cooked and chopped to bits
1 cup dill pickles, chopped
2 cups cheddar cheese, shredded
mayonnaise (not Miracle Whip)
pickle juice
paprika
salt & pepper

Directions:

- Bake potatoes until fork tender.
- Once cooled down, scoop out the inside of the potatoes and adding the hard-boiled eggs, smash together, leaving smaller chunks of potato and egg.
- To the mix, add sautéed onions, cooked bacon, chopped pickles, and shredded cheese.
- Stir in enough mayonnaise and pickle juice to reach your desired consistency.
- Season to taste, top with shredded cheese, and serve cold.
- This salad is my most requested for picnics, potlucks, parties, and even a wedding. You will notice the intentional lack of celery and mustard. I tell those who ask for the recipe that if they choose to add those two ingredients, it should no longer be called Sheila's Potato Salad.

Sheila's Alfredo Sauce

Serves 6

Ingredients:

1/2 cup butter
2 cups heavy cream
2 cloves garlic, crushed
3 cups parmesan cheese, freshly grated
1/2 cup parsley, finely chopped
1/2 cup basil, finely chopped
1 pkg cream cheese, softened

Directions:

- Melt butter in Dutch Oven.
- Add heavy cream and simmer for 5 minutes.
- Add garlic, parmesan cheese, and cream cheese; whisk until bubbly.
- Take off heat and stir in the herbs.
- Serve hot over your pasta of choice.
- Optional stir-ins: cooked chicken, cooked shrimp, sautéed mushrooms or vegetables.
- This dish is a tradition in our home for Valentine's Day, served alongside a heaping bowl of salad and warm crusty bread.

Mom's Brownies

Cook time: 20-25 min

Ingredients:

Brownies

1 cube butter, softened
1 cup sugar
4 eggs
1 tsp. vanilla
1 can Hershey's Chocolate Syrup
1 cup flour
1 tsp. salt

Frosting

1 1/2 Tbsp. butter
2 Tbsp. milk
1/2 cup sugar
1/2 pkg chocolate chips

Directions:

Brownie Directions:

- Cream butter and sugar together.
- Mix in eggs, separately.
- Add chocolate syrup and vanilla and mix well.
- Mix in flour and salt.
- Pour into a greased 9 x 13 pan.
- Bake at 350° for 20-25 minutes.

Frosting directions:

- In a medium saucepan, bring butter, milk, and sugar to a gentle boil. Be careful not to scorch, by stirring continually.
- Remove from heat and stir in the chocolate chips, until melted.
- Pour over warm brownies and allow frosting to set before serving.
- These are best served warm with a scoop of your favorite ice cream.

"I love each of you with the same love that the Father loves me.
You must continually let My love nourish your hearts.
If you keep My commands, you will live in My love,
just as I have kept My Father's commands, for I
continually live nourished and empowered by His love.
My purpose for telling you these things is so that the joy that I
experience will fill your hearts with overflowing gladness!"

(John 15:9-11, TPT)

The Misfit Doll

By Faith Morgan

When I was a little girl, I could not stand to play with Barbies. I could not relate to Ken and Barbie and their perfect little house, three kids, and dog. I related more to Dolly from the Island of the Misfit Toys.

Dolly Sue was a doll on the Island of the Misfit Toys, on the original Rudolph the Red Nose Reindeer.

At quick glance she seemed fine, no eyes missing, no tear in her dress, no stains on her body. But you see Dolly Sue was on The Island of Misfit Toys because of her broken identity.

My own identity was broken.

Dolly looked normal from the outside. I am sure when I was a child; I must have looked normal from the outside too. I was very smart, talkative and the best in my class at school. I laughed and played like kids my age. But, behind closed doors, in my tiny trailer, in the trailer park, my life was anything but normal.

Dolly Sue, like me and so many others, was broken on the inside. This brokenness presented as psychological problems, severe depression, low self-esteem, and a deep-rooted belief of being unlovable.

Dolly Sue had been abandoned by her mistress. That abandonment made her believe there was something deeply wrong and flawed in her. It was nothing Dolly Sue did by her own doing that caused such unbelievable damage to the inside of her soul. It was a result of not being loved, protected, or cared for by those she belonged to.

It was that abandonment that caused Dolly Sue to develop psychological and emotional issues.

My life was anything but normal growing up. I was so broken as a young girl. I lived in a home filled with chaos and fighting, violence, and abuse. Shame and secrets were my close friends. I had been sexually abused by my close family members and a friend of the family. My mother had been an incest survivor, and so, we didn't talk about it much. I had no place to run and was very alone.

My parents had broken childhoods too. They were teen parents and had many mouths to feed. I felt very unseen because I had five younger siblings that needed me. I found myself huddling with them in corners reciting The Lord's Prayer, that I had learned at Sunday school in our bedroom. Meanwhile, listening to our parents screaming and beating on each other.

Life was so unstable and unpredictable. We moved at least six times a year when my parents couldn't pay rent. I remembered one time living in a van at the creek and washing my clothes in the creek bed.

Childhood, for me, was a scary time. I remember pretending we were camping with flashlights and candles when our electricity would be cut off. My mom would heat up soup in a pot outside in the sun. The food stamps never seemed to last for the month, and it was not uncommon for us to depend on strangers for handouts.

As an adult, I now see why I related so much to Dolly Sue. I felt unseen, unloved, and abandoned. I tried all my life to fit in, fix myself, and to conform. I too wanted a place to belong even if it meant that in trying to belong, I had to constantly invent different versions of myself, and wear a different mask.

I still remember when abandonment and rejection entered into my story as an 11-year-old girl. I found myself custody of the state. I inherited the title of foster child and a ticket on the orphan train. I was taken from all and any family I had ever known. It seemed I would always have the identity of Dolly Sue. Something felt very broken in me, and I believed the lie of the enemy that I was unlovable.

Over the next 7 years, I would go through a string of homes, a stint at a mental hospital and even a short time at a woman's homeless shelter. I was a scared Dolly Sue for sure. I would cry out to Jesus. He was the man I was told about in the little children's Bible I had been given from Sunday school. "Jesus, please be my family."

What was worse was when I was finally adopted at fourteen. My new home turned out to be an avenue of more abuse. It was the worst kind, religious abuse. It left me so confused about God and His love for me. Again, I felt like Dolly Sue. I was deeply flawed damaged and therefore, unlovable.

Believing those lies of the enemy caused me to behave in ways that were reactive. It caused me to push away people that loved me because I would wonder what do they see in me? I would worry about them leaving me, and so I would end relationships and friendships first.

Fear and anxiety laid claim on my soul. Fear of rejection was real and not imagined. I had a fear of being vulnerable or speaking the truth. Shame and false guilt became my identity. I was lost for sure.

That early abandonment caused me to seek out wrong relationships, and unhealthy ways to fill up the emptiness in my little soul.

Not having a family of my own, or knowing my roots, history, or story caused a lot of pain and confusion in my life and sent me down a lot of broken dead-end roads.

I had very little and then eventually no contact with my birth family or any of my siblings, so I would cry at night wondering where they were and if they remembered me? Would I ever see them again?

Looking back, I now realize just how much these incidents changed me and the course of my life.

BUT…GOD.

Don't you love that? There is always a " but God" lined up for us in our stories. It is when God steps into your chaos, your confusion, your pain, and those shameful memories, and He holds out His hand and says, "COME, CHILD, let me show you something." He digs in the piles of our mess and lifts us up and out of the rubble.

That is what happened to me. When I got older, after a failed attempt at an abusive marriage, (broken people break people), I had run out of anyone that I thought could fill that deep void in me. I was desperate for the truth, to be set free, for a place of belonging.

That's when I found Jesus. I heard about a place for all the misfits. I heard of a table I was invited to just as I was. I learned God had adopted me, and He was a father to the orphans. Hallelujah!!!

God started to take my hand and walk me out of the darkness and into His glorious light.

I learned in His Word that I was not a foster child or unloved.

I was a daughter of the King. I was a daughter of the Star Breather, the Uncreated One.

He loved me and sent His Son to die for me. I was a daughter of the Light of the World. The Lord had called me His own.

Since then, I have been on a journey to rediscover who I was created to be; Before all the pain and brokenness. I am (I AM)'s.

Dear souls, what happened in your life to cause you to doubt who you are in your Father? Maybe it was a trespass of your innocence during childhood, and it makes you unable to look at yourself in the mirror? Maybe it's something that happened in your first relationship, or on a college campus? What is the thing that changed how you saw yourself?

Your Father wants you to step into the light. Jesus did not make broken things, but He specializes in fixing them.

The truth I needed to know and maybe you need to hear from one former misfit to another is there is a place for you at our Father's table. You have never been alone or left. You are not lost. Here His Truth, precious girl.

"He has carved you on the palms of His hands" (Isaiah 49:16 NIV).

"The hairs on your head are numbered" (Luke 12:7 NIV).

"He knows the plans He has for you, and they are for good, not evil" (Jeremiah 29:11 NIV).

"You formed my innermost being, shaping my delicate inside and my intricate outside,

and wove them all together in my mother's womb" (Psalm 139:13 TPT).

And my favorite,

"My father and mother abandoned me. I'm like an orphan! But you took me in and made me yours" (Psalm 27:10 TPT).

No matter what has tried to define you in life, in childhood, your adulthood or even now, shake it off in the Light of your Father.

Let His love define you.

The broken childhood, the lies, the opinions of others, the failed marriage, the broken dreams, your mistakes, they don't get to tell you who you are unless you allow it.

That addiction, the scale, the mirror, the abusive one-sided relationship, the loss of the job, none of them change who you are in your soul.

Wake up dear ones from the illusion of what happened to you, or what someone has said or thought about you.

Only one person gets to tell you who you are, and that is the one who imagined you and then created you. You are the Dreamers dream, the bride of a King.

You belong beloved, in your Father's Kingdom. COME. There is a place for you, and all the so-called deemed misfits of the world. Come to the table. He has saved a seat for you. Step into the Light Child. Let the truth of who He is, define who you are. God is not afraid of your mess. He wants to make it into a message of His grace and power of restoration. Amen

Recipe from the Kitchen of

Faith Morgan

Not Yo Mama's Banana Pudding

Serves 8

Ingredients:

1 (14-ounce) can sweetened condensed milk
1 (12-ounce) container frozen whipped topping thawed, or equal amount sweetened whipped cream
2 bags Pepperidge Farm Chessmen cookies
6 to 8 bananas, sliced
2 cups milk
1 (5-ounce) box instant French vanilla pudding
1 (8-ounce) package cream cheese, softened

Directions:

- Line the bottom of a 13 by 9 by 2-inch dish with 1 bag of cookies and layer bananas on top.
- In a bowl, combine the milk and pudding mix and blend well using a handheld electric mixer.
- Using another bowl, combine the cream cheese and condensed milk together and mix until smooth.
- Fold the whipped topping into the cream cheese mixture.
- Add the cream cheese mixture to the pudding mixture and stir until well blended.
- Pour the mixture over the cookies and bananas and cover with the remaining cookies.
- Refrigerate until ready to serve.

*"My father and mother abandoned me. I'm like an orphan!
But you took me in and made me yours."*

(Psalm 27:10 TPT)

Jesus the Redeemer

By Antoinette Martinez

My mother was one of 10 kids and was 15 when she got pregnant with me. I was born in the Westwood Projects in Denver, CO, on April 18th. I had young parents, and my mom and dad were still trying to figure out who they were. My dad was a drug dealer and professional thief, he has spent most of his life and mine in prison. My mom left him when I was 6 and began to date a new man, and I got a new brother as a result of that relationship. My mom dated this man for well over 8 years, and for those 8 years, I saw my mother get physically, mentally, and verbally abused by him pretty much every day.

As the oldest child, it became my responsibility to protect my younger sister and brother; it was also my responsibility to call the cops and my grandparents almost daily because he would beat my mom so bad it would leave her unconscious in most cases. I used to hate to go home with them because I already knew what was going to happen. I used to cry and cry and beg my Grandma to let me stay with her, and she used to always tell me, "Mija you need to go take care of your sister and your brother." So very reluctantly I would go, and I would end up having to call 911 and my Grandpa, and he would come to pick us up.

I spent most of my younger years living with my grandparents because my mom was young, and her dysfunctional relationship would result in us moving in and out of my grandparents' house several times a year. By the time I was in 6th grade, I had already been enrolled in and out of 21 different schools. I never had the chance to develop friendships because as soon as I would try, we would have to move again.

I had a very tough childhood, and at the age of 7, my mom's sister began to take me to church with her. It was an old-time Pentecostal church. This is where I had my first experience with Jesus. I was saved and began to attend church with my aunt and uncle as often as I could. I can remember times where I would be home with my grandparents, and my mom would be gone, and it would be late at night, and my stomach would hurt because I was so worried about her. Was she okay? Was she hurt? Was she coming home? I would look out the window and pray and ask God to bring her home safe.

During these years my grandparents were so special to me. My grandma always showed me love, and I developed such a bond with her. I can remember my grandma waking up every morning to make tortillas for the family. She would make them for breakfast, lunch, and dinner. I can recall all of us grabbing tortillas from her stack to enjoy with butter. She used to get so mad and holler at us because she couldn't keep her stack of tortillas because we were eating them as fast as she was making them.

She would spend all day in the kitchen cooking, cleaning, doing laundry, and taking care of all of us kids. She was the hardest working woman I knew. She never complained, and she did everything in love. It was because of her that I am who I am today. She taught me how to be a great cook and how to love.

My grandpa was my dad. He was the only consistent father figure I had in my life. He took care of me. He taught me how to take care of my car. He would take me with him in the garage while he would be working on his cars, and I would assist him by giving him the tools he asked for. I knew all the tools in the garage. He loved fishing, and whenever he and my uncles would go, I would cry to go with them, and he always gave in and took me. I was the only girl with all my uncles and cousins in the mountains camping and fishing. I loved those times.

As a teenager, unfortunately, I became rebellious. I began to drink and do drugs at the age of 13. I would stay out all night with my friends, and at the age of 15, I was jumped into my first gang and arrested for the first time. In the midst of all of this, my mother was still trying to figure out who she was, and I looked to my grandparents for love and guidance. I knew God, and I talked to him all the time, but I was no longer attending church or seeking Him. I began a downward spiral until 1996 when I had hit rock bottom and lost everything.

I decided to become sober and moved back in with my mom. Jesus slowly began to restore who I was. I began dating my now-husband in October of 2000, and we started to change our lives.

On April 16th, 2001, I lost my Grandpa to a massive heart attack. I was devastated and overwhelmed with emotion. I can remember crying out to God to please not let him suffer and if he was going to take him home to please help me get through it. I found out I was pregnant with my son 3 weeks later. He was born on December 14th, 2001, and I named him Paul after my Grandpa. I then had my daughter on April 11, 2003.

My kids were lucky enough to develop a relationship with my grandma. My grandmother never recovered from losing my grandpa, and she developed dementia and began to forget who we were. My kids got to know her as "little gramma," and they would play with her like their playmate. They would all three play together, paint and color. My grandma would take my kids to her room and tell them to keep a secret, and she would go to her dresser drawer and pull out her stash of candy and share with my kids.

My grandma was so brave throughout this battle with her mind; she never forgot her tortillas. She would ask daily if she could make them. It was the one thing she never forgot, and I will always cherish the memory of her and her tortillas.

That is why I chose to share her recipe. It reminds me of family, love, and hard work. God is so faithful; He never left my side He brought through so much pain and hurt and helped me heal from so many hardships in my life. He gave me a wonderful husband and two beautiful children, and I faithfully will follow Him all the days of my life.

Recipe from the Kitchen of

Antoinette Martinez

Homemade Flour Tortillas

Ingredients:

4 cups flour
4 Tbsp. manteca (lard) or shortening
2 tsp. salt
1 1/2 cups warm milk, approximately
2 tsp. baking powder

Directions:

- Combine dry ingredients in a medium-sized mixing bowl and cut in shortening.
- Make a well in the center of dry ingredients.
- Add milk, a small amount at a time, and work the mixture into a dough.
- Knead dough until smooth, cover, and set aside for 10 minutes.
- Form dough into balls the size of an egg. Roll each ball of dough into a circle 6 inches in diameter.
- Heat a griddle or skillet over medium-high heat. Place each tortilla on griddle and cook for approximately 1 minute on each side. (Tortilla should be lightly speckled.)

*"Thou has made known to me the ways of life;
thou shall make me full of joy with thy countenance."*

(Acts 2:28 NKJV)

Redeeming Love: Lacking Nothing

By Amie Koronczok

Satan is a very busy man. He is busy telling you that you don't have a story to tell. Why bother, you aren't a writer….

Satan is a very busy man.

When I was 10 or 11, my dad began to move in and out of the home, he couldn't decide if he wanted to stay or go. My mom was my rock. When my dad left, my mom fell into a deep depression. My heart cried out, praying for God to help my family, to help me. He didn't come. Satan is a very busy man…" You are forgotten."

Two months after my mom, brothers, and I moved out of my family home, my dad moved his new family in. I have a vivid memory of when I first noticed that my stepmom had placed things in the "wrong" place in my mother's kitchen. I quickly began to move things back to where they "belonged." My dad saw me and told me that "this was no longer your mother's house." Amie, the 12-year-old heard, "this is no longer your house." My dad then looked me in the eye and told me that my heart was full of hate and ugliness.

This is just one of many times I was continuously shown that I was not important. I was not worthy of love. My stepfamily was continuously forced on me and chosen before me. I was not allowed to have a voice or my own feelings. My feelings were always wrong, not valid. My voice was never heard. My identity became my excelling grades, athletic ability, and my "perfect body."

Satan is a very busy man…

I lived a lie of who I was for 21 years. Twenty-one years of trying to perfect myself into being loved, 10 of those years looking for a man to tell me I was chosen and lovable.

After college, I dated my first boyfriend; let's call him my low self-esteem boyfriend. I remember him telling me that he would have to find "an angel to accept and love him" because he had a brain injury. I thought to myself, "I can be that angel." When he broke up with me, I recognized that the way I reacted to a breakup was not normal. The sadness overtook me. I've come to understand that every time a boy broke up with me, it brought me back to that 12-year-old little girl whose life began to spin when her father walked away.

Then along came oilfield guy. Oilfield guy and I had dated a few years before, but he literally disappeared. I used to think he was, "the one who got away." When he came back into my life, I thought with every bit of my being that God had brought him back, it was fate. After about 5 months he disappeared again. I prayed and prayed for God to help my pain go away, for Oilfield guy to come back. I didn't understand why God would take him away again, didn't God bring him back? I thought maybe if I prayed enough, worshiped enough. He would hear me. Nothing happened. I became hopeless and very sad. I drank to help the emptiness. I often found myself drinking too much and then finding intimacy with men to feel wanted. Then I finally came to the reality that Oilfield was not going to happen.

Satan is a very busy man…

I heard a voice tell me, "you are so foolish to think that God would hear your prayers and actually answer them? This was when my trust in God vanished.

When I moved to Houston, I decided to get my yoga teacher certification, which helped me gain some self-confidence and find a community. I innocently began to live out the New Age belief system that was taught at the yoga studio. I began a relationship with Yoga Boy, who I later found was an agnostic alcoholic. I fell back into drinking more than I needed to. Deep down I knew he was not right for me; I often wondered if this is all there was to be loved and then would chalk it up to, "at least I am not alone." I look back and see that I had forgotten who I was. I let my standards disappear. I had forgotten the qualities I was looking for in a significant other. For the longest time, I felt like I had an abounding amount of light and joy hidden inside me, which I could never fully let out.

In 2013, my yoga certification brought me to MD Anderson Cancer Hospital, a true blessing. The second day after my new job, my live-in boyfriend, Yoga Boy, broke up with me. This was when God started pulling on me. Through my stages of grief, I had patient after patient testify to me about God's love. These women were sick, yet they were joyous. I wanted what they had. One patient gave me a Bible; another gave me the book Redeeming Love. She said Redeeming Love reminded her of God's love for her. She wanted me to find that love. She then told me that she knew I was going through something painful and that God could be my friend when I was lonely. This was interesting to me because I never told this woman about my current heartbreak, but somehow, she knew.

About a year or so later, I felt happy again, and I met Hollywood. Hollywood was the guy who I thought only existed in fairytales. The guy my mom told me not to expect because you will never find everything you are looking for in one person. I realized that I had been settling with past relationships. I couldn't believe that God would send me the man of my dreams, and he actually wanted me! Hollywood was a devoted Christian. This is the only thing that scared me because I knew I wasn't as devout as he was. He used words that I didn't understand, like obedience and submission to God. After a few conflicting conversations on faith, he soon realized my faith did not have a solid foundation, and I was not walking with the Lord. Let's be honest; I had never heard the term. He told me he could not date me seriously because we were not on the same path, not equally yoked. I was devastated. Hurt and confused, I began my search to validate myself.

As I searched for answers, I ran across the Joyce Meyer ministry site. I saved the page to look into at a later date. The next morning, I received an email from my stepmom. She asked if I could come to South Carolina for the weekend. She told me Joyce Meyer was going to be there and she felt it would be good for my dad and me to go. She offered to buy me a flight.

Things to consider:

I had never heard of Joyce until the day before.

They have never offered to buy me a ticket to visit them.

I would normally say no because I already felt bad, so why would I go somewhere I was uncomfortable being?

I decided to go because I felt it was too much of a coincidence for it not to be God's work. The day I left, I in the shower thinking about how mad I was at Hollywood for judging (I later figured out he wasn't judging me at all) me without really knowing my heart. I was mad that a man who called himself a strong Christian would cast someone aside instead of leading and showing the way. I then heard, "you are no better than he is; you have not forgiven your father and stepmom." I was taken back; I thought I had forgiven them, but, in reality, I hadn't. At that moment, I knew I had forgiven them.

That weekend I spent a lot of time with my dad. Talking and asking questions about my faith and the things Hollywood had challenged me with. As my dad referred to parables and stories of the Bible, I soon realized that maybe Hollywood was right, I needed to read the Bible. Before the weekend was over, I verbally forgave my dad, stepmom, and stepsister. For 21 years, I felt a terrible anxiety and sadness every time I was around them, that weekend, I physically felt all the darkness and heaviness lift off of me.

Satan is a busy man, **BUT GOD….**

At the airport I was holding a book, The Case for the Resurrection of Jesus Christ, the man in front of me at the security point asked me about it. He then told me that Jesus' resurrection was so significant that He made 12 apostles into disciples. As I waited to board the plane, yet another man asked me about the book. I told him what had happened and why I was reading it. He then gave me a small booklet about the story of Jesus's resurrection and forgiveness of our sins. He said to ask "the guy" if this is what he was talking about.

The next week, I sat at my desk heartbroken from the loss of Hollywood, feeling completely lost and needing answers. Why God? Then I got a Facebook message from my cousin. This is a cousin I only really speak to when we have family funerals. She sent me a devotional about submitting to God's timetable, in order to "experience the joy of watching Him make all things beautiful in His timing." When I asked her how she knew I needed to read this, she said, "I was reading that today and a picture of you came to my mind, that's how I knew you somehow needed that. I prayed about it because I was not sure if I should send it. It's a God thing! A good thing!" One thing she said that helped me is that when we pray to God, sometimes He says yes, sometimes He says no and sometimes He says to wait. My cousin then mailed me the book, The God I Never Knew. This book taught me that I didn't know the full measure of God's love and purpose in my life.

As my search for answers continued, I decided I needed to find a church. As I walked into the church, my whole body shook. The second week of church, the sermon was on the Samarian woman at the well. The pastor spoke of all the things in this life we grasp for to fill our void, to fill the hole in our heart. And Jesus said, "If you only knew the gift God has for you and who you are speaking to, you would ask me, and I would give you living water"(John 4:10). I was thirsty, and I thought to myself, "I need that living water."

With all this going on, I had been having trouble finding my identity in teaching secular yoga. How could I teach yoga and teach self-reliance, it was a lie? I realized I had been trying to do life on my own, looking inside my broken self for answers. I was then led to Houston's First Baptist fitness ministry. My friend told me they might need a yoga teacher. I walked in thinking I would talk to the director about my yoga experience, but instead, she wanted to know my story. I broke down. I told her what I had been going through and what brought me to her office. She prayed for me. I then noticed a paper that had the title of a book I had just ordered; Twelve Extraordinary Women. I told her I had just ordered that book. My friend Heather knew I had been seeking and looking for a Bible study group, she told me about another friend who was planning a book club with this book. The fitness ministry director then told me that they had just started the book and invited me to join the next day for the book club/bible study.

The next day, I went to the book club, and at the end of the ending prayer, I just started sobbing. I told them I didn't know why, but I just couldn't stop crying. The ladies all came around me and held me and prayed for me. They asked me why I was crying. I couldn't bring myself to tell them what was in my heart. That next morning, I woke up around 5 and felt that the only way out of this discomfort was to find the answers to the questions haunting my heart, was I a Christian? I met with Debbie that same night, and I was able to find the peace I was looking for.

One thing I find I continue to struggle with is trusting God. Trusting that my prayers could actually be answered. I wrote in my journal on October 18, 2016, "today I remember that God did grant me the chance to see Hollywood again and to talk about what had happened. This was something I prayed for. Why do I not give this credit to God? It was His doing. Therefore, God will do it again. Believe, trust, and commit." That same very day, I had a doctor's appointment downtown and came out an hour earlier than usual, and Hollywood (who lives in a different city) drove by me. He was here for business. We met up that evening. The next day as I read my journal, I realized that God did answer my prayer.

Through my walk with Christ, I have learned that although I am fairly a good person, I am a sinner, and I need a savior. After a night of hard-drinking, I woke up one morning convicted of who I was the night before. I got down on my knees and begged God to change me. I haven't had a problem ever since. I used to think God punished me. I used to yell at Him to leave me alone. I've learned to identify the deceiving voice of Satan. I have found self-worth not because of who I am or anything that I have done, but because God loves me. I have found my identity not in the things I do but as a Child of God.

I realized that being wanted by a man was an idol to my heart. In May of 2016, as I longed to have a husband and family of my own, I heard God tell me, "my grace is sufficient for you." As much as I didn't want to hear this, I knew that my purpose in my next few single years was to allow God to be first in my life and for Him to be my source of living water. I took a year oath to only date Jesus. I told God that I was no longer going to look for my husband, that I was going to trust Him to intervene in that area of my life divinely. The only area I have not seen Him move in my life.

In October of 2016, I was visiting a church, and during praise and worship, they called for people to come forward if they need healing. I did not go forward, but then they looked at me. I was told they had a word for me, " God is going to heal you completely; He will not stop at a little. He is going to give you back what He has taken. God will be glorified when you are glorified in your life."

In 2018, I was worshiping in church, wondering if I was foolish to rely on God to divinely intervene and place my husband in my path. A woman came up to me and said she had a word for me, “God is not worried about you, and He is still working on your husband. God knows the pain from your past and wants your husband to be fully prepared to love you the way you should be loved. And you do not have to do anything, He sees you.”

Following Christ does not always mean you will be on a mountain top high. Sometimes we must pick up our cross. The enemy is stronger than ever when he knows of the glory God has for His daughters. I currently find myself in a wilderness as I wait for God's promises. God has revealed to me that I have a wall built around my heart, scared to fully trust Him because of all the disappointment in my past. Recently it occurred to me that Satan is a very busy man...Satan would like me to believe that all those disappointing times, God was not there… He forgot me.

BUT GOD...

"Now faith is the assurance of things hoped for, the conviction of things not seen" (Hebrews 11:1 NASB).

I tell of these prophetic words in *faith*, *believing* and *standing* on the promises of God.

“For we know that when your faith is tested, your endurance has a chance to grow. So, let it grow, for when your endurance is fully developed, you will be perfect and complete, lacking nothing” (James 1:3-4 NLT).

God showed me a brick wall being chiseled down one brick at a time. He told me that He was my shield and shelter. He had me in His hands the whole time, and He would shine a light of redemption on all my disappointments, trust Him.

Your will be done…

Recipes from the Kitchen of

Amie Koronczok

Jell-O Cookies

Cook time: 12-20 min • Prep time: 15-30 min

Ingredients:

4 cups flour
1 tsp. baking powder
1 1/2 cups butter
1 1/2 cups sugar
1 egg
1 tsp. vanilla
1 box red or green Jell-O

Directions:

- Cream butter, sugar, egg, and Jell-O.
- Add dry ingredients.
- Chill the dough for 30 mins so they will roll out easier.
- Roll out the dough and cut with cookie cutters
- Bake at 350° until almost brown around the edge

These are my favorite cookies to use for valentines. Use red Jell-O and cut out with valentine hearts

Big Nanny's Noodles

Serves 6-8 • Cook time: 30-45 min • Prep time: 5 min

Ingredients:

12 oz bag of noodle
2 sticks of butter
1-1 1/2 bags of saltine crackers

Directions:

- Cook noodles according to the directions on the bag
- Drain noodles
- On low heat melt the butter in a saucepan.
- Crunch crackers into the butter.
- Cook on low heat, occasionally stirring, to a slightly brown color.
- Pour over noodles.

Banana Coffee Bread

Cook time: 30-35 min • Prep time: 10 min

Ingredients:

1/2 cup shortening
1 cup sugar
2 eggs
3/4 cup mashed ripe banana
1 1/4 cups sifted all-purpose flour
3/4 tsp. soda
1/2 tsp. salt

Directions:

- Cream shortening and sugar until fluffy
- Add eggs, one at a time, beating well after each.
- Stir in banana.
- Sift together dry ingredients
- Add to banana mixture; mix well.
- Pour into greased 9x9x2-inch pan.
- Bake at 350 degrees for 30 to 35 minutes

"For the Lord God is a sun and shield;
The Lord gives grace and glory;
No good thing does He withhold
from those who walk uprightly."

(Psalm 84:11 NASB)

My Story, My Song

By Shari Finkler

"In the beginning was the Word, and the Word was with God, and the Word was God. And the Word became flesh and dwelt among us, and we have seen His glory, glory as of the only Son from the Father, full of grace and truth" (John 1:1, 14 ESV).

From my earliest memory, I have loved words. I am the only child of school teacher parents who cherished me and surrounded me with books of every kind. Some of my fondest memories are of my sweet mother reading to me from the Children's Illustrated Bible. I loved the descriptions, the action, and adventure, the heroes, and poetry, and I loved the pictures. (Daniel in the lion's den was my favorite picture!)

This is my story.

God blessed me with Christian parents who trained up this child in a small town in North Carolina. We attended a church down the street from my house, and I was there every time the doors opened. I went to Sunday school, where I learned that Jesus loved me, and I loved vanilla wafers. I went to the "big church" where I would read from the hymnal while the pastor preached.

I was surrounded by my favorite companions: Words and music. You could say that my brain is stitched together with books, Bible verses, and song lyrics.

I lived this storybook childhood until junior high when my church hosted a revival weekend, and during one of the small group sessions, I had a long talk with the group leaders and realized that my vanilla wafer belief system was flawed. I could not live my life in the protective bubble of my Christian parents or my church family. I was a sinner. I could never, ever, not with pages of creeds or a row of gold stars beside my name; Never could I earn salvation. Never could I win my way to heaven. I was lost. I needed a Savior. And I knew from the cardboard fans in my grandma's country church that His name was Jesus.

That weekend I renewed my love for Jesus, this time with the understanding that it was a relationship, a lifelong commitment to remain with Him, in Him, following Him. I could no longer equate church membership or church activities with my faith. But while I knew church participation was not the key to the kingdom, my love for the Bride of Christ, His Church, remains vibrant to this day.

I left home to prepare for the only career I ever considered, and the only one I would choose over and over: teaching. My years at UNC were filled with reading great literature, singing anywhere and everywhere my acapella group gathered, and spending weekends in a tiny Methodist church outside Chapel Hill playing piano for the ragtag choir, always digging deeper in the Word. I prayed over how to integrate my love for literature and writing and to teach with my dedication to the Lord. I began my teaching career in 1987 with more high ideals than common sense, and I still love the classroom as much today as I did 32 years ago.

But this, too, is my story:

Fast forward years later; I was a mom to a young baby and wife to a very sick husband. I was struggling. Struggling to juggle a full teaching load at a small college plus tutoring to help with medical expenses, struggling with taking care of my young son while my husband underwent hospitalizations and treatments, struggling to understand God's plan for my life.

Many days I would awaken and sit on the side of my bed and talk to God.

"God, there's nothing left of me. I am depleted. Financially, emotionally, physically, spiritually, intellectually. There's nothing left of me. If I am to function at all in this world today, Lord, it's gonna have to be You. All You. You will have to be my energy, my words, my steps, my actions, my very breath. All You."

Looking back, that was one of the sweetest seasons of my life. That sounds odd, I'm sure. Obviously, it was a dark and difficult time. My father's health was failing, and my husband passed away, leaving me alone in a new city with a young child. But I felt God's hand in mine during that dark season like never before. He sustained me, strengthened me, and fed me daily from His Word.

And He's with me still. Time passed, and I met a wonderful man who made me smile again and loved my little boy. During our courtship, we visited a church on the very Sunday that the choir debuted a commissioned anthem that echoed Jesus' very words to me when I was struggling, "In this world, you will have trouble…Take heart! I have overcome the world!"

The sweet seasons are my story.

The dark days are my story.

The everyday moments are my story.

My story is written daily through His love and His Word and the sweet spirit of His grace.

"This is my story; this is my song,
Praising my Savior all the day long!"

Recipes from the Kitchen of

Shari Finkler

Pineapple Au Gratin

Serves 8 • Cook time: 30 min • Prep time: 10 min

Ingredients:

2 16-oz. Cans pineapple chunks, drained (reserve 6-8 Tbsp. juice)
6 Tbsp. self-rising flour
1/4 cup granulated sugar
1 sleeve Ritz crackers, crumbled
1 stick butter, melted
1 cup shredded cheddar cheese (we prefer sharp)
6-8 Tbsp. reserved pineapple juice)

Directions:

- Preheat oven to 350°
- Spray casserole or baking dish with Pam and set aside.
- Drain pineapple chunks (remember to reserve 6-8 Tbsp. of the juice)
- In a bowl, combine flour and sugar.
- Fold in pineapple chunks, cheese, and juice.
- Pour into prepared dish and sprinkle with crumbled Ritz crackers.
- Pour melted butter evenly on top.
- Bake at 350° for approx. 30 min.
- This is my family's favorite side dish for Easter. It's the perfect accompaniment to ham! Refrigerate the leftovers (we rarely have any) and reheat to enjoy with cold ham sandwiches the next day.

Caramel Apple Salad

Serves 6-8 • Cook time: chill • Prep time: 30 min

Ingredients:

3 oz. dry instant butterscotch pudding mix
8 oz. Cool Whip, thawed
8 oz. crushed pineapple with juice
3 cup chopped Red Delicious apples with peel
1 cup mini marshmallows
1 cup dry roasted peanuts, chopped (optional)

Directions:

- Chop apples, leaving peel.
- In a bowl, combine dry pudding mix and pineapple with juice.
- Stir until well-blended.
- Fold in Cool Whip.
- Stir in apples, marshmallows, and peanuts (if desired) until thoroughly combined.
- Refrigerate until ready to serve.

I had made this recipe for years (without the peanuts) as a refreshing summer treat. When my husband and I moved to a new town near the coast, there was a peanut festival, including a recipe contest. I added the chopped peanuts and won first prize! I served my winning dish in stemmed wine glasses with an apple slice on the side (in the style of a cocktail lemon) and a colorful plastic spoon to top. Your family will enjoy this tasty and fun salad.

Easy Taco Dip

Serves 6-8 • Cook time: 30 min • Prep time: 10 min

Ingredients:

1 8 oz. block of cream cheese, softened
1 can Hormel chili with beans
1 small can green chiles (drain slightly)
1 small can mushroom pieces, drained
1-2 cups shredded mozzarella cheese
a few chopped jalapeno slices (optional)
sturdy corn chips like Scoops

Directions:

- Preheat oven to 350°
- Spread softened cream cheese to make a layer in the bottom of a glass or ceramic pie pan
- Layer on the can of chili, the green chiles, the mushrooms, jalapenos (opt) and top with shredded mozzarella cheese (as much or little as you like)
- Bake about 30 min. until bubbly and the cheese is browned to your liking
- Serve as a dip with sturdy corn chips.

I first had this dish at an impromptu gathering at my best friend Jerrianne's house. She said she almost always has these ingredients around to throw together for a fun and friendly dish to share. Using a pretty glass or ceramic pie pan makes this simple, toss-together dip a memorable appetizer or side dish. Enjoy!

"I will sing to the LORD as long as I live.
I will praise my God to my last breath!"

(Psalm 104:33 NLT)

Recently I have begun reading all of Psalm 138 from The Passion Translation every evening before I fall asleep. Beautiful and so peaceful!

The Divine Presence

[1] I thank you, Lord, and with all the passion of my heart
I worship you in the presence of angels!
Heaven's mighty ones will hear my voice
as I sing my loving praise to you.
[2] I bow down before your divine presence
and bring you my deepest worship
as I experience your tender love and your living truth.
For the promises of your word and the fame of your name
have been magnified above all else!
[3] At the very moment I called out to you, you answered me!
You strengthened me deep within my soul
and breathed fresh courage into me.
[4] One day all the kings of the earth
will rise to give you thanks when they hear the living words
that I have heard you speak.
[5] They too will sing of your wonderful ways,
for your ineffable glory is great!
[6] For though you are lofty and exalted,
you stoop to embrace the lowly.
Yet you keep your distance from those filled with pride.
[7] By your mighty power I can walk through any devastation
and you will keep me alive, reviving me.
Your power set me free from the hatred of my enemies.
[8] You keep every promise you've ever made to me!
Since your love for me is constant and endless,
I ask you, Lord, to finish every good thing that you've begun in me!

The Days Ordained for Me

By Susan Lee Horton

Psalm 139 is one of my most loved psalms, especially verses 5 and 16. They tell me God's got my back. He knows me before and after. Some seasons of life are harder than others, yet my Sovereign Lord is always with me, comforting, bringing me hope. I haven't always recognized that.

One of those seasons was encased in sorrow.

From the time I was very young, I had a deep desire to be a wife and mother. But once out of high school, with no marital prospects, I settled on teaching as a way of enjoying children while waiting on my dream.

When I finally met the man I would marry, he wanted kids, too–lots of them! Ed and I decided to waste no time; we were mid-30's, and we weren't getting any younger. But time marched on, each pregnancy test was negative, and our younger siblings all began their families. We were deeply hurt.

We sought medical help and learned I wouldn't have children without surgery. About that time, we moved to another state and a new doctor. He believed I could conceive and put me on medication. It didn't work, and Ed and I were increasingly discouraged. Now past 40, time was against us. In spite of many prayers, bargains with God, tears, and pleading, my womb remained closed.

Nine years into our marriage, and with encouragement from friends and family, we decided to try adoption. Because of our ages, I felt little hope of being chosen by a birth mother to raise her child. We would seem like the baby's grandparents! To my surprise, we were chosen, and we received a tenth anniversary present with the birth of our daughter.

Now I can look back on the years of waiting as preparation time. Ed and I grew in our faith and our commitment to each other. We had to realize we were a family--just the two of us. I believe we became better equipped to parent a lively, strong-willed youngster, and later a teen with difficult challenges.

We are far from perfect parents. In the intervening years, our daughter has benefitted from our wisdom and had to endure our mistakes. Our girl deals with some special situations: mental illness, learning disabilities, and a few other problems. Her suffering has molded her into a young woman I am so proud to call my own. She is well-spoken, fiercely loyal, and kind. She is the child of my heart, and I have often told her, "If I could have birthed a child, I'd want her to be you."

Seasons of my life have come and gone. Presently, I am the mom of a grown-up reaching for independence. But I now treasure the years of infertility and desire for parenthood. I've appreciated motherhood more because of my longing, and I know I was meant to be my girl's mom. Because God had a different, better plan. God had my back.

Recipe from the Kitchen of

Susan Horton

My Girl's Favorite Blueberry Muffins

Serves 12 • Cook time: 20 min • Prep time: 15 min

Ingredients:

1-1/2 cups all-purpose flour
1/2 cup wheat germ
1/2 cup sugar
1/2 cup Splenda
2 tsp. baking powder
1/2 tsp. salt
1 large egg
1/2 cup sour cream
1/2 cup milk
1/2 cup butter, melted
6 oz. fresh blueberries, rinsed and drained

Directions:

- Preheat oven to 350°. Fill 12-cup muffin tin with foil liners and spray with cooking spray.
- In a large bowl, whisk together dry ingredients and set aside.
- In a medium bowl, whisk egg and butter, then add milk and sour cream.
- Whisk until well combined.
- Pour all at once into dry ingredients and stir just until combined.
- Fold in blueberries.
- Spoon evenly into muffin tin and top with a sprinkling of sugar, if desired.
- Bake about 20 minutes. Tops will spring back when touched.
- Cool 5 minutes, then move to rack.
- Serve warm with a dollop of butter.
- Store in refrigerator.
- Note: Recipe works well with frozen berries.

"All the days ordained for me were written in your book before one of them came to be."

(Psalm 139:16)

A Good Life

By Arline Robertson

I came to know the Lord in 1981. I was going through a very toxic marriage. During this time, I flew to San Antonio, TX, because of my father's illness. I visited Castle Hills Church while I was there. The words that Pastor Hagee spoke made a tremendous impact on me. Five years after I returned home, and fresh off of a tumultuous divorce, I packed my four children up and moved to San Antonio from Cleveland, OH, permanently. After finding a place to live and a job, I met a wonderful man. I first saw this man when I was working in a coffee shop. He had come in with his father to get a small bite to eat while his mother was in the hospital. During this visit, this man came back into the line several times. Finally, before he left, he asked me if I would go to dinner with him. I accepted his invitation. He asked where I would prefer to go, and I told him to meet me at church. To my great surprise, he accepted. It was then that I knew that the Lord had planted me in that time for a great reason. This was the first happy and pure relationship that I had ever had in my life. I had been raised a truly dysfunctional home. This was different from all of that. I dated that man for 7 years before we married in 1993.

We had many years of happiness. Five years after we married, we moved to Hondo, TX. We renovated a small home and settled into what we thought was going to be the place where we would spend the rest of our lives. The good times were really good. My husband and I were truly content and joyful in these years. It wouldn't last forever. In September 2004, my husband was diagnosed with Glioblastoma. Before he was diagnosed, he passed out in our home. I remember praying to God to help him. I can remember feeling His presence in those moments as if to remind me that He had always been there and would never leave. Once my husband was diagnosed, he had two brain surgeries in four months. He almost died during one of them. My husband never lost hope. He always looked at his chemo time as a time to pray with his fellow patients. He refused to allow anyone to pity him. He used this rough time to spread the word of the Lord. In October 2005, his son passed away. My husband was lost in grief. In August 2006, after a long battle, my husband went home to Jesus. I remember turning over and looking at the clock as I received the phone call. At that moment, before I picked up the phone, I sensed the presence of God telling me that my husband had passed away. After the funeral, I sat in my home looking at all of our memories. I looked at the home that he and I had renovated and repaired. I loved our memories, but I knew that if I was going to stay behind in this life, I couldn't be in that home without him.

I lived in various places throughout the next ten years. I never found a home at that time. I moved from one place to another, one house to another. In August 2016, my daughter Melisa called and told me that I needed to come to live with her and her sons. She said that God had put it on her heart to do this. I had been praying for this very phone call for six years. By the strength of God, I packed up my entire house and readied for the long drive to my daughter's home. I couldn't have done all of that on my own. I know that the Lord was with me because I am a cardiac patient and have had multiple procedures. I could feel God pulling me to my daughter's house. I could feel Him pulling me to my new home.

Recipe from the Kitchen of

Arline Robertson

Gold Brick Pie

Serves 6-8 • Cook time: Chill 1 hr • Prep time: 30 min

Ingredients:

1 1/2 sticks of unsalted butter...cold
1 cup sugar
3 squares unsweetened baker's chocolate
1 Tbsp. vanilla
4 eggs
1/2 cup pecans
1 ready-made pie shell

Directions:

- Slice and place butter in mixer and add sugar.
- Mix ingredients.
- Heat chocolate in the microwave until melted (approx. 2 mins and 40 secs).
- Once completely melted, add to butter/sugar mixture in the mixer.
- Mix all together, starting on medium and finishing on high.
- Begin adding one egg after every five minutes of mixing until all eggs are used.
- Fold in nuts.
- Pour contents into pie shell and chill.

"And we know that all things work together for the good of those that love God and are called according to His purpose."

(Romans 8:28 NKJV)

Loosening My Grip

By Melissa Custer

I have been divorced for seven years. It all seems like a blur now, but I can remember when I first started down this path. I felt overwhelmed. Here I was again. This was my second divorce. This time, instead of two sons, I now had four. I can remember being crushed under the weight of the unknown. My former spouse and I were not on good terms, at all. It truly seemed like he got to live the "free" life while I was staring down the path of responsibility. I had no idea how I was going to juggle the entire thing. I had no clue how I was going to keep my children thriving and maintain a full-time job. I had grown accustomed to having someone there to help. It was a tense moment in my life.

When I remarried in 2006, I thought that this was going to be my happily ever after. I will say that, for a time, it was. We were very happy with our marriage and even happier when we found out that we were expecting a baby. My former spouse had adopted my two oldest sons, and we were all anxiously awaiting our third son's arrival. Life had settled into a pattern. I have always liked patterns. I love the routine actions of a day by day life. It makes me feel secure. We were all very secure within our little tight-knit routine.

Things only got busier and busier as we welcomed our third and fourth sons within two and a half years after we wed. This was the life that I had long dreamt of. I never thought I would be signing divorce papers again. I never even imagined that we would end up 180 degrees from where we were in the beginning. When our divorce was final, we were just shy of our sixth anniversary.

No matter how I reflected on the events that led to my divorce, I soon realized that it wasn't going to help anything to live in the past. So, I compartmentalized the hurt and pressed on. I charged figuratively forward with my kids practically strapped to my back. I shut away my pain and created a new routine for our lives. I learned to rely on myself to do everything. I started believing that I was the only one that could do what we needed the right way. If I needed to be both mom and dad, then I would do it. If I needed to be a hard charger at work, then I would do it. If someone was ill, I would nurse them back to health. If the house needed to be clean, then I would be the maid.

I,I,I,I,I,I,I…Little did I know that "I" was running myself into the ground. "I" was literally sapping myself dry from the inside out. "I" had no energy. "I" wasn't even doing a great job at doing all the things "I" was so self-reliant about. My veil of self-reliance came crashing down on me about 3 years ago. After four years of being divorced and trying to do everything on my own, my house of cards was demolished. Over the course of four years, I had literally destroyed my body. I had no energy. I had no want to leave my home. I was wracked with anxiety over what I had to do, how perfect everything had to be, and whatever was yet to come that I hadn't planned for. My expertise in routine-making had turned into an addiction to control. I had to be the one that had everything under control. I had to be the one that got everything perfect. If someone criticized me, they quickly didn't matter and were easy to forget. Nothing and no one was going to get in the way of my carefully planned and quiet existence. I thought that everything that I was doing was in the best interest of my sons and their happiness. I never even considered my own. I wasn't working all of this for me; I could have cared less about me. I thought that I was doing all of it for them. I had to be SUPER SINGLE MOM.

Well, over the course of the first four years after my divorce, super single mom worked herself into depression, hopelessness, and chronic fatigue. It's funny the things that you realize when you give yourself the time to study the texture in your ceiling while lying in bed. There I was, August 2016, unable to get out of bed. I was completely depleted of any energy. I was only able to look up at my ceiling. My oldest son, who was 19, demanded that I take the weekend to rest. He would make sure the three youngest were well cared for while I took time for me. I can remember looking up at my ceiling, thinking about how I could have possibly gotten myself to this point. I wondered where my plan had gotten off track. I was so frustrated. I felt I had failed everyone. This was when I heard a still, small voice in my gut telling me that I couldn't do this on my own.

My thin veil of self-reliance had to come off. In order for me to keep going, I had to admit that I needed help. I had to admit something that I never wanted to realize. I had to admit that I was…weak. I had to let go of the self-reliance that I had come to anchor my life upon. It was in these moments, staring at my ceiling, that I allowed myself to break. I allowed the thin veneer of perfection that I displayed to the whole world to crack.

When I did this, all of the emotions that I had bottled up for so many years came rushing out like a waterfall. I cried. I cried hard for endless moments. I cried out and allowed my heart to open. I allowed my heart to feel. I allowed whatever emotions I had bottled up to flow out like a river. All the hurts, betrayal, self-hate, anger, sadness, numbness, inadequacy, and disappointment that I had cultivated in the garden of my soul for four long years came pouring out of me in one weekend. That Sunday, I was still quite weak but forced myself to get up and out of bed. I can tell you that it was very different being in my own skin after letting all of that out. I felt empty. I now understand that what I thought was empty and void, was really a vessel that God could fill. From that point on, I was the fertile ground that He needed. The weeds of my self-reliance were stripped away, and I was now a clean patch of soil for Him to plant in. In the three years since I let it all go, my relationship with God has revived and thrived.

He has completely wiped away my expectations and upset any well-laid plans I may have toiled over before. I wish that I could say that I have been able to turn it all over completely and that I am no longer a perfectionist. I would be lying it if I did. I can say that I am a lot better off then where I was. What I am is someone who is now completely aware of my shortcomings. Instead of hiding them, I am learning to find great joy in the fact that I have them. These are the areas that I know He will show His great strength in.

Additionally, I am no longer planning every second of my life. I have learned that sometimes the unplanned events are the sweetest surprises. Living in these moments allows me to smile more. I have found that these surprise moments can bring great joy. Finally, I have hung up my cape. The super single mom I was trying to be was really a hot mess of high self-expectation. I am now content in the fact that I am a child of God, who is a mother, who is single. I am not perfect. I cannot do everything on my own. I am content in the fact that I am already a whole person relying on an all-powerful God.

Recipe from the Kitchen of

Melisa Arreche-Custer

Baked Mac & Cheese

Serves 6-8 • Cook time: 80 min • Prep time: 30 min

Ingredients:

1 1/2 boxes of elbow noodles
3 - 2 cup bags of shredded cheddar cheese
1 cup full-fat half and half
4 Tbsp. of butter cubed
1 cup full-fat sour cream
1 tsp. salt

Directions:

- Preheat oven to 350°.
- Boil noodles, drain and rinse.
- Set noodles off to the side to cool.
- In a small bowl combine sour cream, half and half, butter, salt, and one cup of cheese.
- Mix all ingredients thoroughly and refrigerate until noodles are cool.
- Once noodles are room temperature, dump into 9 X 13 baking dishes. (I always have enough to make a smaller batch in another dish, as well).
- Once all noodles are in a dish, add sauce mixture. If you are using more than one baking dish, you will need to eyeball the appropriate amount based off of the size of the dishes you are using.
- Once the mixture has been added, mix the noodles thoroughly until all noodles are covered in the sauce.
- Level off noodles and sauce within your dish so that it appears flat.
- Use remaining cheese to top the recipe. I heap on enough cheese to cover all the noodles from being seen.
- Once the oven is heated, place dishes in and allow to bake for 45 minutes.
- When baking has completed, remove dishes and allow mac and cheese 10 minutes to stand for 10 mins before serving.

"My bretheren, count it all joy when ye fall into diverse temptations: Knowing this, that the trying of your faith builds patience. But let patience have her perfect work, that ye may be perfect and whole: wanting nothing."

(James 1:2 NKJV)

Throughout My Life

By Judy Jorgensen

Where do I begin? I met my Beautiful Savior 44 years ago, and I can't imagine life without Him. I was raised in an alcoholic household. Mom and Dad drank, and it was not a secure environment. I had a brother nine years older than me and a sister seven years younger. While my brother was home, he was my safety and security net. He left for college, and it was up to me to take care of my sister. To this day, she says, I was like her Mother! We didn't go to Church at all, except for a short period in my younger years. My Dad's family were Reorganized Latter Day Saints, but not that dedicated. It's amazing how we cope with our past by not remembering things. It was truly the Lord watching out for me.

We frequently moved because my Dad was a mechanic and would change jobs frequently, and now that I look back on, it was probably due to his drinking problem. Always being the new kid on the block, I was shy, and so I didn't make friends very easily! I know that my parents loved me with all their hearts, but they used alcohol to deal with life. There were lots of instances in which the Lord protected me and kept me from any harm throughout my whole life. I remember praying to Him and feeling like; I knew who, and how powerful, He was.

I grew up, got married in 1968 to an Air Force soldier. he went to Vietnam for a year, and I remember praying all the time for his safety! He came home, and we started our family. I was happy with my life, but I knew there was something missing. We didn't attend church, but I had a dear friend who was on Fire for Jesus. She would call or come by and ask me to come to church. I would have a reason not to go, always! The more I was around her, the need to find out what this was all about making me more curious. Our girls were young, and my husband was out of town, she called and said she had some books and music tapes for them. We spent hours talking about the Lord and how He had made a difference in her life. She was the one the Lord had chosen before I was even in existence to bring me to Him.1 John 1:9 says, If we confess our sins, He is faithful and just to forgive us {our}sins, and to cleanse us from all unrighteousness.

Throughout my life, I know I have let Him down, but He has been and is still so faithful to me. I was so happy to learn that He was and is my Heavenly Father, and I could call Him my Daddy. Just being able to talk to Him and share my deepest thoughts and needs was such a blessing. I began to feel secure in knowing who I was in Him. Insecurities of who I was, were gone, I was a child of the Almighty King.

I am 70 years old, and I look back and see how I gave in to some things of the world, but you know what, those days are gone, and I am going to spend the rest of my life serving my Lord. He has blessed me with a husband that loves me, and children and grandchildren that love me. I am here to follow you, Jesus, wherever you want me to go!

Deuteronomy 31:6 Be strong and courageous. Do not be afraid or terrified of them, for the Lord, your God, goes with you; He will never leave or forsake you.

Recipe from the Kitchen of

Judy Jorgensen

Gluten-Free Banana Bread

Ingredients:

4 bananas (mashed) 1 1/2 cups, very ripe
2 eggs
1 tsp. baking powder
1 tsp. baking soda
2 cups gluten-free flour
1/2 cup chocolate chips
1/4 tsp. salt
1/2 cup sugar
1/2 tsp vanilla
1 cup butter (1 stick)
2 tbsp. milk

Directions:

- Preheat oven 350°, lightly grease the pan
- In a larger bowl combine flour, baking soda, baking powder, and salt, set aside.
- In a separate bowl cream together butter and sugar.
- Stir in eggs, milk, vanilla, and mashed bananas until well blended.
- Stir the banana mixture and chocolate chips into the flour mixture, stir just to moisten.
- Pour batter into prepared loaf pan.
- Bake in the preheated oven for 50 to 55 minutes.
- Let it cool in pan before you turn it out
- Enjoy, my mom loved to make her Banana Bread!!

"Be strong and courageous. Do not be afraid or terrified of them,
for the Lord your God goes with you;
He will never leave or forsake you."

(Deuteronomy 31:6)

The Cat of Burden

By Tammy Freeman

I was raised Catholic, a cradle Catholic some may call me. I was faithful as a child to the Church's teachings: I went to mass on Sundays, I prayed, I feared our Lord, I completed the Sacraments. I even served the Church at the Altar, during special events and any other ways I could. Yet I felt unfulfilled, uninspired, unattached to my faith. As such, I left: my Church, my community, my faith.

My behavior certainly was not showing the light of Christ to the world. How could it? I left Him behind.

Years went on, I felt happy; I was married, had a good job as a registered nurse, and we had two healthy sons. At the time, I was working in community mental health and addictions as a case manager. Much of my role was to help people in crisis, complete intakes with new referrals, and liaise with our local hospitals. I was burning out. I had nothing left to give to my clients, my husband, my children, and most of all, me! I was dealing with serious postpartum depression and anxiety at the same time. I had also reached out to my biological father, knowing he wanted a relationship with me as well.

It all became too much.

I disclosed to a good colleague my symptoms, and she implored me to get some help. So, I did by leveraging my connections at work and saw a psychiatrist within a couple of weeks. The doctor advised me that I would need time off work due to the severity of my symptoms. In all, I was off work for 6 months.

Throughout this ordeal, I had an office mate - a beautiful friend - who ministered to me. I'm not sure she understands the degree to which she helped me. One day, quietly, Kate handed me a business card. Pictured on it was a butterscotch colored cat, lying on its back, all four paws sprawled out, exposing its belly. On it read, "Come to me all you who are weary, and I will give you rest" (Matthew 11:28).

I thanked her profusely, eyes watery, probably looking a wreck! Sitting on my office chair, sprawled out much like the cat depicted on the card, I bowed my head.

I was humbled.

Here I thought that I could deal with my burdens alone. Truly believing, insisting, that *I* would be the one to solve my problems, deal with postpartum depression and anxiety, and overcome the fear of meeting my father independently. With her simple act of handing me a cleverly illustrated Bible verse, Kate renewed my Faith, reminded me that God the Father holds me, that Jesus willingly carries my burdens if I would simply hand them over.

With four children, from teen to toddler, there are many trials encountered along my walk of Faith. Some days I gladly "drop" my burdens at the foot of the cross. Some days they are ripped from my closed-fisted hands. Many days, I still feel compelled to manage autonomously. Then I see the cat and remember I need not be burdened if I come to Jesus.

Recipes from the Kitchen of
Tammy Freeman

Fudgey Chocolate Greek Yogurt Zucchini Cake

(adapted from www.parsleysagesweet.com Chocolate Sour Cream (or Greek Yogurt) Zucchini Fudge Cake)

Serves 9x13 cake • Cook time: 30-40 min • Prep time: 15 min

Ingredients:

2 1/2 cups of whole wheat flour
1 tsp. of baking soda
1/2 tsp. baking powder
1/2 tsp. salt
3/4 cup of unsweetened cocoa powder
1/2 cup of butter
1/2 cup of vegetable oil (may sub unsweetened apple sauce)
1 1/2 cups of granulated sugar
2 large eggs
1 tsp. vanilla
1/2 cup of Greek yogurt, plain
3 cups of grated zucchini – use all the 'juice' with it
1 1/2 cups of chocolate chips

Directions:

- Preheat the oven to 325° F. Grease the 9 x 13 pan
- In one bowl, mix the dry ingredients (except for the granulated sugar and the chocolate chips)
- In a second bowl, cream the butter, oil, and sugar together until the mixture is well combined.
- Add in the eggs, one at a time, making sure each one is mixed well into the creamed oil/sugar mixture.
- Add the vanilla next.
- Into the wet ingredients, add 1/3 of the dry ingredients, then half of the yogurt.
- Mix gently.

- Repeat the dry and yogurt addition, mixing after.
- Finally, add the last 1/3 of the dry ingredients to the bowl.
- Gently fold the zucchini and the chocolate chips into the batter. Be careful not to overmix as the batter becomes 'tough.'
- Pour the batter into your pan and bake for 30 to 40 minutes. Test the cake at 30 minutes by inserting a cake tester into the middle of the cake. Set the cake on a cooling rack while you prepare the ganache topping.

The 'icing' for your cake:

- Place your chocolate (chopped or chips) in a heat proof bowl.
- Heat the cream in a saucepan over medium heat.
- Once the cream is simmering, remove the pan from the heat and pour the cream over the chocolate.
- Cover the bowl for 4-5 minutes to ensure the chocolate is melted.
- Stir the cream and chocolate together until they are well combined.
- The ganache will thicken as it cools.
- Once it is only warm, pour the ganache over the cake.
- To ensure coverage of the whole cake, I spread it with a butter knife, or the back of a spoon for a rustic look.
- Allow the whole cake to cool for at least 30 minutes; this ensures the ganache has set.

Serve as it is (so delicious!!!) or add some whipped topping or ice cream for a much more decadent dessert. I will omit the ganache topping as well, sprinkle with icing/powdered sugar. My kids love it either way.

I brought this as a dessert for a dinner we were attending. Our friends had a teenage boy who devoured the cake and said to me, "it tastes like a high-end bakery cake." It's a great cake.

Christmas Leftover Casserole

Serves 6-8 • Cook time: 45-60 min • Prep time: 20 min

Ingredients:

4 cups of diced turkey (I prefer white meat here)
1 cup of gravy
2 cups of leftover cooked veggies you have: I use cooked carrots, cooked broccoli/cauliflower, brussel sprouts.
1 cup of frozen peas and/or corn (may use a mix, not greater than 1 cup)
4-6 cups of mashed potatoes (enough to cover the 9x13 pan with potatoes approximately 1-2" thick)
Salt and pepper to taste
Dehydrated parsley sprinkled on the potatoes
1 cup of grated cheddar cheese, to garnish the top of the potatoes (optional)

Directions:

- Lightly grease a 9 x 13 pan and preheat the oven to 350° F
- Mix the diced turkey and gravy together then spread in the pan. If you prefer more gravy, add to your liking. Season with salt and pepper, to taste
- Cover the meat layer with the cooked vegetables that you wish to use
- Cover the casserole with the mashed potatoes, scooping with a tablespoon to ensure even coverage.
- Garnish with the parsley and cheese if desired
- Cover with foil and put in the oven for 45 minutes, or until the gravy is hot and bubbling.
- Remove foil and bake another 10-15 minutes, until the cheese is melted
- Remove the casserole dish from the oven and let stand 10-15 minutes before serving
- Serve with cranberry sauce, leftover stuffing if you have it, and dinner rolls.
- I usually prepare this as I am cleaning up from dinner. I put it in the fridge overnight and serve 1-3 days after the initial dinner. This is when I enjoy my turkey dinner – when I had very little prep and minimal cleaning up!

"Come to me, all you who are weary and burdened, and I will give you rest. Take my yoke upon you and learn from me, for I am gentle and humble in heart, and you will find rest for your souls. For my yoke is easy and my burden is light."

(Matthew 11:28-30)

I Would Not Be Alive if it Was Not for God

By Angela Danielson

I did not grow up in a Christian home, but our neighbors were devout Christians and invited me to some church events like camp from time to time. One Saturday afternoon, when I was 15, I was home alone and heard God tell me that I needed to go to church. So, I called my mom when she was at work and told her what had happened. She told me to find out what time church was, and the next day we went. The service was amazing, and both my mom and I were drawn by the Holy Spirit to the altar call at the end to meet Jesus. That day she re-dedicated her life, and I met Jesus. I was on fire for God all through High School, and then when I was 18, I started to hang out with the wrong people while trying to walk with God. I got pulled into the club scene and started drinking and partying.

Then I went into the Army at 21, and that didn't slow the partying down. I ended up in an unhealthy relationship, and I had a friend that was going to let me move in with her and pay half of the utilities to get out of the situation I was in. At that time, I had not been walking with God and really had no reason to say no, but deep inside my gut, I lacked peace and decided against moving in. Not long after that, one day she didn't show up for formation, which in the military is huge and it's like going Absent Without Leave (AWOL). So, a friend and I went to her apartment off-post to check on her. When we got there, her car was there, but the front door was locked. We went around back, and I crawled through the window of her bedroom and unlocked her back door to let my friend into her apartment. We walked right past the bathroom into the living room, and the TV was on. Another person from our unit showed up, and then I went into the bathroom, and I found her murdered with her throat cut in the tub. I ran outside, screaming and almost threw up. It was so traumatizing. The enemy then tried to make it seem like all my fears were going to come true, and I walked in a very real paralyzing fear of death and destruction for a very long time. I know it was God that saved my life and kept me from moving in. The night before this all happened my new roommate, and I stayed up late talking about how we had walked with God when we were younger and reminiscing about our relationship with Jesus. Jeremiah 29:11 says, "For I know the plans I have for you, to give you a hope and a future." Even though I was currently on the fence, and not walking with God wholeheartedly; it was a planted seed in that direction. Then, about a year later, God put some amazing people in my path that loved on me and led me back to Jesus. They invited me to church and when I finally went, a traveling pastor basically "read my mail" and this really got ahold of me. It pierced through to my soul, woke me up, and changed my life forever.

This is just a snapshot. God has been there for me through so many trials. He never leaves us or forsakes us. He is truly dependable and trustworthy and will use everything for our good to give us a future and a hope. Amen

Recipes from the Kitchen of
Angela Danielson

Mizithra Cheese and Noodles

Ingredients:

Noodles (Your choice, cook to package instructions)
4 Tbsp. butter
Mizithra cheese

Directions:

- Cook Spaghetti Noodles (I use gluten-free ones)
- While the noodles are cooking brown butter in a pan.
- Then shred mizithra cheese into a bowl
- After the noodles have cooked, drain noodles and put back in the pot
- Pour browned butter over noodles and then add cheese and plate it.

We usually eat grilled chicken with it and a side salad with garlic bread that I make out of sliced bread in the oven.

"Having hope will give you courage."

(Job 11:18)

All Because of My Beloved Nephew, Patrick

By Elsie De Luca

I have always loved the month of my birth, September, because of it fresh smells, so each and every year I anxiously await the arrival of the fall season in Michigan. Yet, of all my many Septembers, one stands out for me because what happened in 1977 literally changed my life forever.

Let me begin my story with I received a call that everyone would dread. There had been an accident, so I was asked if I could immediately come to the hospital less than a half-hour away. I was told by a strange voice on the other end of the line that my beloved nephew had been driving on a local expressway when his truck careened out of control. He was in surgery. End of information! To this day, I cannot understand how they had my phone number.

My husband Phil and I frantically left home, not as a couple who would first turn their eyes heavenward, but as an aunt and uncle who had agreed to take care of my sister's four children if anything were to happen to her. Her husband had died at a young age of leukemia, which had prompted her to move up north and try to start a new life with four children to take care of on her own.

On the way to the hospital, we talked about how hard it would be to contact my sister if Patrick's injuries were fatal. What could we possibly say to her that would ease the burden of her pain? We decided to wait until we had more information to give her as we drove along, heartbroken, hoping for the best, yet anticipating the worst.

When we arrived at the hospital, my nephew Patrick was still in surgery. We were asked to wait until they had some news for us. This was the longest wait that I have ever experienced in my life. Yet sadly, God was certainly not my Companion at this moment in time. I was completely relying on the doctor on call to perform a miracle.

I cannot even remember today who came and talked to us when we received the news that this precious 21-year-old had died on the operating table. How can this be? I had just seen

Patrick when he had stopped by to visit us after he moved away from home. He had so much charm and a smile that made my heart literally melt. He was named after a dear family friend who looked like Santa Clause and whose full name was Patrick Kelly. Mr. Kelly had the perfect rosy Irish face, and my sister adored him.

The next thing I can remember as I look back with a very sad heart was that I was asked to identify Patrick's body. When I walked into the room where they had taken him after surgery, he looked like he had just fallen asleep. The fatal injury was to the back of his head; this head which now rested against the sterile white sheet seemingly without a mark on it.

I wanted to shout, "Patrick, wake up! Please, please wake up!"

My next thought was, "What in the world am I going to say to my sister and his siblings when I called them? I was in such a state of shock that I couldn't even cry. I couldn't even utter one word.

Yet at the very moment, as I looked down into Patrick's beautiful face, I looked up to heaven, not knowing what to say to "The God of my Catholic faith." I so desperately needed a "Daddy," yet sadly, I didn't know my Heavenly Father intimately. I really didn't know Him at all.

That lightning bolt moment was the very moment that I began my search for Him Who my soul now truly loves! He is called "The Hound of Heaven," and I became "The hound of earth."

Going back to that very sad moment, the following questions were racing through my mind as I stood there looking into Patrick's serene face. Why did the God that I learned about as a child seem to be beyond my reach? Where was the God of my childhood when I needed Him the most? The Whys? I uttered a million "Whys" as I looked up to heaven.

I called my sister, who immediately let out a cry that I shall never forget. We then waited hour upon hour for her to come from Alpena to the hospital to see her son, her youngest son, her cherished son who had just left her recently to strike out on his own. What was she thinking as she drove those hundreds of miles to see Patrick for the last few times on earth after already suffering the loss of his daddy?

I cannot fully explain what happened when my sister and Patrick's siblings arrived, but I do know from the look on her face, that this precious woman had seen more than her share of suffering. She had carried many babies to full term when they died in her womb because her blood warred against hers because of the RH Factor.

Patrick's funeral was then planned, but how do you reconcile in your heart that one so young, so very precious is no longer with you? One question piled upon another until I realized how much I needed the God that I had learned about growing up, and I needed Him so desperately that I couldn't even sleep at night.

In December of that same year, I finally came to a breaking point where I cried out for my Heavenly Father to reveal Himself to me. I felt like life was crashing in around me because I was also suffering from physical problems along with this grief that held me tightly in its grip.

I went to lie down on my bed one night with the weight of the world on my shoulders when my last final cry drifted up to Heaven.

I cannot even find the words to explain what happened next, except that I fell into a deep sleep as God's Holy Spirit hovered over me. I woke up feeling really strange; a strangeness that I couldn't explain, except to say that I fell asleep in my home in Lapeer and woke up in a strange land filled with peace.

At about this same time, my Heavenly Father had so lovingly sent a neighbor to minister to me. This was highly unusual because we lived in a state game area where our neighbors were few and far between. I was invited to come with her to her church to learn more about God and how He works in our lives.

The following Spring, I attended the classes she had mentioned, yet became fearful of going to the one that she kept saying would literally change my life. Curiosity, however, got the best of me, so I went and received The Baptism of The Holy Spirit. I drove home in the dark that night singing praises to the God that I had been searching and longing for. Yet my next question was this, "How am I going to explain all of this to my husband?" I felt like one of the believers at Pentecost who were accused of being drunk, except that I was just so overwhelmed with the love of my LORD, that I was almost delirious.

Not too long after this encounter, I went to a retreat with friends that I have always referred to as "My Honeymoon with Jesus!" I had become so in love with Him that I only wanted to be hidden away with Him that weekend. And hidden away I was! There was a beautiful garden on the property where I found my secret place among the blue sky, the clouds, and the beautiful flowers.

It has been over forty years since my first true encounter with the God that I so love and adore, and I know that I shall sing His praises forevermore as He reveals more of Himself to me! Jesus is truly, "The Lover of my soul!"

Recipes from the Kitchen of
Elsie DeLuca

Polichenta

Ingredients:

1 1/2 cups flour
2 cups of milk
2 Tbsp. of vanilla
1/2 tsp. of salt and baking powder
2 Tbsp. butter melted
2 eggs (if small, add 3)
2 Tbsp. of sugar

Directions:

- Mix all of the dry ingredients together in a bowl.
- Mix wet ingredients in a separate bowl.
- I add the vanilla at the end; butter not too hot, please! (If you are a meticulous chef, you may want to separate the eggs, and beat the whites separately. Am I considered lazy if I don't?)
- Fry batter until it is a gentle brown.
- Add peanut butter in the middle, roll the crepe, and then cover with real maple syrup.
- My Grandkids beg to have these for breakfast when they visit me. They are also yummy with whipped cream and strawberries! Just use your imagination and enjoy!

"One thing I have desired of my LORD, that I will seek:
that I may dwell in The House of The LORD all the days of my life,
to behold The Beauty of the LORD, and to inquire in His Temple."

(Psalm 27:4 NKJV)

I'm Going, I'm NOT Staying

By Tami Parker Theobald

I used to think my story was boring. I used to wish I had some fancy words I could say and that I had a wild life that turned tame kind of a story. I thought that would make my story sound more interesting and that more people would want to hear me tell it.

I was raised in a Christian family. My parents were Christians. All four of my grandparents were Christians. I became a Christian at an early age sitting on my bed with my mama and my sister huddled around me and a Bible in the center of the three of us. We both prayed for Jesus to forgive us and to come into our hearts and live forever in and through us.

I was a "good" girl. We always went to church. We went every single time those doors did open - Sunday and Wednesday and other days for other things. Then, one day in Sunday School in 2000, a teacher told me that no one's story was ever boring. That gave me hope. That made me think. What exactly is my story? I didn't stop that day and write it out. But I talked it up in my head, and now 19 years later, I pick up my favorite Pentel Energel pen and a composition book my husband gave me, and I go to the window seat in my upstairs library, and I begin to write words down on paper.

My mind drifts back to Sunflower, Mississippi, where I was born and raised. I see myself sitting in that church - Sunflower Baptist Church. I can still recall the exact seats where we all sat. My Daddy. My Pappy and my Mimi. My Paw Paw and my Parkie. Me and my two sisters and my brother. And my Mama. She played the organ and/or piano. So, she sat there – always upfront.

My Mama still plays the organ and/or piano there in Sunflower Baptist Church. One of my sisters still sits in that same pew where she sat as a black-haired little girl. My other sister and also my brother both sit in pews in other churches now as well as myself. My hero, my Daddy, went to Heaven 18 years ago where he was reunited with all four of my grandparents.

You have my background. You can see how I was taught. I hope you realize that this precious family I belong to is so, so important to me and so, so important to them, also, because it is.

Now, let us begin. I'm about to ride you through my life to where I fly around right now in the year 2019. I say fly around because I'm always on the go. Going here and going there. Never staying in one spot. Didn't Jesus tell us all to "Go?" The answer is yes. Yes, He did. Get your Bible and turn with me to Luke 9-10. I am always flabbergasted by the times that Jesus says, "Go." Three times. His last instructions before leaving earth included "Go and make disciples of all nations." That motivates me! How about you? "Go!" is a command to action. You cannot follow Jesus and stay in one comfortable little spot. It's not possible. Going requires movement. That is why I do not stay. I go. Going is a verb. It requires action. Therefore, following Jesus must be seen in your life, NOT just read in your words.

I followed Jesus all my life. What does that even mean? I knew I was supposed to tell others. But did I? No. I did not. Oh, sure I talked about Jesus with my Christian friends. And I prayed for God to protect me and heal the sick, and I prayed for God to forgive me. And I went to all those "churchy" events. Y'all I was that good girl who didn't get into trouble or do bad things. I kind of kept my God to my family, my friends, and myself. I didn't "Go." I didn't do what the Bible commanded us to do. I didn't share the joy I had inside my heart with this broken, crazy, tired, and weary ole world. All these people I would see day after day were the very ones I needed to be going to and sharing with the words of my story. My not boring story. My story of how we have a God who sent His only son to planet earth to walk amongst us and then to crucified and crushed on a cross for our transgressions and to be raised again to life to save us from eternal death, to give us life in the Light of Heaven forevermore. Oh no, my story is not boring. My Jesus saved me from the fires of Hell. And I want to tell you how He can do that for you right this minute. You don't need to dress up in a brand-new outfit from your favorite store and fix your hair all pretty. You can do it now with your hair not combed and wearing old torn pajamas like my sister and I did that night with my Mama on a double bed that wasn't even made up yet.

Well, here I am out of college now from Ole Miss and Delta State and through an internship at Methodist Hospital in Memphis and now working where I still work today at Baptist Hospital in Memphis, Tennessee. I married a Christian man who loves the LORD. And 28 years later what God joined is still a blessed and beautiful life. We have a beautiful daughter. She's now living 5 hours away in the mountains. We love her with all our heart. She loves Jesus and has from an early age. I thank God for my people. I thank God every morning at 6 am for blessing my life with my Carl and my Kate. And that they love the God I love.

Let's push ahead to 2009. I had been staying all these years, not going. I had been keeping all these years and not sharing, as Jesus commanded. I told you we always went to church. We always prayed. We had Jesus, and we read His Word. And that's very good, but He asks us for more. He wants us to share, not keep; He wants us to go, not stay. I was sitting in my Sunday School class in the year 2009 when a girl came in to make an announcement. She was advertising a bible study called "Wisdom for Moms" that was going to start soon and be taught by 5 women in our church. I had never been involved with a women's bible study. So, I listened. The Holy Spirit told me to go to this and to invite a girl I knew from my work. This girl wasn't like a close friend, and she wasn't even a Christian. I kind of pushed that thought away. And added my own thought. I invited a friend, but she said that she couldn't come. I invited another friend who also couldn't come. So, I scooped up what the Holy Spirit had originally told me. I asked this girl. She was much younger than me and not like me, and she had 5 kids and a struggling marriage. She said she would come with me. Wow! The kids could all come with her because my church had Awanas at that same time, that would be perfect. It started in August. We went. We listened. We talked. We prayed. She asked Jesus into her heart in November. The kids started learning Bible verses. All of their lives changed. And guess what? So, did mine. My life changed because I said yes, and I went. It took a girl who was not a Christian to teach me how to live like a Christian. Wow!

I'm still in a weekly study nine years later with about 5 of these same girls. I've been going ever since. I have never stopped. We pray together. We praise together. We rejoice together. We share tears together. God has shown me what a powerful thing women's ministry can be, and He has put me slap dap in the middle of it. And for that, I will never stop thanking Him. God has shown me in Titus that I must always be discipling younger women and that I must always be being discipled by older women. That's exactly what is going on even today. I have two older women who disciple me. I'm involved in community ministry with all ages of women finding my niche to be women about ages 28 to 40. I've helped with women's retreats. I've helped with big women's weekends. I've helped one on one. I am now helping with a single's ministry in a home bible study. I've helped with Christian book launches. And I've simply taken women one by one to lunch, and I've found that time around the table with another human being is perfect because I do believe our tables are becoming our churches. I have a home bible study now meeting around a table in my den weekly. I promised God I'd spend as long as He wants me to do just this. Going. Not staying. Inviting people to come to my table.

He commanded me to go. That's what I'll always do. Will you fly with me? Let's "GO."

I scribbled this not boring story down just for you because I can testify to the fact that I have seen God-glory. And now I live in awe. Our Maker wants us to find Him. This God has now intertwined Himself into my story. And my hope is that you, too, will see Him through my story. And soon you will write about Him being inside your days, too.

And for now, I fly away.

Recipes from the Kitchen of
Tami Theobald

Dorito Casserole

Serves 6 • Cook time: 35 min • Prep time: 20 min

Ingredients:

3 cups of cooked chicken
1 can Original Rotel tomatoes
1 can Fiesta Nacho Cheese soup
1 can cream of mushroom soup
1 can cream of chicken soup
2 cups of shredded taco cheese blend
1 small bag of tortilla chips, crushed

Directions:

- Blend chicken, tomatoes, and all three soups in a bowl. Set aside.
- Grease a 9 x 13 casserole dish.
- Add crushed (about 3/4 of the chips) to the bottom of the greased casserole dish.
- Then add your mixture.
- Bake in a preheated 350° oven for 35 minutes until bubbly.
- Take out and garnish by adding shredded cheese to the top and the remainder (1/4) of the crushed chips.
- This is very good with a tossed green salad and yellow corn.
- Your family will love this cheesy casserole.

Chicken Poppyseed Casserole

Serves 6 • Cook time: 35 min • Prep time: 15 min

Ingredients:

3 cups cooked chicken
2 cans cream of chicken soup
16 ounces sour cream
3 tsp. poppy seeds
Salt
Pepper
1 sleeve of Ritz crackers (crushed)
1 stick of real butter, melted (I use Kerrygold)

Directions:

Blend the chicken, soups, sour cream, poppy seeds in a bowl.

Salt and pepper to taste.

Add to greased 9 x 9 casserole dish.

Melt the butter and add crushed Ritz crackers in another bowl.

Put this on top of the casserole. I sprinkle on some extra poppy seeds on top as well as a little more black pepper.

Bake in a preheated oven at 350° for 35 minutes.

Then enjoy this with a tossed green salad, whole green beans, and sourdough rolls.

Jezebel Sauce

Serves 12 • Cook time: 15 min • Prep time: 10 min

Ingredients:

1 (12 ounce) jar pineapple preserves
1 (16 ounce) jar apple jelly
3/4 cup prepared yellow mustard
2 tsp. black pepper,
3/4 cup prepared horseradish.

Directions:

- Combine all ingredients in a medium saucepan.
- Heat and stir until jellies are melted.
- Cool in a bowl in the refrigerator before serving.
- Store in a sealed container.

For best flavor, prepare a day or two in advance and keep chilled. This can be stored in your refrigerator for up to two weeks. Jezebel sauce is sweet yet spicy. It has a kind of a "wicked" taste, and that's probably where its name comes from. Put it over cream cheese and serve it with crackers - a popular thing to eat in the South. Also, it is tasty served with ham just out of the oven. It is also a great flavor as a topping for burgers. In the Deep South, we always say, "Where there is ham, there is Jezebel Sauce. Now, let the party begin."

"Delight yourself in the LORD; and He will give you the desires of your heart."

(Psalm 37:4 NASB)

My Plumb Line

By Tiffany Brinkman

My Jesus story doesn't come with specific dates and times. It is filled with layers of moments, brokenness, continuous acts of surrender, and an ever-evolving deliverance from the approval of man, or anyone telling me who I was and what I was worth. I hope until I see Jesus, and I am on my face before Him. These acts of surrender will always be of a little girl running to her Daddy.

It sounds so odd to have the heart to run to my Daddy when my earthly father never was on the list for who I would run to when I was hurt or when I did something wrong. His presence was never comforting. It was full of a tyrannical rage. From my earliest memories, I was so afraid of him. Like every little girl though, I wanted his approval, and I wanted him to think I was beautiful and smart. But he was a broken man that did not approve of himself. He was riddled with self-hate from the abuse he received as a child. He was mean and bound by the same generational strongholds as his dad. He took all that anger out on each of us in different ways.

My older siblings caught the brunt of most of his wrath. It was more mental toward me. My mom really got the worst of him though. I am the fourth of five children. There are eleven years between my sister and me. It seems I was an attempt to lure my father home from whatever bar he found himself in or whoever he was spending his time with. My younger brother came just over two years later. My mom used to say that my dad loved the sound of little feet. Little feet grow up and the responsibilities with them, I suppose. Eventually, it wasn't enough. We were never enough to fill the hole inside of him.

My mom was reclusive. Depression from my dad's unfaithfulness and abuse broke her heart and stole her joy. I never saw my mom fully alive. I knew she was in there. Her creativity wanted to come out, her comedic side, but she had been so beaten down emotionally and physically that all she could feel were the lies. The same lies my dad believed about himself he projected onto our whole family. My older sister and brothers all left home at young ages.

They wanted out.

My sister Kelly, oldest brother Mike and his wife Kim would take my little brother Jeremy and I to church when they could. I remember being in church and singing so loud, hoping God would hear me….and approve of me. Being in His presence was like nothing I ever experienced at home. I wished I could live in the four walls of the church.

I just wanted normal. I still wish that somedays. I am learning at new depth every day, that what I felt in His presence is in me. Even in the shaking legs and inner turmoil, I have access to peace. I just didn't know it then. My dad's anger did not lessen when my siblings moved out. His drinking and unfaithfulness worsened, but he was home much less. I remember my mom being so hurt on her anniversary because he didn't even come home. She loaded my brother and me up, and we left to stay in a motel. I remember doing this more than once and always because of my dad. But on this trip to the motel, we came home the next day to broken glass all over the living room. Her trinkets had met his rage. Turmoil and eggshells were an everyday thing. You just had to learn to navigate it and keep your head down. I always kept my head down.

When I was ten years old, we lost our home. I remember the sheriff coming to the house; I know there were others with him. They carried our belongings out the front door. Our toys, furniture, our lives, now were on the lawn. I can still see the lock going on the door when they were finished. We were locked out. I could never go back into my home. This day was the day my dad left. Our lives strewn about, no shelter for the night, no plan, and my dad left my mom with two kids to figure it out.

Something inside of me felt free, and I think my mom did too, maybe just a spark of it mixed with the fear of the unknown. My oldest brother Mike and his wife Kim came to help with their little's in tow. Mike has been my protector and proxy dad all my life. That night he and I slept under the giant oak tree in the front yard. We were trying to keep watch, so nothing was stolen in the night. I felt bigger, stronger, and more convinced of who I was when I was with them. They knew the lies and abandonment I felt as a child. To this day, they speak truth and love to me and come against those lies and point me to the word of God. They taught me to make Jesus my plumb line. Even in my wandering and reckless adolescence, I knew how to return to that.

They have taught me to pray even in the face of hopelessness. Unfortunately, I was a forgetful girl. I didn't know where my dad went that day when he left until I was almost an adult. We still saw him, and despite the situation, he and my mother never divorced. He lived with another woman. But he still made sure we had a roof over our head and groceries as well as a vehicle (though they usually resembled something from the movie *Uncle Buck* starring John Candy). He did this for the rest of my mom's life. The installments were always handed to her with ridicule, disdain, and disappointment in my brother and I. He was good to remind us that we weren't worth much. I believed him. I hated him for it, but I believed it all to be true.

Despite the best efforts of my brother and sister in love, I was still looking to the wrong things to fill me as an awkward teenage girl. Trying to outrun my dad's voice over me. "Someone, please love me, call me beautiful, tell me I am enough." However, what I thought was love was skewed by what I had been given growing up. I was such a mess. Head over heels for anyone who paid me a bit of attention thinking they would love me and make me whole. What I thought was normal, was not being pretty or smart enough to be worthy of love.

Mind you, all the while, Jesus was making himself available to me. I still found my way to church. I would hear the truth and feel His presence and believe it for about a minute until I was alone again. I made so many mistakes. Things I would be appalled for anyone who loves me to know. Things that I relive in my mind to this day. Nights that I gave pieces of myself to things that were not worthy of my innocence. Times that I thought life was not worth living, and I pictured ways to make it all stop. Darkness hung on me like a shroud. Drinking and worse to be numb to my mind. I was failing in school, but I wanted to learn. I couldn't focus on anything. My poor mom was so bound by her own sadness that she could not function and could not help me. Who was I to make things worse for her? I felt like such a waste. Shame.

So, I ran away when I was fifteen years old. I walked almost 15 miles to get to where I could reach my brother. After some hiccups and detours, my mom consented to let me move in with him almost an hour away. Their house was structured, and his four, fair-haired, freckled face girls were like my sisters. Kim made dinner every night. We played in the surrounding fields and took walks as a family. We went to church every Sunday. I lapped it up like a thirsty dog. They weren't at all perfect, but they were real, and they loved me real. All that empty hole, where family was supposed to be, was filling up. The plumb line was where it was supposed to be, but I felt guilty knowing my hurt was lessened, and my brother and mom were back home heavy under it. I couldn't help them.

I was enrolled in 8th grade at the middle school. It was small and country. My bus was K-12. That is when I laid eyes on the boy who would completely change my life. He was a much older 9th grader, and so he walked right on by me. To my giddy joy, when I reached 9th grade that boy shared enough classes with me that we became the best of friends. I mean, he was my absolute best friend. I could be silly or ugly or sappy. He didn't care that I didn't have money, that my family dynamic was not normal. He didn't even care that I had freckles and red hair, in fact, he preferred it. Given my beliefs about myself, I didn't know how to handle all that. I really liked him, but I could not imagine that he could be real when what I believed about myself was not what he saw. Walls went up around my heart. I ran again. It so happened that we had to move, and I had to go back home.

So, Kevin and I said goodbye. I mean, who meets the love of their life at 15? All the while, Jesus was pleading with me to come to Him with all my broken ugly. I gave Him pieces. I let Him into parts of my heart but compartmentalized the rest. Kevin and I continued to cross paths but never made any plans or commitments to each other until after he graduated High School. Then he began to pursue me. He made his heart very known. He scared me to death. I didn't know how to receive his love, but he loved deeply, and he loved real. He looked at me like I was the only girl in the world. (he still does). I was completely undone with him. I believed he would fill the void. We will be married 23 years this May.

It has been a long road. One filled with years of my daddy issues, his addictions, three babies, and all of our brokenness. We have fought ugly, hurt one another, and said horrible things in our heads and out loud. I treated Kevin as if he was like my dad. I thought he would give up and leave, and I gave him plenty of reasons to go because I was so unreasonable about some things. I would heap shame on him that I felt. He stayed and made it clear he loved me more than what my mind believed I deserved.

By grace, I would drag our 3 babies to church while he stayed home. I would pray, and I would nag. I hindered God so much in the process. I would parent my kids through distorted eyes and fear of becoming my parents. FEAR. It took me coming to the end of myself, really coming to the end of myself, and giving Jesus all the stuff, for me to allow my Daddy God to heal my vision and perception of who I was. He came in fully and began to rewrite who Tiffany was. He began to show me who He is as a father. To see His love in how my husband loved our kids and me. I got quiet. God began to move without my help or input. God is still healing me from the rejection of my father. He is still teaching me to love who He made me to be, and how He made me love the people He gives me each day. He is healing my misconceptions of who He is as a Father. He has blessed me with the love of my life, three beautiful kids, and two grandbabies. Where I felt like I fell short in so many areas of my life, they are my joy.

Daddy God is teaching me family, all over again. I want His heart. I want to love like Him in everything I do. Not in fear, not as an orphan, but His daughter.

Recipes from the Kitchen of
Tiffany Brinkman

Smokey Sweet Potato Harvest

Serves 6-8 • Cook time: 35 min

Ingredients:

3-4 medium sweet potatoes peeled and cubed
6-8 red potatoes washed and quartered
2 large tart apples peeled and diced
1/2 of a red onion quartered
1-2 smoked sausages sliced in 1-inch chunks (we like Private Selection brand-Peppered)
1/2 tsp. salt
1/2 tsp. cinnamon
1/2 tsp. pepper
1/4 tsp. smoked paprika
5-6 Tbsp. olive oil
1 Tbsp. minced garlic
1/2-3/4 cup feta cheese (reserve until broil)

Directions:

- Heat oven to 375°
- Toss vegetables in a large mixing bowl until coated by olive oil
- Sprinkle and toss dry spices onto vegetables and meat
- Spray a large casserole pan with cooking oil
- Pour mixture into the pan and cover with aluminum foil and bake for about 35 min at 375°.
- Uncover, if sweet potatoes are tender, sprinkle with feta and broil until golden and bubbly.

"The Spirit you received does not make you slaves,
so that you live in fear again; rather,
the Spirit you received brought about your adoption of sonship.
And by Him we cry, "Abba Father."

(Romans 8:15)

King of My Heart

By Caroline Atuzarirwe (from Uganda)

I want to start by saying thank you, Lord, for this far, you have brought me.

I have been through many highs and lows, and only You have kept me afloat up to this moment. Knowing I can trust You, Lord. Knowing I have a friend in You Lord is the one thing that really keeps me going forward, it's the one thing that keeps me still, knowing You are my refuge. Knowing in Your Word, I find hope and, in Your presence, I am renewed.

Right from when I was a child, from as far back as I can remember, growing up without my mother, I always felt like I was always fighting to be loved, always trying to be good, always going out of my way to work so hard in the home, with my siblings, we tried so hard to work so hard and be so good to be loved but we ended up being hurt by the people we trusted the most, the people we sought love from

Even when I grew up and was hosting prayer meetings in my home, I always had to work so hard to make everything perfect, perfect to the standards of this world and this reminds me of a friend who pointed this out to me recently, that I always want things to be perfect all the time which is not possible. What I didn't know was that God loves me just the way I am. All I have to do is surrender my heart fully to Him. All I had to do was seek Him with all my heart, and then I would find Him, and He would dwell with me and work His ways in me and through me.

One day I was crying so hard in the night from all the heartache that I was feeling. I looked back on my life and asked myself. Does true love really exist? You see, I felt like I had been on a journey, looking for true love in vain. I had given so much of myself, compromised so much and denied myself so much in the name of searching for love and acceptance from man. You see, I gave up so much, even when I had so much to lose, I would still go out of my way hoping the act of love, of loyalty, would speak volumes and create a lasting bond.

One night, I dreamt that the person I loved so much and had sacrificed so much for was stabbing me in the back and in the head with a big knife. Not long after that, I was surprised and shocked by the betrayal that would later follow, that I wasn't prepared for. It was after it happened that I remembered the dream. Then what followed after that was the pain in my heart; it became so much that I started to feel it physically; the pain lasted for several months. I also got terrible headaches and constant dizziness.

What I didn't fully comprehend, even though I heard it all the time is the fact that the Word of God is power. It washes me clean, and it purifies me. The only thing I understood was that whenever I read the Word of God, I regained my strength. So, I decided to bury myself in the Word of God; I became more discerning of what steps I needed to take in my workplace, in my personal life, and in ministry. I suddenly made decisions effortlessly concerning anything. I understood that, whenever I started to read the word of God, it washed my mind clean of all the stress and confusion that I had, and all I had left was a determined resolve.

I suddenly had a resolve to serve the Lord with all my heart, to follow Him all of my days. I decided I was going to let Him truly come into my heart and transform me and show me His ways. I decided to dwell in the power of His love. I decided to trust in His saving grace. So, one of the sleepless nights, I switched on my laptop and decided to look for anything on Facebook with Holy, Holiness, or Purity. I searched until I came upon the HOLY BEAUTIFUL MINISTRY! This caused my heart to skip a beat! I wondered could this be what I am looking for. You see, I had made a resolve in my heart to seek God in holiness and purity, but I knew that I couldn't do it alone, I needed the Holy Spirit to guide me and lead me to the right way to take. And He led me to the Holy Beautiful Ministry! This caused a total turnaround in my life! I read through the devotionals from the Holy beautiful team, and I found them so amazingly real! They ministered to the deepest part of my heart.

Today I can confidently say the pain in my heart is gone and I am so strong in the Lord, I am so sure of who I am in Christ. The Holy Spirit has shown me how important it is to dwell in the Presence of God. I have found great love in writing for God. Whenever I am writing for God, I feel His mighty power, and I am comforted and renewed! In the presence of God; I am filled with so much love and so much peace. I am so thankful to God for bringing me to this beautiful Ministry and for connecting me with a wonderful group of women with whom I can share and grow in the love of Christ.

Recipe from the Kitchen of

Caroline Atuzarirwe

Eshabwe

Serves 7 • Cook time: 30 min • Prep time: 5 min

Ingredients:

1/2 liter of ghee
3 Tbsp. of ground rock salt
400 ml of water
A ladle to use for mixing
A clean round saucepan or big dish
A clean cotton cloth
A spoon

Directions:

- Boil the water
- Crush the rock salt and add 3 Tbsp. of the rock salt to the hot water and stir until it dissolves in the water
- Leave the mixture to cool to almost room temperature
- You can add more rock salt to your desired taste
- Put the ghee in the saucepan
- Stir the ghee in a clockwise direction
- Add bits of water in short intervals as you stir
- Continue to stir for about 15 mins as you add the water until the sauce turns pure white, thick and doubles in volume.
- Cover the sauce with the clean white cloth
- The sauce is ready to be served.
- Can be served as an independent sauce or a side sauce with any food

"For the word of God is quick, and powerful, and sharper than any two-edged sword, piercing even to the dividing asunder of soul and spirit, and of the joints and marrow, and is a discerner of the thoughts and intents of the heart."

(Hebrews 4:12)

"But who may abide the day of His coming? and who shall stand when He appeareth? for He is like a refiner's fire, and like fullers' soap: And He shall sit as a refiner and purifier of silver: and He shall purify the sons of Levi, and purge them as gold and silver, that they may offer unto the LORD an offering in righteousness."

(Malachi 3:2-3)

God's Grace and Goodness

By Jacqueline Landeau

I wouldn't be able to touch on everything in my life at this point, but this will sum up a small measure of God's grace and goodness to me.

I wasn't raised in the church but grew up hearing about Jesus Christ and God from my loving devoted father who made a tremendous impact on my life and my other siblings who are also serving God. He died at age 82, forty years ago, when I was 16 years old. That broke me. My mom was still pretty young, but she migrated to Canada to join her mom and her siblings. She has always been a gifted homemaker but needed a change after my dad passed. She accepted Christ into her life the year he died and never looked back or remarried.

I accepted Christ into my life and got baptized at age 17. I was fervently serving God as a Worshipper, Sunday School teacher, Singing, and Evangelizing. The church had a vibrant Youth Ministry. After about 2 years, the church split suddenly because of irregularities with the leadership.

My life has been a rollercoaster in between because of some very poor choices that I made, and the enemy has tried on countless times to destroy me "But God," has always been good and faithful to my family and me in spite of me being so distant sometimes. As is said, "I have given God countless reasons not to love me. None of them changed His mind.

I always felt God drawing me to Himself which is one of the reasons I always wanted to know Him in a real and personal way. Like, who is this 'God' that keeps showing up in my life, even from a tender age and getting my attention in so many ways, where I will just touch on a couple.

I remembered going home one night with my younger sister and friends around Christmas season. A car driven by a drunk driver crashed into me from behind and picked me up to where witnesses said I was like flying through the air and landed on my back a distance away. Everyone thought I was dead, but all I remembered was floating peacefully and then opening my eyes to people over me, saying rush her to the hospital. They were so scared. I never felt the impact, though. At the hospital, after being examined, the Doctor was so confused and kept asking everyone if they were sure I was in an accident. He couldn't understand how come there were no bruises whatsoever, and all the test results and x-rays came back showing nothing. I walked out of the hospital with a second chance at life, not even understanding what really happened. I was just thankful to God for sparing my life.

Also, in a club partying with friends and family and suddenly everything stood still. I couldn't hear anyone or the music. Everything was like moving slowly, and all I could hear was this voice saying, "my child, this is not what I planned for your life." These are the same people you were called to minister to; they need you. This life is not yours. I was amazed and just stood there not moving until others came across concerned and asked me 'what's up.' All I could do and say was I have to leave here and go home.

I was also attacked by two men who tried to kidnap me forcefully with a huge knife to my neck, forcing me into their vehicle. I was frightened at first, but then I cried out with all my might "Jesus Help Me" and not to this day sure what happened, but I had the knife in my hands, and they were trying to wrench it from me, but God miraculously saved me from that situation unharmed. People heard the commotion and came out and intervened. Glory to God.

In my rebellious times away from God, I always came to realize that there was no way I could live without God in my life. It never, ever worked out. There was never any real peace, especially when I tried to do things in my own strength.

I always came back to God after every experience, but the enemy was so determined to take me out God's hands. I must say my Heavenly Father always fought for me.

One of the other experiences that made an important impact on me was a few years back. I got sick both spiritually and physically. I was struggling and not finding my way and had a few setbacks in my life that I felt I couldn't handle. This caused me to feel empty. This emptiness went so deep that I fell into a life of depression (unknown to most) because I was never without a smile and was always a people person. So, no one suspected. God was seemingly also so distant and silent in those times. I thought and asked God, "where are you?" Most times, I was just crying out to God for help and not feeling Him in anything or in any way. So, I actually thought this time, God had left me, and that was the worst feeling in my life. I felt an emptiness so deep just thinking that God had forsaken me this time. (A place I would never want to be in again). Things got so bad that I had to see a specialist and had to rely on tablets to function daily, but the pills had so many side effects that it wasn't working for me and I came to the point that I had enough, I couldn't go on like this anymore and it was affecting my kids. They were pretty young at that time, the youngest not even a year yet. My sister, who passed really helped me with them.

One day, after work, eager to reach home almost in tears, I came home, opened the door and dropped to my knees broken and in tears, crying hysterically, determined to get God's attention. I had had enough. It was almost time to take the tablets, or I would not be able to function. My body relied on it. I remember sobbing and talking to God and quoting scriptures back at Him and telling God to take these pills; I don't want them anymore; I only wanted Him back in my life. I threw the pills down and continued crying out to Him asking Him to take away this sickness. I wasn't aware of the time. I was in that same position when I dropped to sleep (something that I couldn't do for a long time) and awoke to realize it was morning and I had not taken the pills. So, I was waiting for that nervous feeling and being unable to have any coordination. It never came. All Glory to my loving miracle-working God. Never had that experience again. Never took pills again. God completely healed me. Forever grateful to Him.

There was no rest for me in my spirit until I surrendered fully to my Savior. God made it His business always to seek me out because He knew who I could become in Him. He gives us an indescribable peace that the world definitely cannot give. I had to learn this the hard way. It made no sense not having God in my life. It did not work for me. Remember, God said, He will never leave us nor forsake us.

Of course, my life now is not without challenges, but the difference is I know who I turn to and I know who I resist. Even as God's word said, "Submit to God and resist the enemy," and I know whose report I believe in and God's report says, I am healed, and I am free.

Recipe from the Kitchen of

Jacqueline Landeau

Chicken Pelau (pay lao)

Serves 6 • Cook time: 35 min

Ingredients:

3 lbs. chicken pieces, skinned
1 tsp. salt
1/2 tsp. black pepper
2 Tbsp. mixed green seasoning (parsley, cilantro, green onions, thyme, etc.)
2 tsp. minced garlic
2 Tbsp. parsley
1 tsp. soy sauce
1 Tbsp. Worcestershire sauce
1 Tbsp. ketchup
2 Tbsp. oil
2-3 Tbsp. brown sugar
2 cups parboiled rice
1/2 cup chopped onion
1/2 cup cooked pigeon peas
1 Tbsp. salt
1 whole hot pepper with stem (Scotch bonnet)
2 cups coconut milk
2 cups chicken broth or water

Directions:

- Season chicken with salt, pepper, green seasoning, minced garlic, parsley, Worcestershire sauce, soy sauce, and ketchup.
- Heat oil in a large, heavy iron pot or skillet.
- Add sugar and allow to burn until brown.
- Add the seasoned chicken and stir until pieces are well coated with burnt sugar; brown for 5 minutes.
- Add rice and turn often until well mixed.

- Cook for 3 minutes more.
- Add onion, sweet peppers and peas and cook for a few minutes, stirring a few times.
- Add salt, hot pepper, coconut milk, and broth.
- Bring to the boil, lower heat, cover and simmer until rice is cooked and all liquid is evaporated (about 20 to 30 minutes).
- Add more liquid if rice is still hard and continue to cook for a few minutes.
- Rice should be moist but not sticky.
- Serve with a side of coleslaw.

"I am crucified with Christ: nevertheless I live;
yet not I, but Christ liveth in me:
and the life which I now live in the flesh I live by the faith
of the Son of God, who loved me and gave Himself for me."

(Galatians 2:20 KJV)

The Power of Faith in Jesus Christ

By Sharon Tull

My testimony began forming in the early stages of my life, but I'll begin my story with when I was around the age of 10. My mother's health had begun to decline until she could no longer take care of me. I was then sent to live with an older cousin and began living a life of servitude.

My cousin had six children of her own, but I was the oldest, so I was responsible for everything. My cousin was a food truck vendor, so every morning at 4am, I had to wake up to help her prepare breakfast for at least 100 employees. On school days, I still had to wash all the dishes (huge pots and pans) and make sure the house was clean before the school bus arrived. After school was the same routine because she cooked breakfast and lunch. There was very little time for being a child and playing with my cousins and friends. I remember crying a lot, especially when she often said that I would never become anything and called me nasty names that I barely understood. I often prayed to Jesus Christ to send me back to my mother, but my situation only got worse.

Despite my unfortunate situation in life as a child and young woman, I slowly found my testimony in my faith in God and books. I know that Jesus was with me during those dark periods of my childhood. He consoled me and kept me from having thoughts of suicide, even in my darkest moments. Whenever I read books, I was transported into another time where there was no pain or hard work. I am now a stronger person through it all. There were tough lessons to learn, but I overcame it all with a few bruises that Jesus Christ's love healed. Amen

I will lift up mine eyes unto the hills, from whence cometh my help.

My help cometh from the Lord, which made heaven and earth.

He will not suffer thy foot to be moved: He that keepeth thee will not slumber.

Behold, He that keepeth Israel shall neither slumber nor sleep.

The Lord is thy keeper: the Lord is thy shade upon thy right hand.

The sun shall not smite thee by day, nor the moon by night.

The Lord shall preserve thee from all evil: He shall preserve thy soul.

The Lord shall preserve thy going out and thy coming in from this time forth, and even for evermore (Psalm 121 KJV).

Recipe from the Kitchen of

Sharon Tull

Amazing Pineapple Jerk Chicken

(Adapted from Caribbeanpot.com)

Serves 6 • Cook time: 90 min • Prep time: 150 min

Ingredients:

3 Tbsp. of jerk seasoning
1/4 tsp. black pepper
2 Tbsp. of dark soy sauce
1/2 scotch bonnet pepper(diced), 4 cloves of garlic(minced),
1 1/2 Tbsp. brown sugar
6 sprigs of thyme
3 scallions(sliced thinly)
1 1/4 cup orange juice
1 Tbsp. olive oil
2 whole chicken (about 5 lbs.)

Directions:

- Prepare chicken by cutting into small pieces and removing fat. Leave the skin intact to prevent from drying.
- Rinse and set aside.
- For the marinade, combine the remaining ingredients in a large bowl and mix well.
- Put the chicken in a large roasting pan and pour marinade over it and combine well. Marinade for approximately 2 hours.
- Preheat oven at 410° then put the roasting pan on the middle rack and cook uncovered for 1 hour and 15 minutes.
- For a more golden color, broil for an additional 5 minutes.
- Can be paired with any sides of your choice.
- Note: If you prefer skinless chicken, cover with foil for the first hour of cooking. Remove foil and cook for an additional 30 minutes to obtain a golden color.

"Yea, though I walk through
the valley of the shadow of death,
I will fear no evil"

(Psalm 23:4 KJV)

Purified By Fire

By The Immaculate Akongo Centre For African Research

In August 2014, my health started deteriorating, and I watched myself becoming frail, pale, weak, and continuously losing weight. I had developed excruciating pain in my abdomen and had been put on pain killers and another medication for ulcers. On a visit to the hospital, I was told I was developing type 2 diabetes, and my sister purchased a supplement from Green World Company. I was told my sugar level would normalize within three months of using the supplement. They kind of worked but I was under too much stress at that time considering the hectic nature of my job that involved riding a motorcycle to the field and locations where I was working with the youth on an economic empowerment project. I grew weaker every day. In November, I applied for sick leave, and my supervisor granted me permission, and I went to Mulago Hospital. It is the National Referral Hospital in Kampala. I was treated and improved a little, but the pain in my abdomen persisted, and my appetite was drastically affected because of the pain I was in. I could not figure out whether what I ate also contributed to my pain.

In May 2015, I lost my maternal aunt to cancer of the colon, the grief weighed on me heavily, and I depreciated further. Then in August 2015, just within the span of three months, my maternal uncle, who took care of us, also passed on. He had been battling hypertension and diabetes. When my sister told me the news, I was devastated and that marked the beginning of my fire purification process. Immediately, the pain in my abdomen intensified, the medication that seemed to reduce the pain a little earlier stopped working. I started vomiting and could not eat or drink anything and not throw up. A week after the burial, I could not move by myself anymore; I needed support to get out of bed, going to the shower and toilet and dressing.

In all of this, my sisters and friends were seeking God and unceasingly praying for me with a prayer team at their church. My youngest sister, who is also the last-born confessed salvation before my other sister and me. We were the only three girls remaining in a family of five. Our eldest sister and brother that I followed passed on after our Dad and our mother passed on the

17th September 1997, leaving me as the eldest and caretaker of my two sisters. My youngest sister came home on the 1st of December 2013 to pray for me. While praying, the pastor asked if I minded being led into salvation, and I didn't have the strength to resist anymore. I was meditating on the words they were sharing; one was "…all you need is Jesus Christ as your personal savior, friend, and confidant." I was born and raised in a very staunch Catholic family, but now I had to change where to pray from and joined one of the Pentecostal churches in January 2014 to date.

In November 2015, my sister took me to the hospital again, and I was admitted and stayed in the ward for two weeks. That was the turning point in my life, and if not by the saving grace of the Lord and the deep trust I had in Him, I would be no more. The doctors, after running several tests, continued treating the ulcers, which later turned out to be a wrong diagnosis. Three days after admission, the attending doctor requested a chest x-ray, and when the results came out, I, of course, did not know most of what was being discussed. After he called my sister and said he wanted to discuss my results with my closest family. I later learned that he told my sister that according to my x-rays I had lymphoma in my lungs, tuberculosis, and meningitis and that meant I was GOING TO DIE IN LESS THAN TWO MONTHS due to the complications that have set in. And that there are tests that they cannot do from the hospital I was in and was referred for specialist treatment. That referral was the dim light at the end of the tunnel that later turned out to be the saving light. I was discharged on the 23rd of December 2015, and the doctors said we should hire an ambulance and go straight to Kampala. However, I could not. I did not have the money immediately nor my sisters, so I came home and while at home I could sense a change in my sister's attitude and thought that probably she was just tired, or it was because of what she was told by the doctor, that I was going to die. Because of the wrong diagnosis, I was deserted and went through very cruel times, but the pastor and his wife kept coming to pray with me and to check on me. Later, when we got the money in early January 2016, we traveled to Kampala. This was a journey which usually takes 5 to 6 hours. It took us the whole day because we had to stop after every two hours' so I could rest for a few minutes. Finally, we reached the hospital. Immediately they started running tests, and the doctor came and told me that I had an infection in the small intestine and that was what had caused the persistent vomiting and most of the elements in my body to be below the standard level. Some were almost zero. My blood level was also very low. The doctors told me I could choose to be admitted with them or go to two other hospitals that could handle my condition. I told the doctor that I was okay with being admitted there. It appeared for the first time I was being told a very different diagnosis and prayed this doctor might help. I was admitted immediately, and they started treatment. I came in a wheelchair weighing 46 kgs, but the doctors were so dedicated and committed to saving my life. The day before we left for Kampala, I requested the pastor to pray for me so that I may get the right doctors and access the right treatment. Three days later, I was taken for an x-ray, and I was told my chest was very clear. In my heart, I knew GOD HAD DEALT WITH THAT. I told the doctor I was earlier told that I had tuberculosis and developing cancer of the lungs. In dismay, he asked me if I was coughing, and I told him no. So, he said, they were going to monitor me closely, and in case of any slight symptom, they would run more tests, but for now, they just wanted to treat the infection, stop the vomiting and put me on multi-vitamins. My sugar level was also now normal. I stayed in the ward for eleven days and was discharged. Though weak, I could walk with support and no longer needed a wheelchair. Everyone who saw me the day of my admission, including the doctors, could not understand how fast I was recovering. However, I knew it was the Lord's miracle, and that stepped up my confidence in prayers because before I left for Kampala, the pastor had told me that I should go and return safely. Of course, at that moment, it sounded more like a consolation but later turned out to be the truth. I returned home, recovered so fast, and one of my close friends said: "…people should stop looking for signs of miracles but look at you, you are a living miracle and God indeed heals". Since, then to date, I am well, spiritually grown, happily serving the Lord, ordained and overseeing hospital and prisons ministry.

In all this, I learned total dependence and trust in God. Obedience and submission, never to believe in the report of man, that no condition is permanent, the divine saving power of prayer and above all that greater is He that is in us than he that is in the world. He is our hope of glory in the face of adversity and through whom ALL things are possible. Looking back at what I went through, I also realize that I was being prepared and purified to serve in the kingdom. After my ordination when I was appointed to oversee prison and hospital ministry, the Presiding Bishop and founder of the ministry did not know what I had passed through and I confirmed God was speaking to me, revealing the purpose of my past pain and teaching me compassion, to love and to care unconditionally, listen and be human to the helpless and vulnerable persons.

These made Psalms 23:4 my favorite scripture verse:

"Yea, though I walk through the valley of the shadow of death, I will fear no evil…." (Psalm 23:4 KJV).

To me, it expresses victory as we are more than conquerors in Christ JESUS!

Recipe from the Kitchen of

Immaculate Akongo

Caramel Lemon Cake

Serves 10-20 • Cook time: 20 min • Prep time: 45 min

Ingredients:

1 cup margarine
1 cup sugar
5 eggs
1 tsp. vanilla
1 tsp. lemon
2 Tbsp. sugar
3 cups baking flour
1 Tbsp. baking powder
Several lemons
1 cup water

Directions:

- Scoop 1 cup of margarine & sugar in a mixing bowl, mix with a ladle until it's fluffy whitish
- Beat the 5 eggs one by one into the mixture until it's evenly mixed & looks like spoilt milk
- Add 1 teaspoon each of vanilla & lemon flavor and stir to mix evenly
- Grate the peel of 1 lemon into the mixture (for stronger flavor, squeeze the juice too into the mixture)
- Heat 2 tablespoons of sugar in a pan until deep brown then add the 1 cup of water & keep stirring until the sugar to dissolves, take it away from the heat & let it cool
- Sieve 3 cups of baking powder together with the 1 tablespoon of the baking powder
- Add the caramel mixture (the heated sugar) & the baking flour & powder in 3 portions and mix evenly

- Grease the baking pan with little quantities of margarine & dust with baking flour & pour the mixture and place in the oven.
- Note: pre-heat the oven to 180° C / 350° F. Leave the cake to bake for about 20 minutes or less but check by thrusting a sharp knife, and if nothing sticks on the blade, then it's ready.
- The serving number varies depending on the size of the portions served & preparation time too can be shorter if using an electric mixer.

"It is for freedom that Christ has set us free.
Stand firm then and do not let yourselves be burdened again
by the yoke of slavery."

(Galatians 5:1)

There is Freedom in Forgiveness

By Sheila Millinder

It was a normal day in the life of a teenager. I returned home from school, and what seemed like a normal day would soon be the day my world CRASHED and changed forever. Immediately arriving home like all 15 yr old girls I go to get on the phone, and it rang. A neighbor called and said my dad was in an accident at work and was hurt. Well, I had not heard from my mother, so I assumed it was nothing since previously he had broken his foot and had a few other incidents. Then my grandfather arrived, telling me I needed to go with him now. Long, long story made short late this night I find out my father was killed in an accident at work. He was a Junior Blaster on a coal stripping job, and the Blaster had called off that day, and my dad took his place. He set the charge, but they did not account for the low electric lines and when he set the charge off the line shot up and caught on the high voltage lines and it surged back to the box my father was using, and he was killed instantly.

I think on that day that I went numb and it wouldn't be until years later that I began to breathe again and live. I remember with every moment that I heard someone telling the story it would ring in my ears that the Blaster called off that day and my father had taken his place. My heart began to fill with such anger that hatred for that man built inside me. I became bitter, and it took deep root in my heart. I was not a Christian and knew nothing of forgiveness, or mercy or what real love was. All I knew was I was 15, and my father was gone forever because someone called off work. It should not have been him. And more anger built.

I began drinking, partying, hanging out with friends, ditching school, and it wasn't long before I dropped out. I ended up married at 17 yrs old. My life just became one bad choice after another. Although I got very good at "appearances," I was angry and bitter on the inside. In these years I did manage to have two wonderful boys who are my whole world, I completed my GED and even went to college, but through it all, I still carried what now had become immense hatred for that man. Years passed, and I divorced. And eventually was united with my husband now, and my journey to forgiveness and healing began.

My husband found us a church, and we began attending, and I gave my heart to the Lord. Slowly week after week, my heart began to soften. The more I felt the love of our new church family, and I began to understand Gods love. One day while at home, my husband and I were talking about things, and he said, “It’s time to forgive him.” I was reluctant at first, but I felt the click in my heart that was saying, “yes, its time.” I will never forget the process that took place that day as my husband was a vessel God used to lead me to a place of forgiveness. As we talked and I cried, which felt like the first time since my father’s passing, my husband said, “now say I forgive him.” I hesitated but then said it and then said it again, and then again and then again. Then suddenly it was though I could see that man and the burden he was carrying knowing that would have been him. Then it was as though God was showing me His family, His wife, His children, and then my heart broke into pieces forever wishing this pain upon another person. That was the beginning of freedom for me. For years I looked through the lens of my loss, my dad missing my growing up, my wedding day, the birth of my sons, my graduation from college. Now the lens had become not self-focused, and my eyes could see this man’s life. Although it would be sometime before the thought of him didn’t provoke negative emotions the day did come. Two years ago, I came face to face with this man, and of course, he had no idea who I was, but I remember feeling whole at that moment. No longer did I want to spew out all my pain upon him. My heart flooded with the thoughts that I have truly forgiven and no longer carried any ill feelings, hatred, or contempt. I actually thanked God that day, not only for freeing me from that prison I was locked in, but I thanked Him that this man’s life carried on. He watched his sons grow up and was living a full life with his family. Ahhhh…I AM FREE. God’s grace, mercy, and love now filled those deep places where that bitter root of unforgiveness once held my heart captive.

Recipe from the Kitchen of

Sheila Millinder

Black Bean and Avocado Salsa

Serves 6 • Cook time: 15 min

Ingredients:

2 jalapeños (seeded for less heat, if desired)
1 clove garlic
1/2 medium white onion
kosher salt
pepper
1 can black beans
2 scallions
2 Tbsp. fresh lime juice
1 Tbsp. olive oil
1 avocado
1/2 cup fresh cilantro

Directions:

- In a large bowl, combine the jalapeños, garlic, onion, 1/2 teaspoon salt, and 1/4 teaspoon pepper.
- Add the beans, scallions, lime juice, and oil and toss to combine.
- Fold in the avocado and cilantro.

Behold, I'm standing at the door, knocking.
If your heart is open to hear my voice
and you open the door within,
I will come in to you and feast with you,
and you will feast with me.

(Revelation 3:20 TPT)

Minding My Own Business

By Kristine Cotterman

I've always loved Jesus for as long as I can remember. My mom even wrote in my baby book that I "giggled and cooed" while I got baptized.

My mom sang in the choir at church while my dad and I sat in the service. I loved watching her walk into the sanctuary to sing. She sang and played piano at home, so I knew how angelic her voice was. "That's my mom!"

I had a wonderful childhood, and my mom and dad created the perfect home for me and my much younger brother and sister. I can't complain about anything while I was growing up. God was good! We were a cute little family of 5, with a huge extended family (23 cousins!), lots of friends, and Barbies, who helped my imagination and dreams about the future form.

Well, at least until someone told me about death. Now, that seemed to be a real big problem I'd have to face when I was "old" and it "wouldn't happen for a long, long time."

Unfortunately, it was not a very long time until I stood face to face with death. Cancer came crashing into our lives when I was 16, in 10th grade, and my mom was diagnosed with Non-Hodgkin's Lymphoma. After some success and remission, it was only 4 years later that my mom died. It was so unbelievable, like a bad dream. I am not sure where I shoved those emotions at the time, but it was deep, deep down. A reality not to be fully grasped until I got a little older, engaged, married, and became a mom who really needed her mom!

I married an incredibly talented intelligent man who swept me off my feet. He had rescued me from the East Side of St. Paul and introduced me to the finer things in life. We had 3 beautiful babes in just under 2 years. Our life was unfolding beautifully.

I had met Rick in a restaurant, back in the day, when he was the manager, and I was the girl who needed a job. Fast forward to our kids all going to school...I went back to work and dragged Rick into working in a restaurant with me. He was the head manager, and I was his assistant.

The pizza restaurant was a well known busy place in our city, so almost everyone eventually walked through the doors. Life and work were clicking along. We were minding our own business. Life was good. I'd even go so far as to say our life was just perfect.

UNTIL...the knock at the door!

You see, we live in a twin home, and the place next door had just been purchased. It was our new neighbor, obviously more outgoing than even us, standing there and knocking on our door. He was the new pastor at the biggest church on the main street through the city. He invited us to come to church and told us about his daughter. As it turned out she needed a job, and we were always hiring. "Tell her to come in and see us!"

We hired her and a few of her friends. We had no idea of WHO we were really letting in the door!

In the afternoons, after the lunch rush, the restaurant was very slow. This is when we'd get everything cleaned up, stocked up, then sit and roll silverware while we watched tv. Little did we know these would end up being the most life-changing afternoons of our life!

We hadn't been to church since the kids were baptized. Not that we didn't want God in our life, but we were pretty busy raising the kids and working. So, when our new waitresses started evangelizing to us...let's just say it stirred up a lot of emotion. I even called my Lutheran pastor from back in the day at the church mom sang in and asked him if some of this stuff was "even in the Bible?" The deeper they dug in, the more I got defensive.

Let's just say; I had no clue what God was going to do in our hearts and lives when we accepted their invitation to go to that church on Easter. It changed everything!

We even got fired from the restaurant when we went in to hang posters for a huge evangelistic presentation at church. That was also a huge life changer. You might even be inclined to think it was terrible to lose our jobs after we gave our hearts to Jesus. But it wasn't really.

What I didn't tell you was that I've always been an artist. Way back in Sunday School, Kindergarten, and all through school and my life...that is my gifting. So when we got fired, I went to college and got a degree in graphic design.

I prayed and begged God to let me be a part of what He is doing.

Now, "Minding My Own Business" is a reality, and we get to do it every day. (I dragged Rick into it, too!) Truly, I believe that Jesus knocked on our door that day. He sat and spoke into our life through those young ladies. I sure am glad I heard the knock and answered the door!

Recipes from the Kitchen of
Kristine Cotterman

Mom's Scalloped Corn

Serves 8-10 • Cook time: 45-60 Min

Ingredients:

2 cans of mixed white & yellow corn
1 can evaporated milk
14 Tbsp. of butter divided
2 eggs
4 Tbsp. of flour
2 tsp of salt
1 tsp of pepper
2 cups of crushed saltine crackers

Directions:

- Pre-heat oven to 350° F.
- Pre-butter inside of oven safe casserole dish with 2 Tbsp of butter (or Non-Stick Spray).
- Open cans of corn then drain and SAVE the corn water in large measuring cup. Set corn aside.
- Open the can of evaporated milk and add to the corn water to equal 2 cups of liquid. Set aside.
- Crush 2 cup of saltine crackers and mix with 1 stick melted butter until absorbed. Set aside.
- Crack 2 eggs and slightly beat. Set aside.
- In a medium sauce pan, heat the 2 cups corn water/evap milk with 4 Tbsp. flour, 4 Tbsp. butter, 2 tsp. salt, and 1/2 tsp. pepper. When thickened, add 2 eggs slightly beaten, stir in then remove from heat.
- Add drained corn into thickened sauce pan and stir, then pour into casserole dish. Top with buttered crushed saltines gently and evenly spread on top, then bake in oven for 45-60+ minutes. Start checking middle at 45 min to see if it's firming up. Middle should be somewhat firm when done.

I hope you enjoy this recipe that has been a part of Thanksgiving celebrations in our family for generations!

Ahma's Pizza Burgers

Serves 6-12 (2 each) • Cook time: 12-15 Min • Prep: 20 Min

Ingredients:

2 lbs. ground beef
1 can of Spam
1 lb of Velveeta Cheese
1 Tbsp. Italian seasoning
2 Tbsp. parsley flakes
1/2 tsp. salt
1 24 oz. jar of spaghetti sauce
1 dozen sliced plain hamburger buns

Directions:

- Pre-heat oven to 350° F.
- Grate Spam into bowl and set aside.
- Slice Velveeta cheese into 1/2 inch cubes and set aside.
- Brown the ground beef until done and drain fat.
- Add grated Spam, spaghetti sauce, cubed cheese, stir until cheese is melted.
- Mix in spices.
- Simmer 5-10 minutes.
- Remove from heat and let thicken for 5-10 minutes.
- Spoon evenly covering open bun half.
- Bake pizza burgers for 12-15 minutes.
- Enjoy!!!

Papa's Melting Moments

2-3 Dozen Two-Tier Cookies • Bake time: 12-14 min • Prep time: 2 hours + Overnight

Ingredients:

1 cup butter
1 cup flour
1/3 cup powdered sugar
3/4 cup corn starch
1 tsp. vanilla

We usually 4x the recipe because you'll wish you had more when they melt in your mouth!

Directions:

- Cream the butter in the mixer.
- Add the vanilla.
- Add powdered sugar.
- Add cornstarch.
- Slowly add flour till all mixed.
- Cool 1/2 hour in fridge then roll into long rolls, 10-12 inches long, about the diameter of a quarter.
- Cool in fridge - apart and covered - overnight.
- Pre-heat oven to 350° F.
- Slice into 1/4 inch slices, try to keep roundness.
- Bake for 12 to 14 min. Best to take out when slight golden starts to show on edges.
- Let cool and then frost with fun holiday colors and sprinkles. Cans of squirt frosting are quick and easy on these tiny cookies.
- Frost 2 cookies and stack to make 1.

These will soon be your family's favorite cookie!

At Your Table
Come those in pain
Those who need Your
Healing Rain.
Are you ready, My Beloved?
The time is near,
no time to worry
no time to fear.

Poetry at the Table

From as early as I can remember, the Lord has always spoken to my heart through the beauty of poetry. And when I found myself speaking to Him, I would always be led to take pen in hand and put to paper what was on my heart.

I find such comfort in doing this for many reasons. The most important is that I am actually able to look back over the years and see the journey we are on together, transform, and take shape.

I am able to look back and see this once shy little girl, growing into this bold woman of God that He is calling me to be. It has brought both tears and joy to my heart to see the changes that have taken place and has, at times, taken my breath away. It has also made me stop at times in amazement that I actually wrote something like that, by His Spirit! Wow! Me!

How did that happen?! But then He gently reminds me as He often does, that He will use anyone who is willing. All it takes is someone who is willing to listen, willing to surrender, willing to be used, and not afraid to speak what He longs to say.

I am so very grateful for any opportunity I have to share His heart in the hopes that it will reach or touch even one person. I pray this collection of poems will not only bless you but challenge you to sit with Him, with Your journal open, pen in hand, listening, for what He wants to share with you today. And that you, in turn, can share with others, to touch and minister to their lives and their hearts.

Will you be willing to listen and share today? I pray each of us always will.

In love and service,
Naomi Krstinic

Are You Ready, My Beloved?

Are you ready, My Beloved?
The time is near,
no time to worry
no time to fear.

Are you ready, My Beloved?
Come away with Me more
abide in My Presence
ask Me for more.

Are you ready, My Beloved?
Can you hear Me calling your name?
Does it bring as much joy to you
as when I hear you do the same?

Are you ready, My Beloved?
For our new life to start?
Where we are joined forever
never again to part?

Are you ready, My Beloved?
Can you hear the Father say,
"Make preparations ready
for the Great Wedding Day?"

Are you ready, My Beloved?
To stand by My side,
with Me as your Bridegroom
and you as My Bride?

Are you ready, My Beloved?
Take hold of My hand.
We'll walk together
into our promised land.

I am ready, My Beloved
I'm here at Your side
From this day forward
I will abide as Your Bride.

At Your Table

At Your Table
Come those in pain
Those who need Your
Healing Rain.

At Your Table
You call Your own
To come now,
To come on home.

At Your Table
You beckon the lost
To sacrifice all
To count the cost.

At Your Table
You draw all near
Those in Your heart
That You hold dear.

At Your Table
You share Your plan
For us to walk
Throughout this land.

At Your Table
We come to share
Of Your Love
And how You care.

At Your Table
Filled with Grace
We join together
To behold Your face.

At Your Table
We come to pray
And with our prayers
The enemy slay.

At Your Table
We become bold
As You reveal
Your stories of old.

At Your Table
We long to stay
As we say Lord
Please have Your way.

At Your Table
May we forever abide
For we belong with You
Right at Your side.

Bread of Life

Bread of Life
Speak to me
Tell me who
I am called to be.

Bread of Life
Reveal Your plan
For how I am to
Walk through this land.

Bread of Life
With You I choose to stay
When You call
I won't delay.

Bread of Life
At Your Table I sit
Our hearts are joined together
Forever we're knit.

Bread of Life
At Your Banquet Table
I find that I am strengthened
I am empowered, enabled.

Bread of Life
I give You my all
Wearing Your armor
I am standing tall.

Bread of Life
I'll be Your Faithful Bride
When they look for me
I'll be at Your side.

Bread of Life
My Glorious King
Thank You for choosing me
And giving me everything!

Come Let Me Behold You

Come partake of the Master's Feast
Prepared just for you
Taste of the delicacies made by His hand
They will fill you through and through.

Come and behold the Glory of the King
As you recline with Him here
Let Him share His heart with you
And all that He holds dear.

Come and drink the wine
Offered from His hand
Let Him show you the Majesty
Of His Divine plan.

Come let Him show you
The secrets in His heart
And as you abide there
He'll show you your part.

Come and let Him soothe you
And take away all pain
For it's only in His Presence
You feel His healing rain.

Come let Him adorn you
As His holy Bride
Daily at His Table
Is where you must reside.

Come holy beautiful one
And take some time today
As together we join hands
And spend some time to pray.

Come feast with Me at the Table
It's where you're called to be
Sitting at This Table
You are truly free.

Come let us dine together
Daily in this place
Come let Me behold you
As we sit face to face.

Come My Child

Come My child
And take your place
At the Table
Filled with Grace.

It holds a Banquet
Made for you
So sit beside
Your Holy Groom.

There are stories
You must know
Each one created
To help you grow.

So come My child
And fill your plate
And of this feast
Come partake!

Eat freely
Until you are filled
You'll walk strong again
Your heart healed.

Even simple morsels
Every day
Will strengthen you
Along the way.

Can you hear Me
Calling you?
To The Table
Prepared for two?

Just you and I
Side by side
Resting where
You should abide.

Come to the Table

Come to the Table
And dine with Me
I'll show you things
You've yet to see.

Come and with Me
Spend some time
I'll reveal jewels
You've yet to find.

Come partake
Of all I give
Words to strengthen
And help you live.

Come and sit
By My side
Eat of the Feast
That I provide.

Come when you're weary
And afraid
Partake of the Banquet
I have made.

Come when it's answers
That you need
Wisdom is here
For you to heed.
Come holy beautiful one
Sit with Me
Let Me show you
Who you're called to be.

Come expecting
Such great things
I'll show you the treasure
Time spent with Me brings.

Come

Come and dine
With Me today
Let Me chase
All fear away.

Come and hear
The Truths I speak
They hold the answers
That you seek.

Come and take hold
Of My hand
I'll reveal to you
My Divine plan.

Come and sit
By My side
And in our secret place
With Me abide.

Come and feast
On My Word
I'll reveal Wisdom
You've never heard.

Come to the Banquet
Made just for you
It will equip you
For what you're called to.

Come holy beautiful one
And you will find
All that I have
Now and always is thine.

Dine with Me

Dine with Me
Not just today
But come My Love
And with Me stay.

Dine with Me
At our Table for two
I love the time
It's just Me and you.

Dine with Me
On days of bliss
For it's your presence
I truly miss.

Dine with Me
When days are bleak
I'll strengthen you
When you are weak.

Dine with Me
At evening tide
Come and sit
Right by My side.

Dine with Me
When evening comes
My heart is calling
Will you come?

Dine with Me
Forever more
And on you
My oil I'll pour.

Dine with Me
At our Table for two.
Can you hear Me,
I'm calling you?

Feast on Me

Feast on Me
At our Table today
Come My child
Don't run away.

Feast on Me
Partake of My Word
I'll whisper Truths
That you've never heard.

Feast on Me
And let My Glory fall
Come My Child
As I release My all.

Feast on Me
At this Banquet today
It will strengthen you
So you will not stray.

Feast on Me
From all that I've made
Partake of the offerings
From the Life I gave.

Feast on Me
As your daily need
It will nourish you
And help you succeed.

Feast on Me
Night and day
Come often my child
Come and stay.

Gather at the Table

Gather at The Table
Join with Me here
There's no need to worry
No need to fear.

Gather at the Table
Partake of My Word
Joy unspeakable released
That you've never heard.

Gather at The Table
Its time to enter in
Clothed in My Glory
Cleansed from all sin.

Gather at The Table
There's a Banquet waiting for you
Every morsel you eat
Will strengthen you for what you do.

Gather at The Table
Its time for you to share
You know how much I love you
You know how much I care.

Gather at The Table
Tell what I have done along the way
It will give others strength
And help them not to stray.

Gather at The Table
And lift your voices high
I can still hear you
If you only sigh.

Gather at The Table
Join together in My Name
Fan the embers in your hearts
Until they become a flame.

Gather at The Table
Let your life story unfold
You'll see My Glory here
And My Presence you'll behold.

Gather at The Table
You become one in this place
It's filled with My Mercy
It's filled with My Grace.

Gather at The Table
Give what you can
As you do, I'll unfold
Even more of My plan.

Gather at The Table
Stay with Me today
I will light the Path
So you can find your way.

Gather at The Table
Call others to join in too
The hour is late
And there is so much more to do.

I Yield to You

I yield to You
All that I am
That I may fulfill Your call
And fulfill Your plan.

I yield to You
All of me
Use me for Your Glory Lord
Have Your way in me.

I yield to You
My whole heart
All I ask Lord
Is never depart.

I yield to You
My time each day
To sit in Your Presence
To hear what You'll say.

I yield to You
My heart and my soul
For its Only You
Who can make me whole.

I yield to You
All my future brings
Knowing daily you fill me
With only good things.

I yield to You
Each night and day
O, come now, my Lord
And have Your way.

My Father Awaits

My Father awaits
To see how the day unfolds
How His beautiful daughter kneels
And what her hand offers and holds.

My Father awaits
To hear what my voice will say
As I kneel before Him,
What will I now pray?

My Father awaits
Will there be a smile on my face?
Excitement knowing in His Presence
I am filled with His Grace?

My Father awaits
To hear what's on my heart
Everything is important to Him
Even the smallest part.

My Father awaits
To lead and guide me today
Knowing that with His Light
I will find my way.

My Father awaits
To heal my pain
To apply the Balm of Gilead
Like Heaven's warm rain.

My Father awaits
With arms open wide
Beckoning to me softly
To come to Him and abide.

My Father awaits
For me to fulfill my call
Filling me with all that I need
To give everything, my all.

My Father awaits
To join me to my Groom
He's already picked the guests
Who will fill the room.

My Father awaits
The day I will be
The Bride of Christ
I was destined to be.

My Father awaits
For me to take hold of His hand
And walk with Him forever together
Into the Promised Land.

My Father awaits
Our forever after
A home filled with love
Joy, peace and laughter.

My Father awaits
And I do too
And I know it will happen
Because His Words are True.

Now is the Time

Now is the time
For Me to be Yours
And you
To be Mine.

Now is the time
To count the cost
So not one minute
Or hour is lost.

Now is the time
To dine with Me here
Encircled in Love
Without any fear.

Now is the time
To enter in
So our new lives together
Now can begin.

Now is the time
To come and rest
You know with Me
You're always blessed.

Now is the time
To fulfill My plan
As you walk with Me
Throughout this land.

Now is the time
At the Table to pray
Come now beloved
Don't delay.

Now is the time
Our day will start
When I give My all
And you give your heart.

Table for Two

Come My child
And take your place
At The Table
Filled with Grace.

It holds a Banquet
Made for you
So sit beside
Your Holy Groom.

There are stories
You must know
Each one created
To help you grow.

So come My child
And fill your plate
And of this Feast
Come partake.

Eat freely
Until you're filled
You'll walk strong again
Your heart healed.

Even simple morsels
Every day
Will strengthen you
On the way.
Can you hear Me
Calling you
To The Table
Prepared for two?

Just you and I
Side by side
Resting where
You should abide.

When you are
Dining here
It empowers you
And dispels all fear.

So come beloved
To our Table for two
Let Me empower you
For all you're called to do.

The Gathering Table

Gather here
From near and far
Come together
Just as you are.

Take your place
Around The Table
Make your way,
I know you're able.

Sit right here
Beside your King
And with voices lifted
Begin to sing.

A song from your heart
That's new
Rejoicing for this day,
Offered to you.

Let Him know
Just how much
You're thankful
For His anointing touch.

The strength He gives you
Every day
As you walk boldly
On your way.

Feast with Him here
In this place
As lovingly He beholds
Your face.

It's time to dwell
And abide
Here with Him
Right at His side.

So come holy beautiful one
Don't be late
Your place is here
Don't make Him wait.

Though your journey here
Required the sword
Come beloved,
Feast on Your reward.

The Gathering Table
Is for all who will
Take the time to be
Expectant and still.

So come and join
With us today
As we come together
To eat, talk, and pray.

Table Prayers

Divine **grace** is a theological term present in many religions. It has been **defined** as the divine influence which operates in humans to regenerate and sanctify, to inspire virtuous impulses, and to impart strength to endure trial and resist temptation; and as an individual virtue or excellence of divine origin.

Grace, in a Christian sense, has so much more meaning. The act of saying grace is a prayer offering thanks to who God is and all that He provides for us. This small but incredibly important part of the Christian faith is derived from the Bible, in which Jesus and Paul pray before meals. Their example reflects the holy and beautiful belief that we should always thank God because He alone is the origin of everything.

Grace itself represents our personal intimacy with our Creator. It is His grace that allows us to be present with Him.

The story of each meal we eat is a rich and complex narrative of human and divine collaboration that results in the new creation we are in Christ Jesus. We are one with Him because of His place at the Table and what He did for us through His suffering. In saying grace, we are admitting that we rely on the grace of God Himself.

I grew up saying this simpler prayer.

"Bless us, O Lord, and these thy gifts, which we are about to receive from thy bounty, through Christ our Lord; Amen."

My prayer for you is that saying grace at your own tables places your focus on the only One we should be eternally thankful for. That person is the person of Jesus Christ.

Grace at the Table Provides a Place of Intimacy

The table is the place of intimacy. Around the table, we discover each other. It's the place where we pray. It's the place where we ask: "How was your day?" It's the place where we eat and drink together and say: "Come on, take some more!" It is the place of old and new stories. It is the place of smiles and tears. The table, too, is the place where distance is most painfully felt. It is the place where the children feel the tension between the parents, where brothers and sisters express their anger and jealousies, where accusations are made, and where plates and cups become instruments of violence. Around the table, we know whether there is friendship and community or hatred and division. Precisely because the table is the place of intimacy for all the members of the household, it is also the place where the absence of that intimacy is most painfully revealed.

Henri J. M. Nouwen

The Lord's Prayer

Our Father,
who art in heaven,
hallowed be thy name.
Thy kingdom come,
thy will be done,
on earth as it is in heaven.
Give us this day our daily bread.
And forgive us our trespasses,
as we forgive those who trespass against us.
And lead us not into temptation
but deliver us from evil.
For thine is the kingdom,
and the power,
and the glory forever and ever.
Amen.

The Prayer of Humble Access

We do not presume to come to this your table, merciful Lord,
trusting in our own righteousness,
but in your abundant and great mercies.
We are not worthy so much as to gather up
the crumbs under your table.
But you are the same Lord,
who always delights in showing mercy.
Grant us, therefore, gracious Lord,
so to eat the flesh of your dear Son Jesus Christ
and to drink His blood,
that our sinful bodies may be made clean by His body,
and our souls washed through His most precious blood,
and that we may evermore dwell in Him,
and He is us.
Amen

The Collect for Purity

Almighty God, to you all hearts are open,
all desires known, and from you, no secrets are hid:
Cleanse the thoughts of our hearts
by the inspiration of your Holy Spirit,
that we may perfectly love you,
and worthily magnify your holy Name;
through Christ our Lord.
Amen

The Ten Commandments

God spoke these words and said:

I am the Lord your God; you shall have no other gods but me.
Lord, have mercy upon us, and incline our hearts to keep this law.

You shall not make for yourself any idol.
Lord, have mercy upon us, and incline our hearts to keep this law.

You shall not take the name of the Lord your God in vain.
Lord, have mercy upon us, and incline our hearts to keep this law.

Remember the Sabbath day and keep it holy.
Lord, have mercy upon us, and incline our hearts to keep this law.

Honor your father and your mother.
Lord, have mercy upon us, and incline our hearts to keep this law.

You shall not murder.
Lord, have mercy upon us, and incline our hearts to keep this law.

You shall not commit adultery.
Lord, have mercy upon us, and incline our hearts to keep this law.

You shall not steal.
Lord, have mercy upon us, and incline our hearts to keep this law.

You shall not bear false witness against your neighbor.
Lord, have mercy upon us, and incline our hearts to keep this law.

You shall not covet.
Lord, have mercy upon us, and write all these, your laws, in our hearts, we beseech you.

(Exodus 20:1-17: Deuteronomy 5:6-21)

My Abba, My God

Heavenly Father who is also Almighty God,

I bow before You humbled by the truth that the God of the universe is my Abba Father. Knowing this causes my knees to bend and my heart to sing.

What a blessing it is to cry out "Abba Father" as Jesus did. You are all powerful, Lord, able to change the worlds with a shout and yet pour out overwhelming love with a whisper.

You are the "Great I Am" who holds back the sea with Your hand and then tenderly gather me into Your arms. Your holiness brings forth the honor You deserve from me while Your gentleness stirs my love for You.

Your power is unchallenged, and Your love is unquenchable. You are my mighty Defender on whom I rely and my Abba whom I trust. You are my God full of glory and my Father full of hugs.

I rejoice knowing that when the enemy aims his fiery darts at me You hide me in the shadow of Your wings where I feel Your heart beating with love for me and all my fears fade away.

Your arms are always open welcoming me and Your Daddy lap is always a perfect fit. I praise You for Your power as my God, and I thank You for Your love as my Father.

You alone are my Abba who is my God, and in that my heart rejoices and my spirit dances with delight.

You are my all in all, and I am fully satisfied and cradled in peace.

Thank You, my Abba, my God.

Written by Connie Barngrover

Lover of my Soul

Lord Jesus, I lift my voice to You proclaiming You are my Lord and Savior.

My heart is overflowing with gratitude to You for giving me the greatest love ever known by laying down Your Deity and taking the form of mere man as You stepped through earth's doorway.

You not only said yes when the Father asked this of You, You said yes with great joy.

You who ride on the wings of the wind and walk on the stormy seas to still them, climbed upon a rough wooden altar and Your love for me.

I pray I always live in a state of thankfulness for the gift of Your heartbeat sacrificed for me.

You are the "Lover of my soul" who never turns Your gaze from me even when I may not deserve Your holiness to surround me.

Lord, may I always remember that You go wherever I go and to never take You anywhere where a shadow could be cast upon Your blessed Name.

O' my Lord Jesus, less of me and more of You in me so that I leave Your fragrance behind wooing others into Your unconditional love.

Face to face, hand in hand dance with me on life's dance floor until Father calls us both back to heaven's bridal chambers.

May the sweet savor of Your holiness fill my lungs with life and my heart with love.

O' Lover of my soul, Your life was Your love and your love is my life, Glory to Your holy Name.

Amen

Written by Connie Barngrover

My Holy Indweller

Holy Spirit, I invite You into my day to be who You are in all Your fullness in, through, and for me today.

My Lord, Jesus, sent You to me because He knew I would have great need of Your power enabling me to walk worthy as a child of God. You are my source of wisdom into the Father's will and my Comforter who caresses the wounds of life.

You have poured Yourself into me sealing me in the Father's love. It is You who reveals Jesus to my heart and guides me in my walk in the Kingdom of God.

It is You, Holy Spirit, who floods me with transforming power that will conform me into the image of Jesus. You dwell in me as my Teacher, my Helper, my Companion, and my Prayer Partner.

I have a great longing for Your anointing to flow in me, enabling me to be strong and courageous in the face of uncertainty.

You are my interpreter of the Father's will and the One who peels and reveals any sin hidden from the eyes of my heart.

I thank You for choosing me as Your temple in which to dwell, making me a vessel fit for the Master's use. I surrender my spirit, soul, and body to Your control, knowing that You would never misuse me but only flow through me bringing glory to God.

Holy Spirit, my Indweller, I pray that I am good ground in which Your fruit may grow in abundance and a place where Your gifts are used wisely to benefit those You send my way.

Take me Holy One, where I have never been before into new experiences in the love of God that changes me forever. Without You, I am but a shell, empty and fragile. Fill me, fuel me, and feed me from Your presence today.

Welcome, Holy Spirit. I pray I make a comfortable dwelling for Your holiness. Come, make Yourself at home. Amen.

Written by Connie Barngrover

Holy God

Holy God,
Thou art within every seed, fruit, and harvest.
Help us to see Thee within our lives
as a source of all that is good, true, and loving.
Guide us in the paths of righteousness
and make us grateful for Thy presence.
Amen.

Dear Lord Be our Holy Guest,
Our morning joy and our evening rest.
And with our daily food impart,
Thy love and peace on every heart.
Amen.

Author Unknown

Blessed Are You

Blessed are you, Lord our God,
Ruler of the universe (the praise),
for you provide nourishing food for all your creatures
and sustain the whole world with your goodness,
kindness and loving favor (the remembrance).

Send your blessing upon this food,
and may it strengthen to serve you and your people,
especially those who do not share our abundance (the request).

All glory and honor to you gracious God,
through Jesus Christ, our Lord (second praise).

Amen.

Author Unknown

Lord Almighty

O almighty God, merciful Father,
Your Word keeps all the blessed on the righteous path
of Your Son, Jesus Christ our Lord.

Give us the true bread of heaven for our souls,
that we may never experience spiritual hunger,
just as You now feed Your creatures
out of Your pure mercy and love.

O Father, may we enjoy all Your gifts
with thanksgiving and contentment,
and keep us from gluttony and all wrong desires.

Amen.

Johannes Bugenhagen, 1485-1558

Source of this version: Translated for A Collection of Prayers. German source: Gebetbuch, enthaltend die sämtlichen Gebete und Seufzer Martin Luther's, Evangelischer Bücher-Verein, 1866, #39.

Lord Jesus, Be Our Holy Guest

Lord Jesus, be our Holy Guest,
Our morning Joy, our evening Rest;
And with our daily bread impart
Your love and peace to every heart.

Amen.

Slightly modified from "Forms of Grace before Meat," The Book of Common Worship, Henry Van Dyke, editor, Presbyterian Board of Publication and Sabbath-School Work, 1906, p. 167.

Interesting Notes: According to The Catholic Prayer Book (Servant Books, 1986, p. 216), this prayer was used by President Dwight Eisenhower.

"Lord Jesus, be our Holy Guest" may be based on a German prayer:

Wir bitten, Herr, sei unserm Haus
ein steter Gast, tagein, tagaus,
und hilf, dass wir der Gaben wert,
die deine Güte uns beschert.

A literal translation:

We pray, Lord, be in our house
a constant guest, day-in, day-out,
and grant that we be worthy of your gifts
which your mercy gives us.

Mealtime prayers are essential conversations with God. Paul tells us to: "Celebrate always, pray constantly, and give thanks to God no matter what circumstances you find yourself in" (1 Thessalonians 5:16-18 VOICE).

A Prayer of Confession

Father, this meal is the work of Your hands.
You have provided for me, again, and I am grateful.

I confess my tendency to forget to ask
Your blessing upon my life,
through the comforts that You have given me to enjoy.

So many people lack these daily comforts,
and it is selfish of me to forget about them in their need.

Show me how to make the most of Your blessing in my life,
for everything I have is a gift from You.

In Jesus' Name,
Amen.

Crosswalk.com

Bless Us, O Lord

Traditional Catholic Prayer

Bless us, O Lord,
And these Thy gifts
Which we are about to receive,
Through Thy bounty
Through Christ, our Lord, we pray.
Amen.

We Give Our Thanks

Traditional

For food that stays our hunger,
For rest that brings us ease,
For homes where memories linger,
We give our thanks for these.
Amen.

Truly Thankful

Traditional

Lord, make us truly thankful for
these and all other blessings.
I ask this in Jesus Christ's name,
Amen.

God Is Great

Traditional

God is great!

God is good!

Let us thank Him

For our food.

Amen.

God Is Great

(Extended Version)
Traditional

God is great, and God is good,

Let us thank Him for our food;

By His blessings, we are fed,

Give us Lord, our daily bread.

Amen.

Give Us Grateful Hearts

Book of Common Prayer

Give us grateful hearts,
O Father, for all thy mercies,
And make us mindful
Of the needs of others;
Through Jesus Christ, our Lord.
Amen.

Make Us Grateful

Traditional

For this and all we are about to receive,

Make us truly grateful, Lord.

Through Christ, we pray.

Amen.

Bless, O Lord

Traditional

Bless, O Lord,
This food to our use
And us to thy service,
And keep us ever mindful
Of the needs of others.
In Jesus' Name,
Amen.

God Our Father, Lord, and Savior

Traditional

God our Father, Lord, and Savior
Thank you for your love and favor
Bless this food and drink we pray
And all who shares with us today.
Amen.

Our Heavenly Father, Kind and Good

Traditional

Our Heavenly Father, kind and good,
We thank Thee for our daily food.
We thank Thee for Thy love and care.
Be with us Lord, and hear our prayer.
Amen.

Moravian Dinner Prayer

Traditional Moravian Prayer

Come, Lord Jesus, our guest to be
And bless these gifts
Bestowed by Thee.
And bless our loved ones everywhere,
And keep them in Your loving care.
Amen.

Dinner Prayer Hymn

Traditional Hymn

Lord, bless this food and grant that we
May thankful for thy mercies be;
Teach us to know by whom we're fed;
Bless us with Christ, the living bread.
Lord, make us thankful for our food,
Bless us with faith in Jesus' blood;
With the bread of life our souls supply,
That we may live with Christ on high.
Amen.

Humble Hearts

Traditional

In a world where so many are hungry,
May we eat this food with humble hearts;
In a world where so many are lonely,
May we share this friendship with joyful hearts.
Amen.

Short prayers from https://www.thoughtco.com/dinner-prayers-and-mealtime-blessings-701303

The Table is a Place of Prayer

A Prayer

Dear Lord, Help me keep my eyes on you.
You are the incarnation of Divine Love;
you are the expression of God's infinite compassion;
you are the visible manifestation of the Father's holiness.

You are beauty, goodness, gentleness, forgiveness, and mercy.
In you, all can be found. Outside of you, nothing can be found.

Why should I look elsewhere or go elsewhere?
You have the words of eternal life;
you are food and drink,
you are the Way, the Truth, and the Life.

You are the light that shines in the darkness,
the lamp on the lampstand, the house on the hilltop.
You are the perfect Icon of God.

In and through you, I can see the Heavenly Father,
and with you, I can find my way to Him.

O Holy One, Beautiful One, Glorious One,
be my Lord, my Savior, my Redeemer, my Guide,
my Consoler, my Comforter,
my Hope, my Joy, and my Peace.

To you, I want to give all that I am. Let me be generous, not stingy, or hesitant.
Let me give you all—all that I have, think, do, and feel.
It is yours, O Lord. Please accept it and make it fully your own.

Amen.

Written by Henri J. M. Nouwen

A Prayer for Weariness

Gracious Father,

You are my light and my hope.
I have been weary and have felt so alone.

There are moments when it feels like the tests and trials come one right after another. The weight of it has been crushing me. I am at the end of my strength, Abba.

I cannot make sense of any of this. I don't know which way to turn.
I am sorry that I tried to take all of this on by myself.
Please forgive me.

I am turning to You. I am weak and cannot do this or anything without You.
My weakness is the point where Your strength will shine at its greatest.
My weariness will be the crevice in the dark where Your blinding light will break through.

You have promised me that You will never forsake me.
I believe in You. I give this and all things to You.

I praise You and You alone.
I give You glory, my King, because Your great hand is already on this situation.

No matter what faces me, I shall trust in You.
You are a good Father. Thy will be done.

In Jesus's name,
Amen.

Written by Melisa Custer

My Holy Table

"You prepare a table before me in the presence of my enemies.
You anointed my head with oil my cup overflows."
(Psalm 35:5 NLT)

Beloved,

I am asking you to trust in My love for you. It is great, and it is continuous. I know exactly what you need every time the enemy comes against you to trap you in fear. If you trust Me in the midst of your trials, you will be able to sit at My table that I set before you and eat in peace of its bounty that I have heaped upon it.

What is it you have need of today? Do you need joy? Come, dine on My laughter. Do you need strength? My strength is laid on My table from end to end, waiting to be consumed. Do you need courage? Come be filled with a heaping serving of bravery as that of the Lion of the tribe of Judah. Do you desire grace to help in time of need or favor to go before you today? They both are within arm's reach on My Holy Table. What of wisdom? It too is there for you to eat to your fill. Are you starving for comfort? Then Come and be filled. What about hope? There is hope enough to cause you to rejoice no matter what things look like. It makes no difference what you need because all needs are fulfilled at My table that I Myself set before you knowing everything you will face today. As it says in Psalm 139:16, "You saw me before I was born. Every day of my life was recorded in Your Book. Every moment was laid out before a single day had passed" (NLT). I have made everything ready for you today even before I created you.

My table is a sight that delights the eye and causes your soul to growl with hunger. The mingling of savory fragrances stirs the senses and draws you near with anticipation. My table is draped in white bridal lace linens and hold candles that shine with the Light of Christ so that you can easily find what you hunger for. Flowers adorn My table that are sweet and edible giving your innermost being beauty to replace your ugly past that the enemy is always trying to remind you of.

Beloved, My table is a feast for your spirit. It is set with My blessings and holds a beautifully scripted tag reading, "RESERVED FOR MY BELOVED" and has been lovingly placed at your chair. So come, take and eat and you will find that you will be fully satisfied with all that you desire and all that you need to be victorious in every situation you face today.

COME, BELOVED, MY TABLE HAS BEEN READIED JUST FOR YOU.

Written by Connie Barngrover

The Confession and Absolution

Most merciful God,
we confess that we have sinned against you
in thought, word, and deed,
by what we have done,
and by what we have left undone.

We have not loved you with our whole heart;
we have not loved our neighbors as ourselves.

We are truly sorry, and we humbly repent.
For the sake of Your Son Jesus Christ,
have mercy on us and forgive us;
that we may delight in Your will,
and walk in Your ways,
to the glory of Your Name.

Amen

The Prayer of Thanksgiving

Heavenly Father,
we thank You for feeding us with the spiritual food
of the most precious body and blood
of Your Son our Savior Jesus Christ:
and for assuring us in these holy mysteries
that we are living members of the body of Your Son,
and heirs of Your eternal Kingdom.

And now Father, send us out into the world
to do the work you have given us to do,
to love and serve you as faithful witnesses of Christ our Lord.

To Him, to You, and to the Holy Spirit,
be honor and glory, now and forever.

Amen

Feasting on Scripture

"When your words came, I ate them"
(Jeremiah 15:16)

"Then the angel said to me, "Write these words:
Wonderfully blessed are those who are invited to feast at the wedding celebration of the Lamb!" And then he said to me,
"These are the true words of God."
(Revelation 19:9 TPT)

The Bible is packed full of the goodness and beauty of food and the holiness of feasting. God in His mercy made His creation a feast for us. He made His Word an invitation for all to dine. He made trees "pleasant to the sight and good for food" (Genesis 2:9 ESV), and created us to eat His Word and His world: "Behold, I have given you every plant yielding seed that is on the face of all the earth, and every tree with seed in its fruit. You shall have them for food" (Genesis 1:29 ESV). Then after the flood, He extended His invitation to eating meat: "Every moving thing that lives shall be food for you. And as I gave you the green plants, I give you everything" (Genesis 9:3 ESV). In addition to the distinct holy and beautiful kindness of God in everyday food, we also find the special holy and beautiful grace of His feast. A place set just for us at His banquet table. Here at this seat, our invitation becomes intimate and personal. As we dine and engage with His Word, He resides within us. His Word, which is eternal and everlasting, transforms us with each bite we take.

Unfortunately, we don't usually recognize the importance of feeding ourselves with His spiritual food. We are usually busy running around trying just to stay ahead of our to-do lists. This is why I encourage you to take time out of your schedule and make a dinner date with Jesus. Learn to savor what He is saying through His Word. As you look at the

Scriptures below, read them, and digest each one. Give yourself permission to slow down and enjoy the presented meal before you.

Read them slowly chewing on each one, then read them out loud, write them down, personalize them, study them, and then let each one resonate with your soul. Ask God what He is saying to you with this meal?

God's Word is life. It is all the nourishment we really need. It is meant for us to satisfy all our desires. As you come to the table, my personal prayer is that you will become completely satisfied. I hope you leave full, content, and knowing you are in the holy and beautiful hands of our Father.

Amen

All of the following verses are from the English Standard Version (ESV)

Acts 2:46
And day by day, attending the temple together and breaking bread in their homes, they received their food with glad and generous hearts,

Acts 2:42
And they devoted themselves to the apostles' teaching and the fellowship, to the breaking of bread and the prayers.

1 Corinthians 10:31
So, whether you eat or drink, or whatever you do, do all to the glory of God.

Ecclesiastes 2:24
There is nothing better for a person than that he should eat and drink and find enjoyment in his toil. This also, I saw, is from the hand of God,

Acts 20:7
On the first day of the week, when we were gathered together to break bread, Paul talked with them, intending to depart on the next day, and he prolonged his speech until midnight.

Genesis 1:29
And God said, "Behold, I have given you every plant yielding seed that is on the face of all the earth, and every tree with seed in its fruit. You shall have them for food.

Revelation 3:20
Behold, I stand at the door and knock. If anyone hears my voice and opens the door, I will come in to him and eat with him, and he with me.

John 6:35
Jesus said to them, "I am the bread of life; whoever comes to me shall not hunger, and whoever believes in me shall never thirst.

Colossians 2:16
Therefore let no one pass judgment on you in questions of food and drink, or with regard to a festival or a new moon or a Sabbath.

1 Corinthians 11:20-22
When you come together, it is not the Lord's supper that you eat. For in eating, each one goes ahead with his own meal. One goes hungry, another gets drunk. What! Do you not have houses to eat and drink in? Or do you despise the church of God and humiliate those who have nothing? What shall I say to you? Shall I commend you in this? No, I will not.

Luke 22:19
And He took bread, and when He had given thanks, He broke it and gave it to them, saying, "This is my body, which is given for you. Do this in remembrance of me."

Psalm 23:1-5
A Psalm of David. The LORD is my shepherd; I shall not want. He makes me lie down in green pastures. He leads me beside still waters. He restores my soul. He leads me in paths of righteousness for His name's sake. Even though I walk through the valley of the shadow of death, I will fear no evil, for you are with me; your rod and your staff, they comfort me. You prepare a table before me in the presence of my enemies; you anoint my head with oil; my cup overflows.

Matthew 6:25
"Therefore I tell you, do not be anxious about your life, what you will eat or what you will drink, nor about your body, what you will put on. Is not life more than food, and the body more than clothing?

Deuteronomy 12:7
And there you shall eat before the LORD your God, and you shall rejoice, you and your households, in all that you undertake, in which the LORD your God has blessed you.

Genesis 9:3
Every moving thing that lives shall be food for you. And as I gave you the green plants, I give you everything.

Malachi 3:10
Bring the full tithe into the storehouse, that there may be food in my house. And thereby put me to the test, says the LORD of hosts, if I will not open the windows of heaven for you and pour down for you a blessing until there is no more need.

Hebrews 10:25
Not neglecting to meet together, as is the habit of some, but encouraging one another, and all the more as you see the Day drawing near.

Philippians 3:19
Their end is destruction, their god is their belly, and they glory in their shame, with minds set on earthly things.

John 6:27
Do not labor for the food that perishes, but for the food that endures to eternal life, which the Son of Man will give to you. For on Him God the Father has set His seal."

Matthew 5:6
“Blessed are those who hunger and thirst for righteousness, for they shall be satisfied.

Matthew 4:4
But He answered, “It is written, “‘Man shall not live by bread alone, but by every word that comes from the mouth of God.’”

Psalm 55:14
We used to take sweet counsel together; within God's house we walked in the throng.

Nehemiah 8:10
Then he said to them, “Go your way. Eat the fat and drink sweet wine and send portions to anyone who has nothing ready, for this day is holy to our Lord. And do not be grieved, for the joy of the LORD is your strength.”

1 Corinthians 11:34
If anyone is hungry, let him eat at home—so that when you come together it will not be for judgment. About the other things I will give directions when I come.

Mark 2:15-17
And as He reclined at table in His house, many tax collectors and sinners were reclining with Jesus and His disciples, for there were many who followed Him. And the scribes of the Pharisees, when they saw that He was eating with sinners and tax collectors, said to His disciples, “Why does He eat with tax collectors and sinners?” And when Jesus heard it, He said to them, “Those who are well have no need of a physician, but those who are sick. I came not to call the righteous, but sinners.”

Revelation 19:9
And the angel said to me, “Write this: Blessed are those who are invited to the marriage supper of the Lamb.” And he said to me, “These are the true words of God.”

3 John 1:2
Beloved, I pray that all may go well with you and that you may be in good health, as it goes well with your soul.

Colossians 3:17
And whatever you do, in word or deed, do everything in the name of the Lord Jesus, giving thanks to God the Father through Him.

1 Corinthians 10:25
Eat whatever is sold in the meat market without raising any question on the ground of conscience.

John 6:51
I am the living bread that came down from heaven. If anyone eats of this bread, he will live forever. And the bread that I will give for the life of the world is my flesh."

Hebrews 10:24-25
And let us consider how to stir up one another to love and good works, not neglecting to meet together, as is the habit of some, but encouraging one another, and all the more as you see the Day drawing near.

Colossians 2:16-17
Therefore let no one pass judgment on you in questions of food and drink, or with regard to a festival or a new moon or a Sabbath. These are a shadow of the things to come, but the substance belongs to Christ.

Philippians 4:6-7
Do not be anxious about anything, but in everything by prayer and supplication with thanksgiving let your requests be made known to God. And the peace of God, which surpasses all understanding, will guard your hearts and your minds in Christ Jesus.

1 Corinthians 8:8
Food will not commend us to God. We are no worse off if we do not eat, and no better off if we do.

1 Corinthians 8:4
Therefore, as to the eating of food offered to idols, we know that "an idol has no real existence," and that "there is no God but one."

1 Corinthians 6:19-20
Or do you not know that your body is a temple of the Holy Spirit within you, whom you have from God? You are not your own, for you were bought with a price. So glorify God in your body.

Romans 14:1-5
As for the one who is weak in faith, welcome him, but not to quarrel over opinions. One person believes he may eat anything, while the weak person eats only vegetables. Let not the one who eats despise the one who abstains, and let not the one who abstains pass judgment on the one who eats, for God has welcomed him. Who are you to pass judgment on the servant of another? It is before his own master that he stands or falls. And he will be upheld, for the Lord is able to make him stand. One person esteems one day as better than another, while another esteems all days alike. Each one should be fully convinced in his own mind.

Acts 1:14
All these with one accord were devoting themselves to prayer, together with the women and Mary the mother of Jesus, and His brothers.

Matthew 11:19
The Son of Man came eating and drinking, and they say, 'Look at Him! A glutton and a drunkard, a friend of tax collectors and sinners!' Yet wisdom is justified by her deeds."

Leviticus 11:3
Whatever parts the hoof and is cloven-footed and chews the cud, among the animals, you may eat.

Revelation 1:1
The revelation of Jesus Christ, which God gave him to show to his servants the things that must soon take place. He made it known by sending His angel to His servant John,

1 Timothy 4:3-5
Who forbid marriage and require abstinence from foods that God created to be received with thanksgiving by those who believe and know the truth. For everything created by God is good, and nothing is to be rejected if it is received with thanksgiving, for it is made holy by the word of God and prayer.

2 Corinthians 9:10
He who supplies seed to the sower and bread for food will supply and multiply your seed for sowing and increase the harvest of your righteousness.

Proverbs 13:25
The righteous has enough to satisfy his appetite, but the belly of the wicked suffers want.

Leviticus 11:1-8
And the LORD spoke to Moses and Aaron, saying to them, "Speak to the people of Israel, saying, These are the living things that you may eat among all the animals that are on the earth. Whatever parts the hoof and is cloven-footed and chews the cud, among the animals, you may eat. Nevertheless, among those that chew the cud or part the hoof, you shall not eat these: The camel, because it chews the cud but does not part the hoof, is unclean to you. And the rock badger, because it chews the cud but does not part the hoof, is unclean to you.

Exodus 24:11
And He did not lay His hand on the chief men of the people of Israel; they beheld God, and ate and drank.

1 John 5:14-15
And this is the confidence that we have toward Him, that if we ask anything according to His will He hears us. And if we know that He hears us in whatever we ask, we know that we have the requests that we have asked of Him.

2 Timothy 3:16
All Scripture is breathed out by God and profitable for teaching, for reproof, for correction, and for training in righteousness,

1 Timothy 4:4
For everything created by God is good, and nothing is to be rejected if it is received with thanksgiving,

Ephesians 6:4
Fathers, do not provoke your children to anger, but bring them up in the discipline and instruction of the Lord.

Romans 14:6
The one who observes the day, observes it in honor of the Lord. The one who eats, eats in honor of the Lord, since he gives thanks to God, while the one who abstains, abstains in honor of the Lord and gives thanks to God.

Romans 14:5-6
One person esteems one day as better than another, while another esteems all days alike. Each one should be fully convinced in his own mind. The one who observes the day, observes it in honor of the Lord. The one who eats, eats in honor of the Lord, since he gives thanks to God, while the one who abstains, abstains in honor of the Lord and gives thanks to God.

Luke 15:2
And the Pharisees and the scribes grumbled, saying, "This man receives sinners and eats with them."

Mark 7:19
Since it enters not his heart but his stomach, and is expelled?" (Thus He declared all foods clean.)

Proverbs 25:27
It is not good to eat much honey, nor is it glorious to seek one's own glory.

Genesis 9:3-4
Every moving thing that lives shall be food for you. And as I gave you the green plants, I give you everything. But you shall not eat flesh with its life, that is, its blood.

Ephesians 5:2
And walk in love, as Christ loved us and gave himself up for us, a fragrant offering and sacrifice to God.

1 Corinthians 11:2
Now I commend you because you remember me in everything and maintain the traditions even as I delivered them to you.

Acts 10:28
And he said to them, "You yourselves know how unlawful it is for a Jew to associate with or to visit anyone of another nation, but God has shown me that I should not call any person common or unclean.

John 3:16-17
"For God so loved the world, that He gave His only Son, that whoever believes in Him should not perish but have eternal life. For God did not send His Son into the world to condemn the world, but in order that the world might be saved through Him.

Luke 9:13-17
But He said to them, "You give them something to eat." They said, "We have no more than five loaves and two fish—unless we are to go and buy food for all these people." For there were about five thousand men. And He said to His disciples, "Have them sit down in groups of about fifty each." And they did so, and had them all sit down. And taking the five loaves and the two fish, He looked up to heaven and said a blessing over them. Then He broke the loaves and gave them to the disciples to set before the crowd. And they all ate and were satisfied. And what was left over was picked up, twelve baskets of broken pieces.

Luke 7:34
The Son of Man has come eating and drinking, and you say, 'Look at Him! A glutton and a drunkard, a friend of tax collectors and sinners!'

Mark 7:2
They saw that some of His disciples ate with hands that were defiled, that is, unwashed.

Isaiah 66:15-17
"For behold, the LORD will come in fire, and His chariots like the whirlwind, to render His anger in fury, and His rebuke with flames of fire. For by fire will the LORD enter into judgment, and by His sword, with all flesh; and those slain by the LORD shall be many. "Those who sanctify and purify themselves to go into the gardens, following one in the midst, eating pig's flesh and the abomination and mice, shall come to an end together, declares the LORD.

Isaiah 25:6
On this mountain the LORD of hosts will make for all peoples a feast of rich food, a feast of well-aged wine, of rich food full of marrow, of aged wine well refined.

1 Samuel 30:16
And when he had taken him down, behold, they were spread abroad over all the land, eating and drinking and dancing, because of all the great spoil they had taken from the land of the Philistines and from the land of Judah.

Exodus 12:14-18
"This day shall be for you a memorial day, and you shall keep it as a feast to the LORD; throughout your generations, as a statute forever, you shall keep it as a feast. Seven days you shall eat unleavened bread. On the first day you shall remove leaven out of your houses, for if anyone eats what is leavened, from the first day until the seventh day, that person shall be cut off from Israel. On the first day you shall hold a holy assembly, and on the seventh day a holy assembly. No work shall be done on those days. But what everyone needs to eat, that alone may be prepared by you. And you shall observe the Feast of Unleavened Bread, for on this very day I brought your hosts out of the land of Egypt. Therefore you shall observe this day, throughout your generations, as a statute forever. In the first month, from the fourteenth day of the month at evening, you shall eat unleavened bread until the twenty-first day of the month at evening.

1 John 1:3
That which we have seen and heard we proclaim also to you, so that you too may have fellowship with us; and indeed our fellowship is with the Father and with His Son Jesus Christ.

1 Timothy 4:2
Through the insincerity of liars whose consciences are seared,

1 Thessalonians 5:11
Therefore encourage one another and build one another up, just as you are doing.

Colossians 2:1-5
For I want you to know how great a struggle I have for you and for those at Laodicea and for all who have not seen me face to face, that their hearts may be encouraged, being knit together in love, to reach all the riches of full assurance of understanding and the knowledge of God's mystery, which is Christ, in whom are hidden all the treasures of wisdom and knowledge. I say this in order that no one may delude you with plausible arguments. For though I am absent in body, yet I am with you in spirit, rejoicing to see your good order and the firmness of your faith in Christ.

Ephesians 5:19
Addressing one another in psalms and hymns and spiritual songs, singing and making melody to the Lord with your heart,

Ephesians 5:1
Therefore be imitators of God, as beloved children.

Ephesians 4:17-21
Now this I say and testify in the Lord, that you must no longer walk as the Gentiles do, in the futility of their minds. They are darkened in their understanding, alienated from the life of God because of the ignorance that is in them, due to their hardness of heart. They have become callous and have given themselves up to sensuality, greedy to practice every kind of impurity. But that is not the way you learned Christ!— assuming that you have heard about Him and were taught in Him, as the truth is in Jesus,

1 Corinthians 11:21
For in eating, each one goes ahead with his own meal. One goes hungry, another gets drunk.

1 Corinthians 10:16
The cup of blessing that we bless, is it not a participation in the blood of Christ? The bread that we break, is it not a participation in the body of Christ?

1 Corinthians 7:25-29
Now concerning the betrothed, I have no command from the Lord, but I give my judgment as one who by the Lord's mercy is trustworthy. I think that in view of the present distress it is good for a person to remain as he is. Are you bound to a wife? Do not seek to be free. Are you free from a wife? Do not seek a wife. But if you do marry, you have not sinned, and if a betrothed woman marries, she has not sinned. Yet those who marry will have worldly troubles, and I would spare you that. This is what I mean, brothers: the appointed time has grown very short. From now on, let those who have wives live as though they had none,

1 Corinthians 7:1-5
Now concerning the matters about which you wrote: "It is good for a man not to have sexual relations with a woman." But because of the temptation to sexual immorality, each man should have his own wife and each woman her own husband. The husband should give to his wife her conjugal rights, and likewise the wife to her husband. For the wife does not have authority over her own body, but the husband does. Likewise the husband does not have authority over his own body, but the wife does. Do not deprive one another, except perhaps by agreement for a limited time, that you may devote yourselves to prayer; but then come together again, so that Satan may not tempt you because of your lack of self-control.

1 Corinthians 1:9
God is faithful, by whom you were called into the fellowship of His Son, Jesus Christ our Lord.

1 Corinthians 1:1-5
Paul, called by the will of God to be an apostle of Christ Jesus, and our brother Sosthenes, To the church of God that is in Corinth, to those sanctified in Christ Jesus, called to be saints together with all those who in every place call upon the name of our Lord Jesus Christ, both their Lord and ours: Grace to you and peace from God our Father and the Lord Jesus Christ. I give thanks to my God always for you because of the grace of God that was given you in Christ Jesus, that in every way you were enriched in Him in all speech and all knowledge

Romans 14:3
Let not the one who eats despise the one who abstains, and let not the one who abstains pass judgment on the one who eats, for God has welcomed him.

John 13:34
A new commandment I give to you, that you love one another: just as I have loved you, you also are to love one another.

Matthew 6:16-18
"And when you fast, do not look gloomy like the hypocrites, for they disfigure their faces that their fasting may be seen by others. Truly, I say to you, they have received their reward. But when you fast, anoint your head and wash your face, that your fasting may not be seen by others but by your Father who is in secret. And your Father who sees in secret will reward you.

Daniel 10:3
I ate no delicacies, no meat or wine entered my mouth, nor did I anoint myself at all, for the full three weeks.

Numbers 13:23
And they came to the Valley of Eshcol and cut down from there a branch with a single cluster of grapes, and they carried it on a pole between two of them; they also brought some pomegranates and figs.

Leviticus 19:19
"You shall keep my statutes. You shall not let your cattle breed with a different kind. You shall not sow your field with two kinds of seed, nor shall you wear a garment of cloth made of two kinds of material.

Exodus 23:25
You shall serve the LORD your God, and He will bless your bread and your water, and I will take sickness away from among you.

Exodus 15:26
Saying, "If you will diligently listen to the voice of the LORD your God, and do that which is right in His eyes, and give ear to His commandments and keep all His statutes, I will put none of the diseases on you that I put on the Egyptians, for I am the LORD, your healer."

Exodus 12:4
And if the household is too small for a lamb, then he and his nearest neighbor shall take according to the number of persons; according to what each can eat you shall make your count for the lamb.

2 Timothy 3:2
For people will be lovers of self, lovers of money, proud, arrogant, abusive, disobedient to their parents, ungrateful, unholy,

Colossians 3:2
Set your minds on things that are above, not on things that are on earth.

Colossians 2:2
That their hearts may be encouraged, being knit together in love, to reach all the riches of full assurance of understanding and the knowledge of God's mystery, which is Christ,

Galatians 2:11-14
But when Cephas came to Antioch, I opposed him to his face, because he stood condemned. For before certain men came from James, he was eating with the Gentiles; but when they came he drew back and separated himself, fearing the circumcision party. And the rest of the Jews acted hypocritically along with him, so that even Barnabas was led astray by their hypocrisy. But when I saw that their conduct was not in step with the truth of the gospel, I said to Cephas before them all, "If you, though a Jew, live like a Gentile and not like a Jew, how can you force the Gentiles to live like Jews?"

1 Corinthians 11:3
But I want you to understand that the head of every man is Christ, the head of a wife is her husband, and the head of Christ is God.

Acts 10:2
A devout man who feared God with all his household, gave alms generously to the people, and prayed continually to God.

Exodus 5:1-5

Afterward Moses and Aaron went and said to Pharaoh, "Thus says the LORD, the God of Israel, 'Let my people go, that they may hold a feast to me in the wilderness.'" But Pharaoh said, "Who is the LORD, that I should obey His voice and let Israel go? I do not know the LORD, and moreover, I will not let Israel go." Then they said, "The God of the Hebrews has met with us. Please let us go a three days' journey into the wilderness that we may sacrifice to the LORD our God, lest He fall upon us with pestilence or with the sword." But the king of Egypt said to them, "Moses and Aaron, why do you take the people away from their work? Get back to your burdens." And Pharaoh said, "Behold, the people of the land are now many, and you make them rest from their burdens!"

1 Timothy 4:8

For while bodily training is of some value, godliness is of value in every way, as it holds promise for the present life and also for the life to come.

1 Corinthians 11:25

In the same way also He took the cup, after supper, saying, "This cup is the new covenant in my blood. Do this, as often as you drink it, in remembrance of me."

1 Corinthians 10:28

But if someone says to you, "This has been offered in sacrifice," then do not eat it, for the sake of the one who informed you, and for the sake of conscience—

Matthew 26:1-5

When Jesus had finished all these sayings, He said to His disciples, "You know that after two days the Passover is coming, and the Son of Man will be delivered up to be crucified." Then the chief priests and the elders of the people gathered in the palace of the high priest, whose name was Caiaphas, and plotted together in order to arrest Jesus by stealth and kill Him. But they said, "Not during the feast, lest there be an uproar among the people."

530 | PROVERBS 4:18
PROVERBS 7:8 | 53
Verse 21 TPT
Fill your thoughts with my words until they penetrate deep into your spirit.
Verse 23 TPT
So above all guard the affections of your heart, for they affect all that you are. Pay attention to the welfare of your innermost being, for from there flows the wellspring of life
Warning Against Adultery
Practical Warnings
Warning Against the Adulteress

Come to the Table Bible Reading Plan

We read the Bible to feast on Christ and who He is and what He did for us on the cross. Just as we hunger for food, so should we thirst for God's Word.

Enjoy the meal!

From the Book of Common Prayer

Blessed Lord, who caused all holy Scriptures to be written for our learning: Grant us so to hear them, read, mark, learn, and inwardly digest them, so that we may embrace and ever hold fast the blessed hope of everlasting life, which you have given us in our Savior Jesus Christ; who lives and reigns with you and the Holy Spirit, one God, forever and ever. Amen

The Come to the Table Bible Reading Plan is designed to help you understand who Jesus is and help you experience Him in your daily life. Set a regular time and place to meet with God that is free from distractions. Pray before you begin, "Lord, please speak to me through what I am about to read today." Mark or highlight meaningful phrases or sentences that God brings to your attention as you read. Record in a journal, a paragraph or two daily, what God reveals to you through your reading. Spend a couple of minutes in prayer, asking God to show you how to respond to what He said to you through your Bible reading time. For example, "Lord, show me how to apply what I have learned today at Your table to my life and give me the strength to do it." Amen

Because Jesus is seated at the head of the table and is our Host, I have provided you with The Passion Translation Book of John.

John 1

The Passion Translation by Dr. Brian Simmons

The Living Expression

1 In the very beginning the Living Expression was already there. And the Living Expression was with God, yet fully God. 2 They were together—*face-to-face*, in the very beginning.

3 And through His creative inspiration this Living Expression made all things, for nothing has existence apart from him! 4 Life came into being because of him, for his life is light for all humanity. 5 And this Living Expression is the Light that bursts through gloom the Light that darkness could not diminish!

6 Then suddenly a man appeared who was sent from God, a messenger named John. 7 For he came to be a witness, to point the way to the Light of Life, and to help everyone believe.

8 John was not that Light but he came to show who is. For he was merely a messenger to speak the truth about the Light. 9 For the Light of Truth was about to come into the world and shine upon everyone. 10 He entered into the very world he created, yet the world was unaware. 11 He came to the very people he created—to those who should have recognized him, but they did not receive him.

12 But those who embraced him and took hold of his name were given authority to become the children of God! 13 He was not born by the joining of human parents or from natural means, or by a man's desire, but he was born of God.

14 And so the Living Expression became a man and lived among us! And we gazed upon the splendor of his glory, the glory of the One and Only who came from the Father overflowing with tender mercy and truth!

15 John taught the truth about him when he announced to the people, "He's the One! *Set your hearts on him!* I told you he would come after me, even though he ranks far above me, for he existed before I was even born." 16 And now out of his fullness we are fulfilled! And from him we receive grace heaped upon more grace!

17 Moses gave us the Law, but Jesus, the Anointed One, unveils truth wrapped in tender mercy.

18 No one has ever gazed upon the fullness of God's splendor except the uniquely beloved Son, who is cherished by the Father and held close to his heart. Now he has unfolded to us the full explanation of who God truly is!

My Notes...

The Ministry of John the Baptizer

19 There were some of the Jewish leaders who sent an entourage of priests and temple servants[j] from Jerusalem to interrogate John. They asked him, "Who are you?"

20 John answered them directly, saying, "I am not the Messiah!"

21 "Then who are you?" they asked. "Are you Elijah?"

"No," John replied. So they pressed him further, "Are you the prophet Moses said was coming, the one we're expecting?"

"No," he replied.

22 "Then who are you?" they demanded. "We need an answer for those who sent us. Tell us something about yourself—anything!"

23 So, John answered them, *"I am fulfilling Isaiah's prophecy:* 'I am an urgent, thundering voice shouting in the desert—clear the way and prepare your hearts for the coming of the Lord Yahweh!'"

24 Then some members of the religious sect known as the Pharisees questioned John,

25 "Why do you baptize the people since you admit you're not the Christ, Elijah, or the Prophet?"

26–27 John answered them, "I baptize in this river, but the One who will take my place is to be more honored than I, but even when he stands among you, you will not recognize or embrace him! I am not worthy enough to stoop down in front of him and untie his sandals!" 28 This all took place at Bethany, where John was baptizing at the place of the crossing of the Jordan River.

The Lamb of God

29 The very next day John saw Jesus coming to him to be baptized, and John cried out, "Look! There he is—God's Lamb! He will take away the sins of the world! 30 I told you that a Mighty One would come who is far greater than I am, because he existed long before I was born! 31 My baptism was for the preparation of his appearing to Israel, even though I've yet to experience him."

32 Then, as John baptized Jesus he spoke these words: "I see the Spirit of God appear like a dove descending from the heavenly realm and landing upon him—and it rested upon him from

My Notes...

that moment forward! 33 And even though I've yet to experience him, when I was commissioned
to baptize with water God spoke these words to me, 'One day you will see the Spirit descend
and remain upon a man. He will be the One I have sent to baptize with the Holy Spirit.' 34 And
now I have seen with discernment. I can tell you for sure that this man is the Son of God."

Jesus' First Followers

35–36 The very next day John was there again with two of his disciples as Jesus was walking
right past them. John, gazing upon him, pointed to Jesus and said, "Look! There's God's
Lamb!" 37 And as soon as John's two disciples heard this, they immediately left John and began
to follow a short distance behind Jesus.

38 Then Jesus turned around and saw they were following him and asked, "What do you
want?" They responded, "Rabbi (which means, Master Teacher), where are you staying?" 39
Jesus answered, "Come and discover for yourselves." So they went with him and saw where
he was staying, and since it was late in the afternoon, they spent the rest of the day with Jesus.

40–41 One of the two disciples who heard John's words and began to follow Jesus was a man
named Andrew. He went and found his brother, Simon, and told him, "We have found the
Anointed One!" (Which is translated, the Christ.) 42 Then Andrew brought Simon to meet him.
When Jesus gazed upon Andrew's brother, he prophesied to him, "You are Simon and your
father's name is John. But from now on you will be called Cephas" (which means, Peter the
Rock).

Jesus Calls Philip and Nathanael

43 The next day Jesus decided to go to the region of Galilee. There he found Philip and said to
him, "Come and follow me." 44 (Now Philip, Andrew, and Peter were all from the same village
of Bethsaida.) 45 Then Philip went to look for his friend, Nathanael, and told him, "We've found
him! We've found the One we've been waiting for! It's Jesus, son of Joseph from Nazareth,
the Anointed One! He's the One that Moses and the prophets prophesied would come!"

46 Nathanael sneered, "Nazareth! What good thing could ever come from Nazareth?" Philip
answered, "Come and let's find out!"

47 When Jesus saw Nathanael approaching, he said, "Now here comes a true son of Israel—an
honest man with no hidden motive!"

My Notes...

[48] *Nathanael was stunned* and said, "But you've never met me—how do you know anything about me?"

Jesus answered, "Nathanael, right before Philip came to you I saw you sitting under the shade of a fig tree."

[49] Nathanael blurted out, "Teacher, you are truly the Son of God and the King of Israel!"

[50] Jesus answered, "Do you believe simply because I told you I saw you sitting under a fig tree? You will experience even more impressive things than that! [51] I prophesy to you eternal truth. From now on you will see an open heaven and gaze upon the Son of Man like a stairway reaching into the sky with the messengers of God climbing up and down upon him!"

John 2

The Passion Translation (TPT)

Jesus Comes to a Wedding

[1] Now on the third day there was a wedding feast in the Galilean village of Cana, and the mother of Jesus was there. [2–3] Jesus and his disciples were all invited to the banquet, but with so many guests in attendance, they ran out of wine. And when Mary realized it, she came to him and asked, "They have no wine, *can't you do something about it?*"

[4] Jesus replied, "My dear one, don't you understand that if I do this, it won't change anything for you, but it will change everything for me! My hour *of unveiling my power* has not yet come."

[5] Mary then went to the servers and told them, "Whatever Jesus tells you, make sure that you do it!"

[6] Now there were six stone water pots standing nearby. They were meant to be used for the Jewish washing rituals. Each one held about 20 gallons or more [7] Jesus came to the servers and told them, "Fill the *pots with water, right up to the very brim*." [8] Then he said, "Now fill your pitchers and take them to the master of ceremonies."

[9] And when they poured out their pitcher for the master of ceremonies to sample, the water became wine! When he tasted the water that became wine, the master of ceremonies was impressed. (Although he didn't know where the wine had come from, but the servers knew.)

My Notes...

10 He called the bridegroom over and said to him, "Every host serves his best wine first until
everyone has had a cup or two, then he serves the wine of poor quality. But you, my friend,
you've reserved the most exquisite wine until now!"

11 This miracle in Cana was the first of the many extraordinary miracles Jesus performed in
Galilee. This was a sign revealing his glory, and his disciples believed in him.

Jesus at the Temple

12 After this, Jesus, his mother and brothers and his disciples went to Capernaum and stayed
there for a few days. 13 But the time was close for the Jewish passover to begin, so Jesus walked
to Jerusalem. 14 As he went into the temple courtyard, he noticed it was filled with merchants
selling oxen, lambs, and doves *for exorbitant prices*, while others were overcharging as they
exchanged currency behind their counters. 15 So Jesus found some rope and made it into a whip.
Then he drove out every one of them and their animals from the courtyard of the temple, and
he kicked over their tables filled with money, scattering it everywhere! 16 And he shouted at
the merchants, "Get these things out of here! Don't you dare make my Father's house into a
center for merchandise!" 17 That's when his disciples remembered the Scripture: "I am
consumed with a fiery passion to keep your house pure!"

18 But the Jewish religious leaders challenged Jesus, "What authorization do you have to do
this sort of thing? If God gave you this kind of authority, what *supernatural* sign will you show
us to prove it?"

19 Jesus answered, "After you've destroyed this temple, I will raise it up again in three days."

20 Then the Jewish leaders sneered, "This temple took forty-six years to build, and you mean
to tell us that you will raise it up in three days?" 21 *But they didn't understand that* Jesus was
speaking of the "temple" of his body. 22 But the disciples remembered his prophecy after Jesus
rose from the dead, and believed both the Scripture and what Jesus had said.

23 While Jesus was at the Passover Feast , *the number of his followers began to grow*, and many
gave their allegiance to him because of all the miraculous signs they had seen him doing! 24
But Jesus did not yet entrust himself to them, because he knew how fickle human hearts can
be. 25 He didn't need anyone to tell him about human nature, *for he fully understood what man
was capable of doing*.

My Notes...

John 3

The Passion Translation (TPT)

Nicodemus

[1] Now there was a prominent religious leader among the Jews named Nicodemus, who was
part of the sect called the Pharisees and a member of the Jewish ruling council. [2] One night he
discreetly came to Jesus and said, "Master, we know that you are a teacher from God, for no
one performs the miracle signs that you do, unless God's power is with him."

[3] Jesus answered, "Nicodemus, listen to this eternal truth: Before a person can perceive God's
kingdom realm, they must first experience a rebirth."

[4] Nicodemus said, "Rebirth? How can a gray-headed man be reborn? It's impossible for a man
to go back into the womb a second time and be reborn!"

[5] Jesus answered, "I speak an eternal truth: Unless you are born of water and Spirit-wind, you
will never enter God's kingdom realm. [6] For the natural realm can only give birth to things that
are natural, but the spiritual realm gives birth to supernatural life!

[7] "You shouldn't be amazed by my statement, 'You must be born from above!' [8] For the Spirit-
wind blows as it chooses. You can hear its sound, but you don't know where it came from or
where it's going. So it is within the hearts of those who are Spirit-born!"

[9] Then Nicodemus replied, "But I don't understand, what do you mean? How does this
happen?"

[10] Jesus answered, "Nicodemus, aren't you the respected teacher in Israel, and yet you don't
understand this revelation? [11] I speak eternal truths about things I know, things I've seen and
experienced—and still you don't accept what I reveal. [12] If you're unable to understand and
believe what I've told you about the natural realm, what will you do when I begin to unveil
the heavenly realm? [13] No one has risen into the heavenly realm except the Son of Man who
also exists in heaven."

God's Love for Everyone

[14] "And just as Moses in the desert lifted up the brass replica of a snake on a pole *for all the
people to see and be healed*, so the Son of Man is ready to be lifted up, [15] so that those who

My Notes...

truly believe in him will not perish but be given eternal life. [16] For this is how much God loved the world—he gave his one and only, unique Son *as a gift*. So now everyone who believes in him will never perish but experience everlasting life.

[17] "God did not send his Son into the world to judge and condemn the world, but to be its Savior and rescue it! [18] So now there is no longer any condemnation for those who believe in him, but the unbeliever already lives under condemnation because they do not believe in the name of God's beloved Son. [19] And here is the basis for their judgment: The Light of God has now come into the world, but the hearts of people love their darkness more than the Light, because they want the darkness to conceal their evil. [20] So the wicked hate the Light and try to hide from it, for their lives are fully exposed in the Light. [21] But those who love the truth will come out into the Light and welcome its exposure, for the Light will reveal that their fruitful works were produced by God."

John, Friend of the Bridegroom

[22] Then Jesus and his disciples went out for a length of time into the Judean countryside where they baptized the people. [23] At this time John was still baptizing people at Aenon, near Salim, where there was plenty of water. And the people kept coming for John to baptize them. [24] (This was before John was thrown into prison.)

[25] An argument then developed between John's disciples and a particular Jewish man about baptism. [26] So they went to John and asked him, "Teacher, are you aware that the One you told us about at the crossing place—he's now baptizing everyone with larger crowds than yours. People are flocking to him! *What do you think about that?*"

[27] John answered them, "A person cannot receive even one thing unless God bestows it. [28] You heard me tell you before that I am not the Messiah, but certainly I am the messenger sent ahead of him. [29] He is the Bridegroom, and the bride belongs to him. I am the friend of the Bridegroom who stands nearby and listens with great joy to the Bridegroom's voice. And because of his words my joy is complete and overflows! [30] So it's necessary for him to increase and for me to be diminished.

[31] "For the one who is from the earth belongs to the earth and speaks from the natural realm. But the One who comes from above is above everything and speaks of the highest realm of all! [32] His message is about what he has seen and experienced, even though people don't accept it. [33] Yet those who embrace his message know in their hearts that it's the truth.

[34] "The One whom God has sent to represent him will speak the words of God, for God has

My Notes...

poured out upon him the fullness of the Holy Spirit without limitation. 35 The Father loves his Son so much that all things have been given into his hands. 36 Those who trust in the Son possess eternal life; but those who don't obey the Son will not see life, and God's anger will rise up against them."

John 4

The Passion Translation (TPT)

A Thirsty Savior

1 Soon the news reached the Jewish religious leaders known as the Pharisees that Jesus was drawing greater crowds of followers coming to be baptized than John. 2 (Although Jesus didn't baptize, but had his disciples baptize the people.) 3 *Jesus* heard what was being said and abruptly left Judea and returned to the province of Galilee, 4 and he had to pass through Samaritan territory.

5 Jesus arrived at the Samaritan village of Sychar, near the field that Jacob had given to his son, Joseph, long ago. 6–8 Wearied by his long journey, he sat on the edge of Jacob's well. He sent his disciples into the village to buy food, for it was already afternoon.

Soon a Samaritan woman came to draw water. Jesus said to her, "Give me a drink of water."

9 Surprised, she said, "Why would a Jewish man ask a Samaritan woman for a drink of water?"

10 Jesus replied, "If you only knew who I am and the gift that God wants to give you—you'd ask me for a drink, and I would give to you living water."

11 The woman replied, "But sir, you don't even have a bucket and this well is very deep. So where do you find this 'living water'? 12 Do you really think that you are greater than our ancestor Jacob who dug this well and drank from it himself, along with his children and livestock?"

13 Jesus answered, "If you drink from Jacob's well you'll be thirsty again and again, 14 but if anyone drinks the living water I give them, they will never thirst again and will be forever satisfied! For when you drink the water I give you it becomes a gushing fountain *of the Holy Spirit*, springing up and flooding you with endless life!"

15 The woman replied, "Let me drink that water so I'll never be thirsty again and won't have to come back here to draw water."

My Notes...

16 Jesus said, "Go get your husband and bring him back here."

17 "But I'm not married," the woman answered.

"That's true," Jesus said, 18 "for you've been married five times and now you're living with a
man who is not your husband. You have told the truth."

19 The woman said, "You must be a prophet! 20 So tell me this: Why do our fathers worship
God here on this nearby mountain, but your people teach that Jerusalem is the place where we
must worship. Which is right?"

Jesus responded, 21 "Believe me, dear woman, the time has come when you won't worship the
Father on a mountain nor in Jerusalem, *but in your heart*. 22 Your people don't really know the
One they worship. We Jews worship out of our experience, for it's from the Jews that salvation
is made available. 23–24 From here on, worshiping the Father will not be a matter of the right
place but with the right heart. For God is a Spirit, and he longs to have sincere worshipers who
worship and adore him in the realm of the Spirit and in truth."

25 The woman said, "*This is all so confusing*, but I do know that the Anointed One is coming—
the true Messiah. And when he comes, he will tell us everything we need to know."

26 Jesus said to her, "You don't have to wait any longer, the Anointed One is here speaking with
you—I am the One you're looking for."

27 At that moment the disciples returned and were stunned to see Jesus speaking with the
Samaritan woman. Yet none of them dared to ask him why or what they were discussing. 28
All at once, the woman dropped her water jar and ran off to her village and told everyone, 29
"Come and meet a man at the well who told me everything I've ever done! He could be the
Anointed One we've been waiting for." 30 Hearing this, the people came streaming out of the
village to go see Jesus.

The Harvest Is Ready

31 Then the disciples began to insist that Jesus eat some of the food they brought back from the
village, saying, "Teacher, you must eat something." 32 But Jesus told them, "Don't worry about
me. I have eaten a meal you don't know about."

33 Puzzled by this, the disciples began to discuss among themselves, "Did someone already
bring him food? Where did he get this meal?"

34 Then Jesus spoke up and said, "My food is to be doing the will of him who sent me and
bring it to completion."

My Notes...

[35] *As the crowds emerged from the village, Jesus said to his disciples*, "Why would you say,
'The harvest is another four months away'? Look at all the people coming—now is harvest
time! For their hearts are like vast fields of ripened grain—ready for a spiritual harvest. [36] And
everyone who reaps these souls for eternal life will receive a reward. And those who plant
spiritual seeds and those who reap the harvest will celebrate together with great joy! [37] And
this confirms the saying, 'One sows the seed and another reaps the harvest.' [38] I have sent you
out to harvest a field that you haven't planted, where many others have labored long and hard
before you. And now you are privileged to profit from their labors and reap the harvest."

[39] So there were many from the Samaritan village who became believers in Jesus because of
the woman's testimony: "He told me everything I ever did!" [40] Then they begged Jesus to stay
with them, so he stayed there for two days, [41] resulting in many more coming to faith in him
because of his teachings.

[42] Then the Samaritans said to the woman, "We no longer believe just because of what you told
us, but now we've heard him ourselves and are convinced that he really is the true Savior of
the world!"

Jesus Returns to Galilee

[43] On the third day Jesus left there and walked to the province of Galilee, *where he was raised.*
[44] Now Jesus knew that prophets are honored everywhere they go except in their own
hometown. [45] Even so, as Jesus arrived in the province of Galilee, he was welcomed by the
people with open arms. Many of them had been in Jerusalem during the Passover Festival and
had witnessed firsthand the miracles he had performed.

[46–47] Jesus entered the village of Cana of Galilee where he had transformed water into wine.
And there was a governmental official in Capernaum who had a son who was very sick and
dying. When he heard that Jesus had left Judea and was staying in Cana of Galilee, he decided
to make the journey to Cana. When he found Jesus he begged him, "You must come with me
to Capernaum and heal my son!"

[48] So Jesus said to him, "You never believe unless you see signs and wonders."

[49] But the man continued to plead, "You have to come with me to Capernaum before my little
boy dies!"

[50] Then Jesus looked him in the eyes and said, "Go back home now. I promise you, your son
will live and not die."

My Notes...

The man believed in his heart the words of Jesus and set off for home. 51 When he was still a distance from Capernaum, his servants met him on the road and told him the good news, "Your son is healed! He's alive!"

52 Overjoyed, the father asked his servants, "When did my son begin to recover?"

"Yesterday," they said, "at one in the afternoon. All at once his fever broke—and now he's well!"

53 Then the father realized that it was at that very same hour that Jesus spoke the words to him, "Your son will live and not die." So from that day forward, the man and all his family and servants believed. 54 This was Jesus' second extraordinary miracle in Galilee after coming from Judea.

John 5

The Passion Translation (TPT)

The Healing at Bethesda

1 Then Jesus returned to Jerusalem to observe one of the Jewish holy days. 2 Inside the city near the Sheep Gate there is a pool called in Aramaic, The House of Loving Kindness. And this pool is surrounded by five covered porches. 3 Hundreds of sick people were lying there on the porches—the paralyzed, the blind, and the crippled, all of them waiting for their healing. 4 For an angel of God would periodically descend into the pool to stir the waters, and the first one who stepped into the pool after the waters swirled would instantly be healed.

5 Now there was a man who had been disabled for thirty-eight years lying among the multitude of the sick. 6 When Jesus saw him lying there, he knew that the man had been crippled for a long time. So Jesus said to him, "Do you truly long to be healed?"

7 The sick man answered him, "Sir, there's no way I can get healed, for I have no one who will lower me into the water when the angel comes. As soon as I try to crawl to the edge of the pool, someone else jumps in ahead of me."

8 Then Jesus said to him, "Stand up! Pick up your sleeping mat and you will walk!" 9 Immediately he stood up—he was healed! So he rolled up his mat and walked again! Now this miracle took place on the Jewish Sabbath.

My Notes...

10 When the Jewish leaders saw the man walking along carrying his sleeping mat, they objected
and said, "What are you doing carrying that? Don't you know it's the Sabbath? It's not lawful
for you to carry things on the Sabbath!"

11 He answered them, "The man who healed me told me to pick it up and walk."

12 "What man?" they asked him. "Who was this man who ordered you to carry something on
a Sabbath?" 13 But the healed man couldn't give them an answer, for he didn't yet know who
it was since Jesus had already slipped away into the crowd.

14 A short time later, Jesus found the man at the temple and said to him, "Look at you now!
You're healed! Walk away from your sin so that nothing worse will happen to you."

15 Then the man went to the Jewish leaders to inform them, "It was Jesus who healed me!" 16
So from that day forward the Jewish leaders began to persecute Jesus because of the things he
did on the Sabbath.

Jesus Responds to the Jewish Leaders

17 Jesus answered his critics by saying, "Everyday my Father is at work, and I will be too!" 18
This infuriated them and made them all the more eager to devise a plan to kill him. For not
only did he break their Sabbath rules, but he called God "my Father," which made him equal
to God.

19 So Jesus said, "I speak to you timeless truth. The Son is not able to do anything from himself
or through my own initiative. I only do the works that I see the Father doing, for the Son does
the same works as his Father.

20 "Because the Father loves his Son so much, he always reveals to me everything that he is
about to do. And you will all be amazed when he shows me even greater works than what
you've seen so far! 21 For just like the Father has power to raise the dead, the Son will raise the
dead and give life to whomever he wants.

22 "The Father now judges no one, for he has given all the authority to judge to the Son, 23 so
that the honor that belongs to the Father will now be shared with his Son. So if you refuse to
honor the Son, you are refusing to honor the Father who sent him.

24 "I speak to you an eternal truth: if you embrace my message and believe in the One who sent
me, you will never face condemnation, for in me, you have already passed from the realm of
death into the realm of eternal life!"

My Notes...

Two Resurrections

25 "I speak to you eternal truth: Soon the dead will hear the voice of the Son of God, and those
who listen will arise with life! 26 For the Father has given the Son the power to impart life,
even as the Father imparts life. 27 The Father has transferred to the Son the authority to judge,
because he is the Son of Man.

28 "So don't be amazed when I tell you these things, for there is a day coming when all who
have ever died will hear my voice *calling them back to life*, 29 and they will come out of their
graves! Those who have done what is good will experience a resurrection to eternal life. And
those who have practiced evil will taste the resurrection that brings them to condemnation!

30 "Nothing I do is from my own initiative, for as I hear the judgment passed by my Father, I
execute judgment. And my judgments will be perfect, because I can do nothing on my own,
except to fulfill the desires of my Father who sent me. 31 For if I were to make claims about
myself, you would have reasons to doubt. 32 But there is another who bears witness on my
behalf, and I know that what he testifies of me is true."

John the Baptizer

33 "You have sent messengers to John, and what he testified *about me* is true. 34 I have no need
to be validated by men, but I'm saying these things so that you will *believe* and be rescued.

35 "John was a blazing, burning torch, and for a short time you basked in his light with great
joy. 36 But I can provide a more substantial proof of who I am that exceeds John's testimony—
my miracles! These works which the Father destined for me to complete—they prove that the
Father has sent me! 37 And my Father himself, who gave me this mission, has also testified
that I am his Son. But you have never heard his voice nor seen his face, 38 nor does his Word
truly live inside of you, for you refuse to believe in me or to embrace me as God's messenger.

39 "You are busy analyzing the Scriptures, frantically poring over them in hopes of gaining
eternal life. Everything you read points to me, 40 yet you still refuse to come to me so I can
give you the life you're looking for—eternal life!

41 "I do not accept the honor that comes from men, 42 for I know what kind of people you really
are, and I can see that the love of God has found no home in you. 43 I have come to represent
my Father, yet you refuse to embrace me in faith. But when someone comes in their own name
and with their own agenda, you readily accept him. 44 Of course you're unable to believe in
me. For you live for the praises of others and not for the praise that comes from the only true
God.

My Notes...

[45] "I won't be the one who accuses you before the Father. The one who will incriminate you is Moses, the very one you claim to obey, the one in whom you trust! [46] If you really believed what Moses has written, then you would embrace me, for Moses wrote about me! [47] But since you do not believe what he wrote, no wonder you don't believe what I say."

John 6

The Passion Translation (TPT)

Jesus Multiplies Food

[1] After this Jesus went to the other side of the Lake of Tiberias, which is also known as Lake Galilee. [2] And a massive crowd of people followed him everywhere. They were attracted by his miracles and the healings they watched him perform. [3] Jesus went up the slope of a hill and sat down with his disciples. [4] Now it was approaching the time of the Jewish celebration of Passover, *and there were many pilgrims on their way to Jerusalem in the crowd.*

[5] As Jesus sat down, he looked out and saw the massive crowd of people scrambling up the hill, for they wanted to be near him. So he turned to Philip and said, "Where will we buy enough food to feed all these people?" [6] Now Jesus already knew what he was about to do, but he said this to stretch Philip's faith.

[7] Philip answered, "Well, I suppose if we were to give everyone only a snack, it would cost thousands of dollars to buy enough food!"

[8] But just then, Andrew, Peter's brother, spoke up and said, [9] "Look! Here's a young person with five barley loaves and two small fish . . . but how far would that go with this huge crowd?"

[10] "Have everyone sit down," Jesus said to his disciples. So on the vast grassy slope, more than five thousand hungry people sat down. [11] Jesus then took the barley loaves and the fish and gave thanks to God. He then gave it to the disciples to distribute to the people. Miraculously, the food multiplied, with everyone eating as much as they wanted!

[12] When everyone was satisfied, Jesus told his disciples, "Now go back and gather up the pieces left over so that nothing will be wasted." [13] The disciples filled up twelve baskets of fragments, *a basket of leftovers for each disciple*.

[14] All the people were astounded as they saw with their own eyes the incredible miracle Jesus had performed! They began to say among themselves, "He really is the One—the true prophet we've been expecting!"

My Notes...

15 So Jesus, knowing that they were about to take him and make him their king by force, quickly left and went up the mountainside alone.

Jesus Walks on Water

16–17 After waiting until evening for Jesus to return, the disciples went down to the lake. But as darkness fell, he still hadn't returned, so the disciples got into a boat and headed across the lake to Capernaum. 18 By now a strong wind began to blow and was stirring up the waters. 19
The disciples had rowed about halfway across the lake when all of a sudden they caught sight of Jesus walking on top of the waves, coming toward them. The disciples panicked, 20 but Jesus called out to them, "Don't be afraid. You know who I am."

21 They were relieved to take him in, and the moment Jesus stepped into the boat, they were instantly transported to the other side!

Jesus, the Living Bread

22–23 The next morning, the crowds were still on the opposite shore of the lake, near the place where they had eaten the bread he had multiplied after he had given thanks to God. Yet Jesus was nowhere to be found. They realized that only one boat had been there and that Jesus' hadn't boarded, and they concluded that his disciples had left him behind. 24 So when the people saw on the shoreline a number of small boats from Tiberias and realized Jesus and the disciples weren't there, they got into the boats and went to Capernaum to search for him.

25 When they finally found him, they asked him, "Teacher, how did you get here?"

26 Jesus replied, "Let me make this very clear, you came looking for me because I fed you by
a miracle, not because you believe in me. 27 Why would you strive for food that is perishable and not be passionate to seek the food of eternal life, which never spoils? I, the Son of Man, am ready to give you what matters most, for God the Father has destined me for this purpose."

28 They replied, "So what should we do if we want to do God's work?"

29 Jesus answered, "The work you can do for God starts with believing in the One he has sent."

30–31 They replied, "Show us a miracle so we can see it, and then we'll believe in you. *Moses took care of our ancestors* who were fed by the miracle of manna every day in the desert, just like the Scripture says, 'He fed them with bread from heaven.' What sign will you perform for us?"

My Notes...

32 "The truth is," Jesus said, "Moses didn't give you the bread of heaven. It's my Father who
offers bread that comes as a dramatic sign from heaven. 33 The bread of God is the One who
came out of heaven to give his life to feed the world."

34 "Then please, sir, give us this bread every day," they replied.

35 Jesus said to them, "I am the Bread of Life. Come every day to me and you will never be
hungry. Believe in me and you will never be thirsty. 36 Yet I've told you that even though you've
seen me, you still don't believe in me. 37 But everyone my Father has given to me, they will
come. And all who come to me, I will embrace and will never turn them away. 38 And I have
come out of heaven not for my own desires, but for the satisfaction of my Father who sent me.
39 My Father who sent me has determined that I will not lose even one of those he has given to
me, and I will raise them up in the last day. 40 For the longing of my Father is that everyone
who embraces the Son and believes in him will experience eternal life and I will raise them up
in the last day!"

41 When the Jews who were hostile to Jesus heard him say, "I am the bread that came down
from heaven," they immediately began to complain, 42 "How can he say these things about
himself? We know him, and we know his parents. How dare he say, 'I have come down from
heaven?'"

43 Jesus responded, "Stop your grumbling! 44 The only way people come to me is by the Father
who sent me—he pulls on their hearts to embrace me. And those who are drawn to me, I will
certainly raise them up in the last day."

45 Jesus continued, "It has been written by the prophets, 'They will all be taught by God
himself.' If you are really listening to the Father and learning directly from him, you will come
to me. 46 For I am the only One who has come from the Father's side, and I have seen the
Father!

47 "I speak to you living truth: Unite your heart to me and believe—and you will experience
eternal life! 48 I am the true Bread of Life. 49 Your ancestors ate manna in the desert and died.
50 But standing here before you is the true Bread that comes out of heaven, and when you eat
this Bread you will never die. 51 I alone am this living Bread that has come to you from heaven.
Eat this Bread and you will live forever. The living Bread I give you is my body, which I will
offer as a sacrifice so that all may live."

52 These words of Jesus sparked an angry outburst among the Jews. They protested, saying,
"Does this man expect us to eat his body?"

My Notes...

53 Jesus replied to them, “Listen to this eternal truth: Unless you eat the body of the Son of
Man and drink his blood, you will not have eternal life. 54 Eternal life comes to the one who
eats my body and drinks my blood, and I will raise him up in the last day. 55 For my body is
real food for your spirit and my blood is real drink. 56 The one who eats my body and drinks
my blood lives in me and I live in him. 57 The Father of life sent me, and he is my life. In the
same way, the one who feeds upon me, I will become his life. 58 I am not like the bread your
ancestors ate and later died. I am the living Bread that comes from heaven. Eat this Bread and
you will live forever!”

59 Jesus preached this sermon in the synagogue in Capernaum.

Many Disciples Became Offended

60 And when many of Jesus’ followers heard these things, it caused a stir. “That’s disgusting!”
they said. “How could anybody accept it?”

61 Without anyone telling him, Jesus knew they were outraged and told them, “Are you offended
over my teaching? 62 What will you do when you see the Son of Man ascending *into the
realm* from where he came?

63 “The Holy Spirit is the one who gives life, that which is of the natural realm is of no help.
The words I speak to you are Spirit and life. But there are still some of you who won’t believe.”
64 In fact, Jesus already knew from the beginning who the skeptics were and who his traitor
would be.

65 He went on to say, “This is why I told you that no one embraces me unless the Father has
given you to me.”

Peter’s Confession of Faith

66 And so from that time on many of the disciples turned their backs on Jesus and refused to be
associated with him. 67 So Jesus said to his twelve, “And you—do you also want to leave?” 68
Peter spoke up and said, “But Lord, where would we go? No one but you gives us the revelation
of eternal life. 69 We’re fully convinced that you are the Anointed One, the Son of the Living
God, and we believe in you!”

70 Then Jesus *shocked them* with these words: “I have hand-picked you to be my twelve,
knowing that one of you is the devil.” 71 Jesus was referring to Judas Iscariot, son of Simon, for
he knew that Judas, one of his chosen disciples, was getting ready to betray him.

My Notes...

John 7

The Passion Translation (TPT)

Jesus at the Feast of Tabernacles

[1] After this Jesus traveled extensively throughout the province of Galilee, but he avoided the province of Judea, for he knew the Jewish leaders in Jerusalem were plotting to have him killed. [2] Now the annual Feast of Tabernacles was approaching. [3] So Jesus' brothers came to advise him, saying, "Why don't you leave the countryside villages and go to Judea where the crowds are, so that your followers can see your miracles? [4] No one can see what you're doing here in the backwoods of Galilee. How do you expect to be successful and famous if you do all these things in secret? Now is your time—go to Jerusalem, come out of hiding, and show the world who you are!" [5] His brothers were pushing him, even though they didn't yet believe in him as the Savior.

[6] Jesus responded, "My time of being unveiled hasn't yet come, but any time is a suitable opportunity for you *to gain man's approval.* [7] The world can't hate you, but it does me, for I am exposing their evil deeds. [8] You can go ahead and celebrate the feast without me—my appointed time has not yet come."

[9–10] Jesus lingered in Galilee until his brothers had left for the feast in Jerusalem. Then later, Jesus took a back road and went into Jerusalem in secret. [11] During the feast, the Jewish leaders kept looking for Jesus and asking around, "Where is he? Have you seen him?"

[12] A controversy was brewing among the people, with so many differing opinions about Jesus. Some were saying, "He's a good man!" While others weren't convinced and insisted, saying, "He's just a demagogue." [13] Yet no one was bold enough to speak out publicly on Jesus' behalf for fear of the Jewish leaders.

[14] Not until the feast was half over did Jesus finally appear in the temple courts and begin to teach. [15] The Jewish leaders were astonished by what he taught and said, "How did this man acquire such knowledge? He wasn't trained in our schools—who taught him?"

[16] So Jesus responded, "I don't teach my own ideas, but the truth revealed to me by the One who sent me. [17] If you want to test my teachings and discover where I received them, first be passionate to do God's will, and then you will be able to discern if my teachings are from the heart of God or from my own opinions. [18] Charlatans praise themselves and seek honor from men, but my Father sent me to speak truth on his behalf. And I have no false motive, because

My Notes...

I seek only the glory of God. [19] Moses has given you the law, but not one of you is faithful to
keep it. So if you are all law-breakers, why then would you seek to kill me?"

[20] Then some in the crowd shouted out, "You must be out of your mind! Who's trying to kill
you?"

[21] Jesus replied, "I only had to do one miracle, and all of you marvel![22] Yet isn't it true that
Moses and your forefathers ordered you to circumcise your sons even if the eighth day fell on
a Sabbath? [23] So if you cut away part of a man on the Sabbath and that doesn't break the Jewish
law, why then would you be indignant with me for making a man completely healed on the
Sabbath? [24] Stop judging based on the superficial. First you must *embrace the standards of
mercy* and truth."

[25] Then some of the residents of Jerusalem spoke up and said, "Isn't this the one they're trying
to kill? [26] So why is he here speaking publicly and not one of the Jewish leaders is doing
anything about it? Are they starting to think that he's the Anointed One? [27] But how could he
be, since we know this man is from Galilee, but no one will know where the true Messiah
comes from, he'll just appear out of nowhere."

[28] Knowing all of this, Jesus one day preached *boldly* in the temple courts, "So, you think you
know me and where I come from? But you don't know the One who sent me—the Father who
is always faithful.I have not come simply on my own initiative. [29] The Father has sent me here,
and I know all about him, for I have come from his presence."

[30] His words caused many to want to arrest him, but no man was able to lay a hand on him, for
it wasn't yet his appointed time. [31] And there were many people who thought he might be the
Messiah. They said, "After all, when the Anointed One appears, could he possibly do more
signs and wonders than this man has done?"

[32] So when the Pharisees heard these rumors circulating about Jesus, they went with the leading
priests and the temple guards to arrest him.

[33] Then Jesus said, "My days to be with you are numbered. Then I will return to the One who
sent me. [34] And you will search for me and not be able to find me. For where I am, you cannot
come."

[35] When the Jewish leaders heard this, they discussed among themselves, "Where could he
possibly go that we won't be able to find him? Is he going to minister in a different land where
our people live scattered among the nations? Is he going to teach those who are not Jews?
[36] What did he really mean by his statement, 'You will search for me and won't be able to find
me. And where I am you can't come'?"

My Notes...

Rivers of Living Water

[37] Then on the most important day of the feast, the last day, Jesus stood and shouted out to the crowds—"All you thirsty ones, come to me! Come to me and drink! [38] Believe in me so that rivers of living water will burst out from within you, flowing from your innermost being, just like the Scripture says!"

[39] Jesus was prophesying about the Holy Spirit that believers were being prepared to receive. But the Holy Spirit had not yet been poured out upon them, because Jesus had not yet been unveiled in his full splendor.

Divided Opinions about Jesus

[40] When the crowd heard Jesus' words, some said, "This man really is a prophet!" [41] Others said, "He's the Messiah!" But others said, "How could he be the Anointed One since he's from Galilee? [42] Don't the Scriptures say that he will be one of David's descendants and be born in Bethlehem, the city of David?" [43] So the crowd was divided over Jesus, [44] some wanted him arrested but no one dared to lay a hand on him.

The Unbelief of Religious Leaders

[45] So when the temple guards returned to the Pharisees and the leading priests without Jesus, they were questioned, "Where is he? Why didn't you bring that man back with you?"

[46] They answered, "You don't understand—he speaks amazing things like no one else has ever spoken!"

[47] The religious leaders mocked, "Oh, so now you also have been led astray by him? [48] Do you see even one of us, your leaders, following him? [49] This ignorant rabble swarms around him because none of them know anything about the Law! They're all cursed!"

[50] Just then, Nicodemus, who had secretly spent time with Jesus, spoke up, for he was a respected voice among them. [51] He cautioned them, saying, "Does our law decide a man's guilt before we first hear him and allow him to defend himself?"

[52] They argued, "Oh, so now you're an advocate for this Galilean! Search the Scriptures, Nicodemus, and you'll see that there's no mention of a prophet coming out of Galilee!" *So with that their debate ended*, [53] and they each went their own way.

My Notes…

John 8

The Passion Translation (TPT)

An Adulteress Forgiven

[1] Jesus walked up the Mount of Olives near the city *where he spent the night.* [2] Then at dawn Jesus appeared in the temple courts again, and soon all the people gathered around to listen to his words, so he sat down and taught them. [3] Then in the middle of his teaching, the religious scholars and the Pharisees broke through the crowd and brought a woman who had been caught in the act of committing adultery and made her stand *in the middle* of everyone.

[4] Then they said to Jesus, "Teacher, we caught this woman in the very act of adultery. [5] Doesn't Moses' law command us to stone to death a woman like this? Tell us, what do you say we should do with her?" [6] They were only testing Jesus because they hoped to trap him with his own words and accuse him *of breaking the laws of Moses*.

But Jesus didn't answer them. Instead he simply bent down and wrote in the dust with his finger. [7] Angry, they kept insisting that he answer their question, so Jesus stood up and looked at them and said, "Let's have the man who has never had a sinful desire throw the first stone at her." [8] And then he bent over again and wrote some more words in the dust.

[9] Upon hearing that, her accusers slowly left the crowd one at a time, beginning with the oldest to the youngest, with a convicted conscience. [10] Until finally, Jesus was left alone with the woman still standing there in front of him. So he stood back up and said to her, "Dear woman, where are your accusers? Is there no one here to condemn you?"

[11] Looking around, she replied, "I see no one, Lord."

Jesus said, "Then I certainly don't condemn you either. Go, and from now on, be free from a life of sin."

Jesus, the Light of the World

[12] Then Jesus said, "I am light to the world and those who embrace me will experience life-giving light, and they will never walk in darkness."

[13] The Pharisees were immediately offended and said, "You're just boasting about yourself! Since we only have your word on this, it makes your testimony invalid!"

My Notes...

14 Jesus responded, "Just because I am the one making these claims doesn't mean they're
invalid. *For I absolutely know who I am*, where I've come from, and where I'm going. But
you Pharisees have no idea about what I'm saying. 15 For you've set yourselves up as judges
of others based on outward appearances, but I certainly never judge others in that way. 16 For
I discern the truth. And I am not alone in my judgments, for my Father and I have the same
understanding in all things, and he has sent me to you.

17 "Isn't it written in the law of Moses that the testimony of two men is trustworthy? 18 Then
what I say about who I am is true, for I am not alone in my testimony—my Father is the other
witness, and we testify together of the truth."

19 Then they asked, "Just who is this 'Father' of yours? Where is he?"

Jesus answered, "You wouldn't ask that question if you knew who I am, or my Father. For if
you knew me, you would recognize my Father too."20 (Jesus taught all these things while
standing *in the treasure room of the temple*. And no one dared to arrest him, for it wasn't yet
his time to surrender to men.)

"I Am Not from This World"

21 One day Jesus said again, "I am about to leave you. You will want to find me, but you will
still die in your sins. You won't be able to come where I am going."

22 This so confused the Jewish leaders that they began to say, "Is he planning to commit suicide?
What's he talking about—'You won't be able to come where I am going'?"

23 Jesus spoke up and said, "You are all from the earth; I am from above. I am not from this
world like you are. 24 That's why I've told you that you will all die in your sins if you fail to
believe that I AM who I AM."

25 So they asked him plainly, "Who are you?"

"I am the One I've always claimed to be." Jesus replied. 26 "And I still have many more things
to pronounce in judgment about you. For I will testify to the world of the truths that I have
heard from my Father, and the Father who sent me is trustworthy." 27 (Even after all of this,
they still didn't realize that he was speaking about his heavenly Father.)

28 "You will know me as 'I AM' after you have lifted me up from the earth as the Son of Man.
Then you will realize that I do nothing on my own initiative, but I only speak the truth that the
Father has revealed to me. 29 I am his messenger and he is always with me, for I only do that
which delights his heart." 30 These words caused many *respected Jews* to believe in him.

My Notes...

The Son Gives Freedom

[31] Jesus said to those Jews who believed in him, "When you continue to embrace all that I
teach, you prove that you are my true followers. [32] For if you embrace the truth, it will release
more freedom into your lives."

[33] Surprised by this, they said, "But we're the descendants of Abraham and we're already free.
We've never been in bondage to anyone. How could you say that we will be released into more
freedom?"

[34] "I speak eternal truth," Jesus said. "When you sin you are not free. You've become a slave
in bondage to your sin. [35] And slaves have no permanent standing in a family, like a son does,
for a son is a part of the family forever. [36] So if the Son sets you free from sin, then become a
true son and be unquestionably free! [37] Even though you are descendants of Abraham, you
desire to kill me because the message I bring has not found a home in your hearts. [38] Yet the
truths I speak I've seen and received in my Father's presence. But you are doing what you've
learned from your father!"

[39] "What do mean?" they replied. "Abraham is our father!"

Jesus said, "If you are really Abraham's sons, then you would follow in the steps of
Abraham. [40] I've only told you the truth that I've heard in my Father's presence, but now you
are wanting me dead—is that how Abraham acted? [41] No, you people are doing what your
father has taught you!"

Indignant, they responded, "What are you talking about? We only have one Father, God
himself! We're not illegitimate!"

[42] Jesus said, "Then if God were really your father, you would love me, for I've come from his
presence. I didn't come here on my own, but God sent me to you. [43] Why don't you understand
what I say? You don't understand because your hearts are closed to my message!

[44] "You are the offspring of your father, the devil, and you serve your father very well,
passionately carrying out his desires. He's been a murderer right from the start! He never stood
with the One who is the true Prince, for he's full of nothing but lies—lying is his native tongue.
He is a master of deception and the father of lies! [45] But I am the true Prince who speaks nothing
but the truth, yet you refuse to believe and you want nothing to do with me. [46] Can you name
one sin that I've committed? Then if I am telling you only the truth, why don't you believe
me? [47] If you really knew God, you would listen, receive, and respond with faith to his words.
But since you don't listen and respond to what he says, it proves you don't belong to him and
you have no room for him in your hearts."

My Notes...

48 "See! We were right all along!" some of the Jewish leaders shouted. "You're nothing but a demon-possessed Samaritan!"

49 Jesus replied, "It is not a demon that would cause me to honor my Father. I live my life for his honor, even though you insult me for it. 50 I never have a need to seek my own glory, for the Father will do that for me, and he will judge those who do not. 51 I speak to you this eternal truth: whoever cherishes my words and keeps them will never experience death."

52 This prompted the Jewish leaders to say, "Now we know for sure that you're demon possessed! You just said that those who keep watch over your words will never experience death, but Abraham and all the prophets have died! 53 Do you think you're greater than our father Abraham and all the prophets? You are so delusional about yourself that you make yourself greater than you are!"

54 Jesus answered them, "If I were to tell you how great I am, it would mean nothing. But my Father is the One who will prove it and will glorify me. Isn't he the One you claim is your God? 55 But in reality, you've never embraced him as your own. I know him, and I would be a liar, like yourselves, if I told you anything less than that. I have fully embraced him, and I treasure his every word. 56 And not only that, Abraham, your ancestor, was overjoyed when he received the revelation of my coming to earth. Yes, he foresaw me coming and was filled with delight!"

57 But many of the Jewish leaders doubted him and said, "What are you talking about? You're not even fifty years old yet. You talk like you've seen Abraham!"

58 Jesus said to them, "I give you this eternal truth: I have existed long before Abraham was born, for I AM!"

59 When they heard this, they picked up rocks to stone him, but Jesus concealed himself as he passed through the crowd and went away from there.

My Notes...

John 9

The Passion Translation (TPT)

Jesus Healed a Man Born Blind

1 Afterward, as Jesus walked down the street, he noticed a man blind from birth. 2 His disciples
asked him, "Teacher, whose sin caused this guy's blindness, his own, or the sin of his parents?"

3 Jesus answered, "Neither. It happened to him so that you could watch him experience God's
miracle. 4 While I am with you, it is daytime and we must do the works of God who sent me
while the light shines. For there is coming a dark night when no one will be able to work. 5 As
long as I am with you my life is the light that pierces the world's darkness."

6 Then Jesus spat on the ground and made some clay with his saliva. Then he anointed the blind
man's eyes with the clay. 7 And he said to the blind man, "Now go and wash the clay from
your eyes in the ritual pool of Siloam." So he went and washed his face and as he came back,
he could see for the first time in his life!

8 This caused quite a stir among the people of the neighborhood, for they noticed the blind
beggar was now seeing! They began to say to one another, "Isn't this the blind man who once
sat and begged?" 9 Some said, "No, it can't be him!" Others said, "But it looks just like him—
it has to be him!" All the while the man kept insisting, "I'm the man who was blind!"

10 Finally, they asked him, "What has happened to you?"

11 He replied, "I met the man named Jesus! He rubbed clay on my eyes and said, 'Go to the
pool named Siloam and wash.' So I went and while I was washing the clay from my eyes I
began to see *for the very first time ever!*"

12 So the people of the neighborhood inquired, "Where is this man?"

"I have no idea." the man replied.

13 So the people marched him over to the Pharisees to speak with them. 14 They were concerned
because the miracle Jesus performed by making clay with his saliva and anointing the man's
eyes happened on a Sabbath day, a day that no one was allowed to "work."

15 Then the Pharisees asked the man, "How did you have your sight restored?"

He replied, "A man anointed my eyes with clay, then I washed, and now I can see for the first
time in my life!"

My Notes...

[16] Then an argument broke out among the Pharisees over the healing of the blind man on the Sabbath. Some said, "This man who performed this healing is clearly not from God! He doesn't even observe the Sabbath!" Others said, "If Jesus is just an ordinary sinner, how could he perform a miracle like that?"

[17] This prompted them to turn on the man healed of blindness, putting him on the spot in front of them all, demanding an answer. They asked, "Who do you say he is—this man who opened your blind eyes?"

"He's a prophet of God!" the man replied.

[18] Still refusing to believe that the man had been healed and was truly blind from birth, the Jewish leaders called for the man's parents to be brought to them.

[19–20] So they asked his parents, "Is this your son?"

"Yes," they answered.

"Was he really born blind?"

"Yes, he was," they replied.

So they pressed his parents to answer, "Then how is it that he's now seeing?"

[21] "We have no idea," they answered. "We don't know what happened to our son. Ask him,
he's a mature adult. He can speak for himself." [22] (Now the parents were obviously intimidated
by the Jewish religious leaders, for they had already announced to the people that if anyone
publicly confessed Jesus as the Messiah, they would be excommunicated. [23] That's why they
told them, "Ask him, he's a mature adult. He can speak for himself.")

[24] So once again they summoned the man who was healed of blindness and said to him, "Swear to God to tell us the truth! We know the man who healed you is a sinful man! Do you agree?"

[25] The healed man replied, "I have no idea what kind of man he is. All I know is that I was blind and now I can see for the first time in my life!"

[26] "But what did he do to you?" they asked. "How did he heal you?"

[27] The man responded, "I told you once and you didn't listen to me. Why do you make me repeat it? Are you wanting to be his followers too?"

[28] This angered the Jewish leaders. They heaped insults on him, "We can tell you are one of his
followers—now we know it! We are true followers of Moses, [29] for we know that God spoke
to Moses directly. But as for this one, we don't know where he's coming from!"

My Notes...

30 “Well, what a surprise this is!” the man said. “You don’t even know where he comes from,
but he healed my eyes and now I can see! 31 We know that God doesn’t listen to sinners, but
only to godly people who do his will. 32 Yet who has ever heard of a man born blind that was
healed and given back his eyesight? 33 I tell you, if this man isn’t from God, he wouldn’t be
able to heal me like he has!”

34 Some of the Jewish leaders were enraged and said, “Just who do you think you are to lecture
us! You were born a blind, filthy sinner!” So they threw the man out in the street.

35 When Jesus learned they had thrown him out, he went to find him and said to him, “Do you
believe in the Son of God?”

36 The man whose blind eyes were healed answered, “Who is he, Master? Tell me so that I can
place all my faith in him.”

37 Jesus replied, “You’re looking right at him. He’s speaking with you. It’s me, the one in front
of you now.”

38 Then the man threw himself at his feet and worshiped Jesus and said, “Lord, I believe in
you!”

39 And Jesus said, “I have come to judge those who think they see and make them blind. And
for those who are blind, I have come to make them see.”

40 Some of the Pharisees were standing nearby and overheard these words. They interrupted
Jesus and said, “You mean to tell us that we are blind?”

41 Jesus told them, “If you would acknowledge your blindness, then your sin would be removed.
But now that you claim to see, your sin remains with you!”

John 10

The Passion Translation (TPT)

The Parable of the Kind Shepherd

1 *Jesus said to the Pharisees*, “Listen to this eternal truth: The person who sneaks over the wall
to enter into the sheep pen, rather than coming through the gate, reveals himself as a thief
coming to steal. 2 But the true Shepherd walks right up to the gate, 3 and because the gatekeeper
knows who he is, he opens the gate to let him in. And the sheep recognize the voice of the true

My Notes...

Shepherd, for he calls his own by name and leads them out, for they belong to him. [4] And when
he has brought out all his sheep, he walks ahead of them and they will follow him, for they are
familiar with his voice. [5] But they will run away from strangers and never follow them because
they know it's the voice of a stranger." [6] Jesus told the Pharisees this parable even though they
didn't understand a word of what he meant.

[7] So Jesus went over it again, "I speak to you eternal truth: I am the Gate for the flock. [8] All
those who broke in before me are thieves who came to steal, but the sheep never listened to
them. [9] I am the Gateway. To enter through me is to experience life, freedom, and
satisfaction. [10] A thief has only one thing in mind—he wants to steal, slaughter, and destroy.
But I have come to *give you everything in abundance, more than you expect*—life in its fullness
until you overflow! [11] I am the Good Shepherd who lays down my life as a sacrifice for the
sheep. [12–13] But the worker who serves only for wages is not a real shepherd. Because he has
no heart for the sheep he will run away and abandon them when he sees the wolf coming. And
then the wolf mauls the sheep, drags them off, and scatters them.

[14] "I alone am the Good Shepherd, and I know those whose hearts are mine, for they recognize
me and know me, [15] just as my Father knows my heart and I know my Father's heart. I am
ready to give my life for the sheep.

[16] "And I have other sheep that I will gather which are not of this Jewish flock. And I, their
shepherd, must lead them too, and they will follow me and listen to my voice. And I will join
them all into one flock with one shepherd.

[17] "The Father has an intense love for me because I freely give my own life—to raise it up
again. [18] I surrender my own life, and no one has the power to take my life from me. I have the
authority to lay it down and the power to take it back again. This is the destiny my Father has
set before me."

[19] This teaching set off another heated controversy among the Jewish leaders. [20] Many of them
said, "This man is a demon-possessed lunatic! Why would anyone listen to a word he
says?" [21] But then there were others who weren't so sure: "His teaching is full of insight. These
are not the ravings of a madman! How could a demonized man give sight to one born blind?"

Jesus at the Feast of Renewal

[22–23] The time came to observe the winter Feast of Renewal in Jerusalem. Jesus walked into the
temple area under Solomon's covered walkway [24] when the Jewish leaders encircled him and
said, "How much longer will you keep us in suspense? Tell us the truth and clarify this for us
once and for all. Are you really the Messiah, the Anointed One?"

My Notes...

25 Jesus answered them, "I have told you the truth already and you did not believe me. The
proof of who I am is revealed by all the miracles that I do in the name of my Father. 26 Yet, you
stubbornly refuse to follow me, because you are not my sheep. As I've told you before: 27 My
own sheep will hear my voice and I know each one, and they will follow me. 28 I give to them
the gift of eternal life and they will never be lost and no one has the power to snatch them out
of my hands. 29 My Father, who has given them to me as his gift, is the mightiest of all, and no
one has the power to snatch them from my Father's care. 30 The Father and I are one."

31 When they heard this, the Jewish leaders were so enraged that they picked up rocks to stone
him to death. 32 But Jesus said, "My Father has empowered me to work many miracles and
acts of mercy among you. So which one of them do you want to stone me for?"

33 The Jewish leaders responded, "We're not stoning you for anything good you did—it's
because of your blasphemy! You're just *a son of Adam*, but you've claimed to be God!"

34 Jesus answered, "Isn't it written in your Scriptures that God said, 'You are gods?' The
Scriptures cannot be denied or found to be in error.35 So if those who have the message of the
Scriptures are said to be 'gods,' then why would you accuse me of blasphemy? 36 For I have
been uniquely chosen by God and he is the one who sent me to you. How then could it be
blasphemy for me to say, 'I am the Son of God!' 37 If I'm not doing the beautiful works that
my Father sent me to do, then don't believe me. 38 But if you see me doing the beautiful works
of God upon the earth, then you should at least believe the evidence of the miracles, even if
you don't believe my words! Then you would come to experience me and be convinced that I
am in the Father and the Father is in me."

39 Once again they attempted to seize him, but he escaped *miraculously* from their
clutches. 40 Then Jesus went back to the place where John had baptized him at the crossing of
the Jordan. 41 Many came out to where he was and said about him, "Even though John didn't
perform any miracles, everything he predicted about this man is true!" 42 And many people
became followers of Jesus at the Jordan and believed in him.

My Notes...

John 11

The Passion Translation (TPT)

Lazarus Raised from the Dead

1–2 In the village of Bethany there was a man named Lazarus, and his sisters, Mary and Martha. Mary was the one who would anoint Jesus' feet with costly perfume and dry his feet with her long hair. One day Lazarus became very sick to the point of death. 3 So his sisters sent *a message* to Jesus, "Lord, our brother Lazarus, the one you love, is very sick. Please come!"

4 When he heard this, he said, "This sickness will not end in death for Lazarus, but will bring glory and praise to God. This will reveal the greatness of the Son of God by what takes place."

5–6 Now even though Jesus loved Mary, Martha, and Lazarus, he remained where he was for two more days. 7 Finally, on the third day, he said to his disciples, "Come. It's time to go to Bethany."

8 "But Teacher," they said to him, "do you really want to go back there? It was just a short time ago the people of Judea were going to stone you!"

9–10 Jesus replied, "Are there not twelve hours of daylight *in every day*? You can go through a day without the fear of stumbling when you walk in the One who gives light to the world. But you will stumble when the light is not in you, for you'll be walking in the dark."

11 Then Jesus added, "Lazarus, our friend, has just fallen asleep. It's time that I go and awaken him."

12 When they heard this, the disciples replied, "Lord, if he has just fallen asleep, then he'll get better." 13 Jesus was speaking about Lazarus' death, but the disciples presumed he was talking about natural sleep.

14 Then Jesus made it plain to them, "Lazarus is dead. 15 And for your sake, I'm glad I wasn't there, *because now you have another opportunity to see who I am* so that you will learn to trust in me. Come, let's go and see him."

16 So Thomas, nicknamed the Twin, remarked to the other disciples, "Let's go so that we can die with him."

17–18 Now when they arrived at Bethany, which was only about two miles from Jerusalem, Jesus found that Lazarus had already been in the tomb for four days. 19 Many friends of Mary and

My Notes...

Martha had come from the region to console them over the loss of their brother. 20 And when
Martha heard that Jesus was approaching the village, she went out to meet him, but Mary
stayed in the house.

21 Martha said to Jesus, "My Lord, if only you had come sooner, my brother wouldn't have
died. 22 But I know that if you were to ask God for anything, he would do it for you."

23 Jesus told her, "Your brother will rise and live."

24 She replied, "Yes, I know he will rise with everyone else on resurrection day."

25 "Martha," Jesus said, "*You don't have to wait until then*. I am the Resurrection, and I am Life
Eternal. Anyone who clings to me in faith, even though he dies, will live forever. 26 And the
one who lives by believing in me will never die. Do you believe this?"

27 Then Martha replied, "Yes, Lord, I do! I've always believed that you are the Anointed One,
the Son of God who has come into the world for us!" 28 Then she left and hurried off to her
sister, Mary, and called her aside from all the mourners and whispered to her, "The Master is
here and he's asking for you."

29 So when Mary heard this, she quickly went off to find him, 30 for Jesus was lingering outside
the village at the same spot where Martha met him. 31 Now when Mary's friends who were
comforting her noticed how quickly she ran out of the house, they followed her, assuming she
was going to the tomb of her brother to mourn.

32 When Mary finally found Jesus outside the village, she fell at his feet in tears and said, "Lord,
if only you had been here, my brother would not have died."

33 When Jesus looked at Mary and saw her weeping at his feet, and all her friends who were
with her grieving, he shuddered with emotion and was deeply moved with tenderness and
compassion. 34 He said to them, "Where did you bury him?"

"Lord, come with us and we'll show you," they replied.

35 Then tears streamed down Jesus' face.

36 Seeing Jesus weep caused many of the mourners to say, "Look how much he loved Lazarus."
37 Yet others said, "Isn't this the One who opens blind eyes? Why didn't he do something to
keep Lazarus from dying?"

38 Then Jesus, with intense emotions, came to the tomb—a cave with a stone placed over its
entrance. 39 Jesus told them, "Roll away the stone."

Then Martha said, "But Lord, it's been four days since he died—by now his body is already
decomposing!"

My Notes...

40 Jesus looked at her and said, "Didn't I tell you that if you will believe in me, you will see God unveil his power?"

41 So they rolled away the heavy stone. Jesus gazed into heaven and said, "Father, thank you that you have heard my prayer, 42 for you listen to every word I speak. Now, so that these who stand here with me will believe that you have sent me to the earth as your messenger, *I will use the power you have given me*." 43 Then with a loud voice Jesus shouted with authority: "Lazarus! Come out of the tomb!"

44 Then in front of everyone, Lazarus, who had died four days earlier, slowly hobbled out—he still had grave clothes tightly wrapped around his hands and feet and covering his face! Jesus said to them, "Unwrap him and let him loose."

45 From that day forward many of those who had come to visit Mary believed in him, for they had seen with their own eyes this amazing miracle! 46 But a few went back to inform the Pharisees about what Jesus had done.

47 So the Pharisees and the chief priests called a special meeting of the High Council and said, "So what are we going to do about this man? Look at all the great miracles he's performing! 48 If we allow him to continue like this, everyone will believe in him. And the Romans will take action and destroy both our country and our people!"

49 Now Caiaphas, the high priest that year, spoke up and said, "You don't understand a thing! 50 Don't you realize we'd be much better off if this one man were to die for the people than for the whole nation to perish?"

51 (This prophecy that Jesus was destined to die for the Jewish people didn't come from Caiaphas himself, *but he was moved by God* to prophesy as the chief priest. 52 And Jesus' death would not be for the Jewish people only, but to gather together God's children scattered around the world and unite them as one.) 53 So from that day on, they were committed to killing Jesus.

54 For this reason Jesus no longer went out in public among the Jews. But he went in the wilderness to a village called Ephraim, where he secluded himself with his disciples.

55 Now the time came for the Passover preparations, and many from the countryside went to Jerusalem for their ceremonial cleansing before the feast began. 56 And all the people kept looking out for Jesus, expecting him to come to the city. They said to themselves while they waited in the temple courts, "Do you think that he will dare come to the feast?" 57 For the leading priests and the Pharisees had given orders that they be informed immediately if anyone saw Jesus, so they could seize and arrest him.

My Notes...

John 12

The Passion Translation (TPT)

Mary Anoints Jesus

1 Six days before the Passover began, Jesus went back to Bethany, the town where he raised
Lazarus from the dead. 2 They had prepared a supper for Jesus. Martha served, and Lazarus
and Mary were among those at the table. 3 Mary picked up an alabaster jar filled with nearly a
liter of extremely rare and costly perfume—the purest extract of nard, and she anointed Jesus'
feet. Then she wiped them dry with her long hair. And the fragrance of the costly oil filled the
house. 4 But Judas the locksmith, Simon's son, the betrayer, spoke up and said, 5 "What a waste!
We could have sold this perfume for a fortune and given the money to the poor!"

6 (In fact, Judas had no heart for the poor. He only said this because he was a thief and in charge
of the money case. He would steal money whenever he wanted from the funds *given to support
Jesus' ministry*.)

7 Jesus said to Judas, "Leave her alone! She has saved it for the time of my burial. 8 You'll
always have the poor with you; but you won't always have me."

9 When the word got out that Jesus was not far from Jerusalem, a large crowd came out to see
him, and they also wanted to see Lazarus, the man Jesus had raised from the dead. 10 This
prompted the chief priests to seal their plans to do away with both Jesus and Lazarus, 11 for his
miracle testimony was incontrovertible and was persuading many of the Jews living in
Jerusalem to believe in Jesus.

12 The next day the news that Jesus was on his way to Jerusalem swept through the massive
crowd gathered for the feast. 13 So they took palm branches and went out to meet him. Everyone
was shouting, "Lord, be our Savior! Blessed is the one who comes to us sent from Jehovah-
God, the King of Israel!"

14 Then Jesus found a young donkey and rode on it to fulfill what was prophesied: 15 "People
of Zion, have no fear! Look—it's your king coming to you riding on a young donkey!"

16 Now Jesus' disciples didn't fully understand the importance of what was taking place, but
after he was raised and exalted into glory, they understood how Jesus fulfilled all the prophecies
in the Scriptures that were written about him.

My Notes...

17 All the eyewitnesses of the miracle Jesus performed when he called Lazarus out of the tomb
and raised him from the dead kept spreading the news about Jesus to everyone. 18 The news of
this miracle of resurrection caused the crowds to swell as great numbers of people *welcomed
him into the city with joy*. 19 But the Pharisees were disturbed by this and said to each other,
"We won't be able to stop this. The whole world is going to run after him!"

True Seekers

20 Now there were a number of foreigners from among the nations who were worshipers at the
feast. 21 They went to Philip (who came from the village of Bethsaida in Galilee) and they asked
him, "Would you take us to see Jesus? We want to see him." 22 So Philip went to find Andrew,
and then they both went to inform Jesus.

23 He replied to them, "Now is the time for the Son of Man to be glorified. 24 Let me make this
clear: A single grain of wheat will never be more than a single grain of wheat unless it drops
into the ground and dies. Because then it sprouts and produces a great harvest of wheat—all
because one grain died.

25 "The person who loves his life and pampers himself will miss true life! But the one who
detaches his life from this world and abandons himself to me, will find true life and enjoy it
forever! 26 If you want to be my disciple, follow me and you will go where I am going. And if
you truly follow me as my disciple, the Father will shower his favor upon your life.

27 "Even though I am torn within, and my soul is in turmoil, I will not ask the Father to rescue
me from this hour of trial. For I have come to fulfill my purpose—*to offer myself to God*. 28 So,
Father, bring glory to your name!" Then suddenly a booming voice was heard from the sky,

"I have glorified my name! And I will glorify it *through you* again!"

29 The audible voice of God startled the crowd standing nearby. Some thought it was only
thunder, yet others said, "An angel just spoke to him!"

30 Then Jesus told them, "The voice you heard was not for my benefit, but for yours—*to help
you believe*. 31 From this moment on, everything in this world is about to change, for the ruler
of this dark world will be overthrown. 32 *And I will do this* when I am lifted up off the ground
and when I draw the hearts of people to gather them to me." 33 He said this to indicate that he
would die by being lifted up on the cross.

34 People from the crowd spoke up and said, "Die? How could the Anointed One die? The Word
of God says that the Anointed One will live with us forever, but you just said that the Son of
Man must be lifted up from the earth. And who is this Son of Man anyway?"

My Notes...

[35] Jesus replied, "You will have the light shining with you for only a little while longer. While you still have me, walk in the light, so that the darkness doesn't overtake you. For when you walk in the dark you have no idea where you're going. [36] So believe and cling to the light while I am with you, so that you will become children of light." After saying this, Jesus then entered into the crowd and hid himself from them.

The Unbelief of the Crowd

[37] Even with the overwhelming evidence of all the many signs and wonders that Jesus had performed in front of them, his critics still refused to believe. [38] This fulfilled the prophecy given by Isaiah:

Lord, who has believed our message? Who has seen the unveiling of your great power?

[39] And the people were not able to believe, for Isaiah also prophesied:

[40] God has blinded their eyes and hardened their hearts to the truth. So with their eyes and hearts closed they cannot understand the truth nor turn to me so that I could instantly cleanse and heal them.

[41] Isaiah said these things because he had seen and experienced the splendor of Jesus and prophesied about him. [42] Yet there were many Jewish leaders who believed in Jesus, but because they feared the Pharisees they kept it secret, so they wouldn't be ostracized by the assembly of the Jews. [43] For they loved the glory that men could give them rather than the glory that came from God!

Jesus' Last Public Teaching

[44] Jesus shouted out passionately, "To believe in me is to also believe in God who sent me. [45] For when you look at me you are seeing the One who sent me. [46] I have come as a light to shine in this dark world so that all who trust in me will no longer wander in darkness. [47] If you hear my words and refuse to follow them, I do not judge you. For I have not come to judge you but to save you. [48] If you reject me and refuse to follow my words, you already have a judge. The message of truth I have given you will rise up to judge you at the Day of Judgment. [49] For I'm not speaking as someone who is self-appointed, but I speak by the authority of the Father himself who sent me, and who instructed me what to say. [50] And I know that the Father's commands result in eternal life, and that's why I speak the very words I've heard him speak."

My Notes...

John 13

The Passion Translation (TPT)

Jesus Washes Feet

[1] Jesus knew that the night before Passover would be his last night on earth before leaving this world to return to the Father's side. All throughout his time with his disciples, Jesus had demonstrated a deep and tender love for them. And now he longed to show them the full measure of his love. [2] Before their evening meal had begun, the accuser had already planted betrayal into the heart of Judas Iscariot, the son of Simon.

[3] Now Jesus was fully aware that the Father had placed all things under his control, for he had come from God and was about to go back to be with him. [4] So he got up from the meal and took off his outer robe, and took a towel and wrapped it around his waist. [5] Then he poured water into a basin and began to wash the disciples' dirty feet and dry them with his towel.

[6] But when Jesus got to Simon Peter, he objected and said, "I can't let you wash my dirty feet—you're my Lord!"

[7] Jesus replied, "You don't understand yet the meaning of what I'm doing, but soon it will be clear to you."

[8] Peter looked at Jesus and said, "You'll never wash my dirty feet—never!"

"But Peter, if you don't allow me to wash your feet," Jesus responded, "then you will not be able to share life with me."

[9] So Peter said, "Lord, in that case, don't just wash my feet, wash my hands and my head too!"

[10] Jesus said to him, "You are already clean. You've been washed completely and you just need your feet to be cleansed—but that can't be said of all of you." For Jesus knew which one was about to betray him, [11] and that's why he told them that not all of them were clean.

[12] After washing their feet, he put his robe on and returned to his place at the table. "Do you understand what I just did?" Jesus said. [13] "You've called me your teacher and lord, and you're right, for that's who I am. [14–15] So if I'm your teacher and lord and have just washed your dirty feet, then you should follow the example that I've set for you and wash one another's dirty feet. Now do for each other what I have just done for you. [16] I speak to you timeless truth: a servant is not superior to his master, and an apostle is never greater than the one who sent

My Notes...

him. [17] So now put into practice what I have done for you, and you will experience a life of happiness enriched with untold blessings!"

Jesus Predicts His Betrayal

[18] "I don't refer to all of you when I tell you these things, for I know the ones I've chosen—to fulfill the Scripture that says, 'The one who shared supper with me treacherously betrays me.' [19] I am telling you this now, before it happens, so that when the prophecy comes to pass you will be convinced that I AM. [20] "Listen to this timeless truth: whoever receives the messenger I send receives me, and the one who receives me receives the Father who sent me."

[21] Then Jesus was moved deeply in his spirit. Looking at his disciples, he announced, "I tell you the truth—one of you is about to betray me."

[22] Eyeing each other, his disciples puzzled over which one of them could do such a thing. [23] The disciple that Jesus dearly loved was at the right of him at the table and was leaning his head on Jesus. [24] Peter gestured to this disciple to ask Jesus who it was he was referring to. [25] Then the dearly loved disciple leaned into Jesus' chest and whispered, "Master, who is it?"

[26] "The one I give this piece of bread to after I've dipped it in the bowl," Jesus replied. Then he dipped the piece of bread into the bowl and handed it to Judas Iscariot, the son of Simon. [27] And when Judas ate the piece of bread, Satan entered him. Then Jesus looked at Judas and said, "What you are planning to do, go do it now." [28] None of those around the table realized what was happening. [29] Some thought that Judas, their trusted treasurer, was being told to go buy what was needed for the Passover celebration, or perhaps to go give something to the poor. [30] So Judas left quickly and went out into the dark night to betray Jesus.

Jesus Predicts Peter's Denial

[31] After Judas left the room, Jesus said, "The time has come for the glory of God to surround the Son of Man, and God will be greatly glorified through what happens to me. [32] And very soon God will unveil the glory of the Son of Man.

[33] "My dear friends, I only have a brief time left to be with you. And then you will search and long for me. But I tell you what I told the Jewish leaders: you'll not be able to come where I am.

[34] "So I give you now a new commandment: Love each other just as much as I have loved you. [35] For when you demonstrate the same love I have for you by loving one another, everyone will know that you're my true followers."

My Notes...

[36] Peter interjected, "But, Master, where are you going?"

Jesus replied, "Where I am going you won't be able to follow, but one day you will follow me there."

[37] Peter said, "What do you mean I'm not able to follow you now? I would sacrifice my life to die for you!"

[38] Jesus answered, "Would you really lay down your life for me, Peter? Here's the absolute truth: Before the rooster crows in the morning, you will say three times that you don't even know me!"

John 14

The Passion Translation (TPT)

Jesus Comforts His Disciples

14 "Don't worry or surrender to your fear. For you've believed in God, now trust and believe
in me also. [2] My Father's house has many dwelling places. If it were otherwise, I would tell
you plainly, because I go to prepare a place for you to rest. [3] And when everything is ready, I
will come back and take you to myself so that you will be where I am.[4] And you already know
the way to the place where I'm going."

[5] Thomas said to him, "Master, we don't know where you're going, so how could we know the way there?"

[6] Jesus explained, "I am the Way, I am the Truth, and I am the Life. No one comes next to the
Father except through *union with me*. To know me is to know my Father too. [7] And from now
on you will realize that you have seen him and experienced him."

[8] Philip spoke up, "Lord, show us the Father, and that will be all that we need!"

[9] Jesus replied, "Philip, I've been with you all this time and you still don't know who I am?
How could you ask me to show you the Father, for anyone who has looked at me has seen the
Father. [10] Don't you believe that the Father is living in me and that I am living in the Father?
Even my words are not my own but come from my Father, for he lives in me and performs his
miracles of power through me. [11] Believe that I live as one with my Father and that my Father
lives as one with me—or at least, believe because of the mighty miracles I have done.

[12] "I tell you this timeless truth: The person who follows me in faith, believing in me, will do the same mighty miracles that I do—even greater miracles than these because I go to be with my Father!

My Notes...

13 For I will do whatever you ask me to do when you ask me in my name. And that is how the Son will show what the Father is really like and bring glory to him. 14 Ask me anything in my name, and I will do it for you!"

Jesus Prophesies about the Holy Spirit

15 "Loving me empowers you to obey my commands. 16–17 And I will ask the Father and he will give you another Savior, the Holy Spirit of Truth, who will be to you a friend just like me—and he will never leave you. The world won't receive him because they can't see him or know him. But you will know him intimately, because he will make his home in you and will live inside you.

18 "I promise that I will never leave you helpless or abandon you as orphans—I will come back to you! 19 Soon I will leave this world and they will see me no longer, but you will see me, because I will live again, and you will come alive too. 20 So when that day comes, you will know that I am living in the Father and that you are one with me, for I will be living in you. 21 Those who truly love me are those who obey my commands. Whoever passionately loves me will be passionately loved by my Father. And I will passionately love you in return and will manifest my life within you."

22 Then one of the disciples named Judas (not Judas Iscariot) said, "Lord, why is it you will only reveal your identity to us and not to everyone?"

23 Jesus replied, "Loving me empowers you to obey my word. And my Father will love you so deeply that we will come to you and make you our dwelling place. 24 But those who don't love me will not obey my words. The Father did not send me to speak my own revelation, but the words of my Father. 25 I am telling you this while I am still with you. 26 But when the Father sends the Spirit of Holiness, the One like me who sets you free, he will teach you all things in my name. And he will inspire you to remember every word that I've told you.

27 "I leave the gift of peace with you—my peace. Not the kind of fragile peace given by the world, but my perfect peace. Don't yield to fear or be troubled in your hearts—instead, be courageous! 28 "Remember what I've told you, that I must go away, but I promise to come back to you. So if you truly love me, you will be glad for me, since I'm returning to my Father, who is greater than I. 29 So when all of these things happen, you will still trust and cling to me. 30 I won't speak with you much longer, for the ruler of this dark world is coming. But he has no power over me, *for he has nothing to use against me*. 31 I am doing exactly what the Father destined for me to accomplish, so that the world will discover how much I love my Father. Now come with me."

My Notes...

John 15

The Passion Translation (TPT)

Jesus the Living Vine

1 “I am a true sprouting vine, and the farmer who tends the vine is my Father. 2 He cares for the branches connected to me by lifting and propping up the fruitless branches and pruning every fruitful branch to yield a greater harvest. 3 The words I have spoken over you have already cleansed you. 4 So you must remain in life-union with me, for I remain in life-union with you. For as a branch severed from the vine will not bear fruit, so your life will be fruitless unless you live your life intimately joined to mine.

5 “I am the sprouting vine and you’re my branches. As you live in union with me as your source, fruitfulness will stream from within you—but when you live separated from me you are powerless. 6 If a person is separated from me, he is discarded; such branches are gathered up and thrown into the fire to be burned. 7 But if you live in life-union with me and if my words live powerfully within you—then you can ask whatever you desire and it will be done. 8 When your lives bear abundant fruit, you demonstrate that you are my mature disciples who glorify my Father!

9 “I love each of you with the same love that the Father loves me. You must continually let my love nourish your hearts. 10 If you keep my commands, you will live in my love, just as I have kept my Father’s commands, for I continually live nourished and empowered by his love. 11 My purpose for telling you these things is so that the joy that I experience will fill your hearts with overflowing gladness!

12 “So this is my command: Love each other deeply, as much as I have loved you. 13 For the greatest love of all is a love that sacrifices all. And this great love is demonstrated when a person sacrifices his life for his friends.

14 “You show that you are my intimate friends when you obey all that I command you. 15 I have never called you ‘servants,’ because a master doesn’t confide in his servants, and servants don’t always understand what the master is doing. But I call you my most intimate friends, for I reveal to you everything that I’ve heard from my Father. 16 You didn’t choose me, but I’ve chosen and commissioned you to go into the world to bear fruit. And your fruit will last, because whatever you ask of my Father, for my sake, he will give it to you! 17 So this is my parting command: Love one another deeply!”

My Notes...

True Disciples Can Expect Persecution

18 "Just remember, when the unbelieving world hates you, they first hated me. 19 If you were to give your allegiance to the world, they would love and welcome you as one of their own. But because you won't align yourself with the values of this world, they will hate you. I have chosen you and taken you out of the world to be mine. 20 So remember what I taught you, that a servant isn't superior to his master. And since they persecuted me, they will also persecute you. And if they obey my teachings, they will also obey yours. 21 They will treat you this way because you are mine, and they don't know the One who sent me.

22 "If I had not come and revealed myself to the unbelieving world, they would not feel the guilt of their sin, but now their sin is left uncovered. 3 If anyone hates me, they hate my Father also. 24 If I had not performed miracles in their presence like no one else has done, they would not feel the guilt of their sins. But now, they have seen and hated both me and my Father. 25 And all of this has happened to fulfill what is written in their Scriptures: They hated me for no reason.

26 "And I will send you the Divine Encourager from the very presence of my Father. He will come to you, the Spirit of Truth, emanating from the Father, and he will speak to you about me. 27 And you will tell everyone the truth about me, for you have walked with me from the start."

John 16

The Passion Translation (TPT)

Jesus Warns His Disciples

1 "I have told you this so that you would not surrender to confusion or doubt. 2 For you will be excommunicated from the synagogues, and a time is coming when you will be put to death by misguided ones who will presume to be doing God a great service by putting you to death. 3 And they will do these things because they don't know anything about the Father or me. 4 I'm telling you this now so that when their time comes you will remember that I foretold it. I didn't tell you this in the beginning because I was still with you. 5 But now that I'm about to leave you and go back to join the One who sent me, you need to be told. Yet, not one of you are asking me where I'm going. 6 Instead your hearts are filled with sadness because I've told you these things. 7 But here's the truth: It's to your advantage that I go away, for if I don't go away the Divine Encourager will not be released to you. But after I depart, I will send him to you.

My Notes...

8 And when he comes, he will expose sin and prove that the world is wrong about God's
righteousness and his judgments.

9 "'Sin,' because they refuse to believe in who I am.

10 "God's 'righteousness,' because I'm going back to join the Father and you'll see me no
longer.

11 "And 'judgment' because the ruler of this dark world has already received his sentence.

12 "There is so much more I would like to say to you, but it's more than you can grasp at this
moment. 13 But when the truth-giving Spirit comes, he will unveil the reality of every truth
within you. He won't speak his own message, but only what he hears from the Father, and he
will reveal prophetically to you what is to come. 14 He will glorify me on the earth, for he will
receive from me what is mine and reveal it to you. 15 Everything that belongs to the Father
belongs to me—that's why I say that the Divine Encourager will receive what is mine and
reveal it to you. 16 Soon you won't see me any longer, but then, after a little while, you will see
me *in a new way*."

17 Some of the disciples asked each other, "What does he mean, 'Soon you won't see me,' and,
'A little while after that and you will see me in a new way'? And what does he mean, 'Because
I'm going to my Father'?" 18 So they kept on repeating, "What's the meaning of 'a little while'?
We have no clue what he's talking about!"

19 Jesus knew what they were thinking, and it was obvious that they were anxious to ask him
what he had meant, so he spoke up and said, 20 "Let me make it quite clear: You will weep and
be overcome with grief *over what happens to me*. The unbelieving world will be happy, while
you will be filled with sorrow. But know this, your sadness will turn into joy *when you see me
again*! 21 Just like a woman giving birth experiences intense labor pains in delivering her baby,
yet after the child is born she quickly forgets what she went through because of the
overwhelming joy of knowing that a new baby has been born into the world.

22 "So will you also pass through a time of intense sorrow *when I am taken from you*, but you
will see me again! And then your hearts will burst with joy, with no one being able to take it
from you! 23 For here is eternal truth: When that time comes you won't need to ask me for
anything, but instead you will go directly to the Father and ask him for anything you desire
and he will give it to you, because of your relationship with me. 24 Until now you've not been
bold enough to ask the Father for a single thing in my name, but now you can ask, and keep on
asking him! And you can be sure that you'll receive what you ask for, and your joy will have
no limits!

My Notes...

[25] "I have spoken to you using figurative language, but the time is coming when I will no longer
teach you with veiled speech, but I will teach you about the Father with your eyes unveiled.
[26] And I will not need to ask the Father on your behalf, for you'll ask him directly because of
your new relationship with me. [27] For the Father tenderly loves you, because you love me and
believe that I've come from God. [28] I came to you sent from the Father's presence, and I entered
into the created world, and now I will leave this world and return to the Father's side."

[29] His disciples said, "At last you're speaking to us clearly and not using veiled speech and
metaphors! [30] Now we understand that you know everything there is to know, and we don't
need to question you further. And everything you've taught us convinces us that you have
come directly from God!"

[31] Jesus replied, "Now you finally believe in me. [32] And the time has come when you will all
be scattered, and each one of you will go your own way, leaving me alone! Yet I am never
alone, for the Father is always with me. [33] And everything I've taught you is so that the peace
which is in me will be in you and will give you great confidence as you rest in me. For in this
unbelieving world you will experience trouble and sorrows, but you must be courageous, for I
have conquered the world!"

John 17

The Passion Translation (TPT)

Jesus Finished the Father's Work

[1] This is what Jesus prayed as he looked up into heaven, "Father, the time has come. Unveil the glorious splendor of your Son so that I will magnify your glory!

[2] You have already given me authority over all people so that I may give the gift of eternal life to all those that you have given to me.

[3] Eternal life means to know and experience you as the only true God, and to know and experience Jesus Christ, as the Son whom you have sent.

[4] I have glorified you on the earth by faithfully doing everything you've told me to do.

[5] So my Father, restore me back to the glory that we shared together when we were face-to-face before the universe was created."

My Notes...

Jesus Prays for His Disciples

6 "Father, I have manifested who you really are and I have revealed you to the men and women that you gave to me. They were yours, and you gave them to me, and they have fastened your Word firmly to their hearts.

7 And now at last they know that everything I have is a gift from you,

8 And the very words you gave to me to speak I have passed on to them. They have received your words and *carry them in their hearts*. They are convinced that I have come from your presence, and they have fully believed that you sent me to represent you.

9 So with deep love, I pray for my disciples. I'm not asking on behalf of the unbelieving world, but for those who belong to you, those you have given me.

10 For all who belong to me now belong to you. And all who belong to you now belong to me as well, and my glory is revealed through *their surrendered lives*.

11 "Holy Father, I am about to leave this world to return and be with you, but my disciples will remain here. So I ask that by the power of your name, protect each one that you have given me, and watch over them so that they will be united as one, even as we are one.

12 While I was with these that you have given me, I have kept them safe by your name that you have given me. Not one of them is lost, except the one that was destined to be lost, so that the Scripture would be fulfilled.

13 "But now I am returning to you so Father, I pray that they will experience and enter into my joyous delight in you so that it is fulfilled in them and overflows.

14 I have given them your message and that is why the unbelieving world hates them. For their allegiance is no longer to this world because I am not of this world.

15 I am not asking that you remove them from the world, but I ask that you guard their hearts from evil,

16 For they no longer belong to this world any more than I do.

17 "Your Word is truth! So make them holy by the truth.

18 I have commissioned them to represent me just as you commissioned me to represent you.

19 And now I dedicate myself to them as a holy sacrifice so that they will live as fully dedicated to God and be made holy by your truth."

My Notes...

Jesus Prays for You

[20] "And I ask not only for these disciples, but also for all those who will one day believe in me through their message.

[21] I pray for them all to be joined together as one even as you and I, Father, are joined together as one. I pray for them to become one with us so that the world will recognize that you sent me.

[22] For the very glory you have given to me I have given them so that they will be joined together as one and experience the same unity that we enjoy.

[23] You live fully in me and now I live fully in them so that they will experience perfect unity, and the world will be convinced that you have sent me, for they will see that you love each one of them with the same passionate love that you have for me.

[24] "Father, I ask that you allow everyone that you have given to me to be with me where I am! Then they will see my full glory—the very splendor you have placed upon me because you have loved me even before the beginning of time.

[25] "You are my righteous Father, but the unbelieving world has never known you in the perfect way that I know you! *And all those who believe in me* also know that you have sent me!

[26] I have revealed to them who you are and I will continue to make you even more real to them, so that they may experience the same endless love that you have for me, for your love will now live in them, even as I live in them!"

John 18

The Passion Translation (TPT)

Jesus in the Garden of Gethsemane

[1] After Jesus finished this prayer; he left with his disciples and went across the Kidron Valley
to a place where there was a garden. [2] Judas, the traitor, knew where this place was, for Jesus
had gone there often with his disciples. [3] The Pharisees and the leading priests had given Judas
a large detachment of Roman soldiers and temple police to seize Jesus. Judas guided them to
the garden, all of them carrying torches and lanterns and armed *with swords and spears*. [4] Jesus,
knowing full well what was about to happen, went out to the garden entrance to meet them.

My Notes...

Stepping forward, he asked, “Who are you looking for?”

5 “Jesus of Nazareth,” they replied. (Now Judas, the traitor, was among them.)

He replied, “I am he.”

6 And the moment Jesus spoke the words, “I am he,” the mob fell backward to the ground!

7 So once more, Jesus asked them, “Who are you looking for?”

As they stood up, they answered, “Jesus of Nazareth.”

8 Jesus replied, “I told you that I am the one you’re looking for, so if you want me, let these men go home.”

9 He said this to fulfill the prophecy he had spoken, “Father, not one of those you have given me has been lost.”

10 Suddenly, Peter took out his sword and struck the high priest’s servant, slashing off his right ear! The servant’s name was Malchus.

11 Jesus ordered Peter, “Put your sword away! Do you really think I will avoid the suffering which my Father has assigned to me?”

Jesus Is Taken before Annas

12 Then the soldiers and their captain, along with the Jewish officers, seized Jesus and tied him
up. 13 They took him first to Annas, as he was the father-in-law of Caiaphas, the high priest
that year. 14 Caiaphas was the one who had persuaded the Jewish leaders that it would be better
off to have one person die for the sake of the people.

Peter’s First Denial

15 Peter and another disciple followed along behind them as they took Jesus into the courtyard
of Annas’ palace. Since the other disciple was well known to the high priest, he entered in,
16 but Peter was left standing outside by the gate. Then the other disciple came back out to the
servant girl who was guarding the gate and convinced her to allow Peter inside. 17 As he passed
inside, the young servant girl guarding the gate took a look at Peter and said to him, “Aren’t
you one of his disciples?”

He denied it, saying, “No! I’m not!”

18 Now because it was cold, the soldiers and guards made a charcoal fire and were standing around it to keep warm. So Peter huddled there with them around the fire.

My Notes...

Jesus Interrogated by Annas

19 The high priest interrogated Jesus concerning his disciples and his teachings.

20 Jesus answered Annas' questions by saying, "I have said nothing in secret. At all times I have
taught openly and publicly in a synagogue, in the temple courts, and wherever the people
assemble. 21 Why would you ask me for evidence to condemn me? Ask those who have heard
what I've taught. They can tell you."

22 Just then one of the guards standing near Jesus punched him in the face with his fist and said,
"How dare you answer the high priest like that!"

23 Jesus replied, "If my words are evil, then prove it. But if I haven't broken any laws, then
why would you hit me?"

24 Then Annas sent Jesus, still tied up, across the way to the high priest Caiaphas.

Peter's Second and Third Denials

25 Meanwhile, Peter was still standing in the courtyard by the fire. And one of the guards
standing there said to him, "Aren't you one of his disciples? I know you are!" Peter swore and
said, "I am not his disciple!" 26 But one of the servants of the high priest, a relative to the man
whose ear Peter had cut off, looked at him and said, "Wait! Didn't I see you out there in the
garden with Jesus?" 27 Then Peter denied it the third time and said, "No!"—and at that very
same moment, a rooster crowed nearby.

Pilate Questions Jesus' Arrest

28 Before dawn they took Jesus from his trial before Caiaphas to the Roman governor's palace.
Now the Jews refused to go into the Roman governor's residence to avoid ceremonial
defilement before eating the Passover meal. 29 So Pilate came outside where they waited and
asked them pointedly, "Tell me, what exactly is the accusation that you bring against this man?
What has he done?"

30 They answered, "We wouldn't be coming here to hand over this 'criminal' to you if he wasn't
guilty of some wrongdoing!"

31 Pilate said, "Very well, then you take him yourselves and go pass judgment on him according
to your Jewish laws!"

My Notes...

But the Jewish leaders complained and said, "We don't have legal authority to put anyone to
death. *You should have him crucified*!" 32 (This was to fulfill the words of Jesus when he
predicted the manner of death that he would die.)

Pilate Interrogates Jesus

33 Upon hearing this, Pilate went back inside his palace and summoned Jesus. Looking him
over, Pilate asked him, "Are you really the king of the Jews?"

34 Jesus replied, "Are you asking because you really want to know, or are you only asking this
because others have said it about me?"

35 Pilate responded, "Only a Jew would care about this; do I look like a Jew? It's your own
people and your religious leaders that have handed you over to me. So tell me, Jesus, what
have you done wrong?"

36 Jesus looked at Pilate and said, "The royal power of my kingdom realm doesn't come from
this world. If it did, then my followers would be fighting to the end to defend me from the
Jewish leaders. My kingdom realm authority is not from this realm."

37 Then Pilate responded, "Oh, so then you are a king?"

"You are right." Jesus said, "I was born a King, and I have come into this world to prove what
truth really is. And everyone who loves the truth will receive my words."

38 Pilate looked at Jesus and said, "What is truth?"

As silence filled the room, Pilate went back out to where the Jewish leaders were waiting and
said to them, "He's not guilty. I couldn't even find one fault with him. 39 Now, you do know
that we have a custom that I release one prisoner every year at Passover—shall I release your
king—the king of the Jews?"

40 They shouted out over and over, "No, not him! Give us Barabbas!" (Now Barabbas was a
robber and a troublemaker.)

My Notes...

John 19

The Passion Translation (TPT)

Jesus Is Flogged

[1] Then Pilate ordered Jesus to be brutally beaten with a whip of leather straps embedded with metal. [2] And the soldiers also wove thorn-branches into a crown and set it on his head and placed a purple robe over his shoulders. [3] Then, one by one, they came in front of him to mock him by saying, "Hail, to the king of the Jews!" And one after the other, they repeatedly punched him in the face.

[4] Once more Pilate went out and said to the Jewish officials, "I will bring him out once more so that you know that I've found nothing wrong with him." [5] So when Jesus emerged, *bleeding*, wearing the purple robe and the crown of thorns on his head, Pilate said to them, "Look at him! Here is your man!"

[6] No sooner did the high priests and the temple guards see Jesus that they all shouted in a frenzy, "Crucify him! Crucify him!"

Pilate replied, "You take him then and nail him to a cross yourselves! I told you—he's not guilty! I find no reason to condemn him."

[7] The Jewish leaders shouted back, "But we have the Law! And according to our Law, he must die, because he claimed to be the Son of God!"

[8] Then Pilate was greatly alarmed when he heard that Jesus claimed to be the Son of God! [9] So he took Jesus back inside and said to him, "Where have you come from?" But once again, silence filled the room. [10] Perplexed, Pilate said, "Are you going to play deaf? Don't you know that I have the power to grant you your freedom or nail you to a tree?"

[11] Jesus answered, "You would have no power over me at all, unless it was given to you from above. This is why the one who betrayed me is guilty of an even greater sin."

[12] From then on Pilate tried to find a way out of the situation and to set him free, but the Jewish authorities shouted him down: "If you let this man go, you're no friend of Caesar! Anyone who declares himself a king is an enemy of the emperor!"

[13] So when Pilate heard this threat, he relented and had Jesus, *who was torn and bleeding*, brought outside. Then he went up the elevated stone platform and took his seat on the judgment bench—which in Aramaic is called Gabbatha, or "The Bench." [14] And it was now almost noon.

My Notes...

And it was the same day they were preparing to slay the Passover lambs.

Then Pilate said to the Jewish officials, "Look! Here is your king!"

15 But they screamed out, "Take him away! Take him away and crucify him!"

Pilate replied, "Shall I nail your king to a cross?"

The high priests answered, "We have no other king but Caesar!"

16 Then Pilate handed Jesus over to them. So the soldiers seized him and took him away to be crucified.

Jesus Is Crucified

17 Jesus carried his own cross out of the city to the place called "The Skull," which in Aramaic
is Golgotha. 18 And there they nailed him to the cross. He was crucified, along with two others,
one on each side with Jesus in the middle. 19–20 Pilate had them post a sign over the cross, which
was written in three languages—Aramaic, Latin, and Greek. Many of the people of Jerusalem
read the sign, for he was crucified near the city. The sign stated: "Jesus of Nazareth, the King
of the Jews."

21 But the chief priests of the Jews said to Pilate, "You must change the sign! Don't let it say,
'King of the Jews,' but rather—'he claimed to be the King of the Jews!'" 22 Pilate responded,
"What I have written will remain!"

23 Now when the soldiers crucified Jesus, they divided up his clothes into four shares, one for
each of them. But his tunic was seamless, woven from the top to the bottom as a single
garment. 24 So the soldiers said to each other, "Don't tear it—let's throw dice to see who gets
it!" The soldiers did all of this not knowing they fulfilled the Scripture that says, "They divided
my garments among them and gambled for my garment."

25 Mary, Jesus' mother, was standing next to his cross, along with Mary's sister, Mary the wife
of Clopas, and Mary Magdalene. 26 So when Jesus looked down and saw the disciple he loved
standing with her, he said, "Mother, look—John will be a son to you." 27 Then he said, "*John*,
look—she will be a mother to you!" From that day on, John accepted Mary into his home *as
one of his own family*.

My Notes...

Jesus' Death on the Cross

28 Jesus knew that his mission was accomplished, and to fulfill the Scripture, Jesus said: "I am
thirsty."

29 A jar of sour wine was sitting nearby, so they soaked a sponge with it and put it on the stalk
of hyssop and raised it to his lips. 30 When he had sipped the sour wine, he said, "It is finished,
my bride!" Then he bowed his head and surrendered his spirit to God.

31 The Jewish leaders did not want the bodies of the victims to remain on the cross through the
next day, since it was the day of preparation for a very important Sabbath. So they asked Pilate's
permission to have the victims' legs broken *to hasten their death* and their bodies taken down
before sunset. 32 So the soldiers broke the legs of the two men who were nailed there. 33 But
when they came to Jesus, they realized that he had already died, so they decided not to break
his legs. 34 But one of the soldiers took a spear and pierced Jesus' side, and blood and water
gushed out.

35 (I, John, do testify to the certainty of what took place, and I write the truth so that you might
also believe.) 36 For all these things happened to fulfill the prophecies of the Scriptures:

"Not one of his bones will be broken," 37 and, "They will gaze on the one they have pierced!"

Jesus' Burial

38 After this, Joseph from the city of Ramah, who was a secret disciple of Jesus for fear of the
Jewish authorities, asked Pilate if he could remove the body of Jesus. So Pilate granted him
permission to remove the body from the cross. 39 Now Nicodemus, who had once come to Jesus
privately at night, accompanied Joseph, and together they carried a significant amount of myrrh
and aloes to the cross. 40 Then they took Jesus' body and wrapped it in strips of linen with the
embalming spices according to the Jewish burial customs. 41 Near the place where Jesus was
crucified was a garden, and in the garden there was a new tomb where no one had yet been
laid to rest. 42 And because the Sabbath was approaching, and the tomb was nearby, that's where
they laid the body of Jesus.

My Notes...

John 20

The Passion Translation (TPT)

The Empty Tomb

1 Very early Sunday morning, before sunrise, Mary Magdalene made her way to the tomb. And
when she arrived she discovered that the stone that sealed the entrance to the tomb was moved
away! 2 So she went running as fast as she could to go tell Peter and the other disciple, the one
Jesus loved. She told them, "They've taken the Lord's body from the tomb, and we don't know
where he is!"

3 Then Peter and the other disciple jumped up and ran to the tomb to go see for
themselves. 4 They started out together, but the other disciple outran Peter and reached the
tomb first. 5 He didn't enter the tomb, but peeked in, and saw only the linen cloths lying
there. 6 Then Peter came behind him and went right into the tomb. He too noticed the linen
cloths lying there, 7 but the burial cloth that had been on Jesus' head had been rolled up and
placed separate from the other cloths.

8 Then the other disciple who had reached the tomb first went in, and after one look, he
believed! 9 For until then they hadn't understood the Scriptures that prophesied that he was
destined to rise from the dead. 10 Puzzled, Peter and the other disciple then left and went back
to their homes.

11 Mary arrived *back at the tomb*, broken and sobbing. She stooped to peer inside, and through
her tears 12 she saw two angels in dazzling white robes, sitting where Jesus' body had been
laid—one at the head and one at the feet!

13 "Dear woman, why are you crying?" they asked.

Mary answered, "They have taken away my Lord, and I don't know where they've laid him."

14 Then she turned around to leave, and there was Jesus standing in front of her, but she didn't
realize that it was him!

15 He said to her, "Dear woman, why are you crying? Who are you looking for?"

Mary answered, thinking he was only the gardener, "Sir, if you have taken his body somewhere
else, tell me, and I will go and . . ."

16 "Mary," Jesus interrupted her.

Turning to face him, she said, "Rabboni!" (Aramaic for "my teacher")

My Notes...

17 Jesus cautioned her, "Mary, don't hold on to me now, for I haven't yet ascended to God, my
Father. And he's not only my Father and God, but now he's your Father and your God! Now
go to my brothers and tell them what I've told you, that I am ascending to my Father—and
your Father, to my God—and your God!"

18 Then Mary Magdalene left to inform the disciples of her encounter with Jesus. "I have seen
the Lord!" she told them. And she gave them his message.

Jesus Appears to His Disciples

19 That evening, the disciples gathered together. And because they were afraid of reprisals from
the Jewish leaders, they had locked the doors to the place where they met. But suddenly Jesus
appeared among them and said, "Peace to you!" 20 Then he showed them the wounds of his
hands and his side—they were overjoyed to see the Lord with their own eyes!

21 Jesus repeated his greeting, "Peace to you!" And he told them, "Just as the Father has sent
me, I'm now sending you." 22 Then, taking a deep breath, he blew on them and said, "Receive
the Holy Spirit. 23 I send you to preach the forgiveness of sins—and people's sins will be
forgiven. But if you don't proclaim the forgiveness of their sins, they will remain guilty."

Jesus Appears to Thomas

24 One of the twelve wasn't present when Jesus appeared to them—it was Thomas, whose
nickname was "the Twin." 25 So the disciples informed him, "We have seen the Lord with our
own eyes!"

Still unconvinced, Thomas replied, "There's no way I'm going to believe this unless I personally see the wounds of the nails in his hands, touch them with my finger, and put my hand into the wound of his side where he was pierced!"

26 Then eight days later, Thomas and all the others were in the house together. And even though
all the doors were locked, Jesus suddenly stood before them! "Peace to you," he said.

27 Then, looking into Thomas' eyes, he said, "Put your finger here in the wounds of my hands.
Here—put your hand into my wounded side and see for yourself. Thomas, don't give in to
your doubts any longer, just believe!"

28 Then the words spilled out of his heart—"You are my Lord, and you are my God!"

My Notes...

29 Jesus responded, "Thomas, now that you've seen me, you believe. But there are those who have never seen me with their eyes but have believed in me with their hearts, and they will be blessed even more!"

30 Jesus went on to do many more miraculous signs in the presence of his disciples, which are not even included in this book. 31 But all that is recorded here is so that you will fully believe that Jesus is the Anointed One, the Son of God, and that through your faith in him you will experience eternal life by the power of his name!

John 21

The Passion Translation (TPT)

Jesus Appears at Lake Galilee

1 Later, Jesus appeared once again to a group of his disciples by Lake Galilee. 2 It happened one day while Peter, Thomas (the Twin), Nathanael (from Cana in Galilee), Jacob, John, and two other disciples were all together. 3 Peter told them, "I'm going fishing." And they all replied, "We'll go with you." So they went out and fished through the night, but caught nothing.

4 Then at dawn, Jesus was standing there on the shore, but the disciples didn't realize that it was him! 5 He called out to them, saying, "Hey guys! Did you catch any fish?"

"Not a thing," they replied.

6 Jesus shouted to them, "Throw your net over the starboard side, and you'll catch some!" And so they did as he said, and they caught so many fish they couldn't even pull in the net!

7 Then the disciple whom Jesus loved said to Peter, "It's the Lord!" When Peter heard him say that, he quickly wrapped his outer garment around him, and because he was athletic, he dove right into the lake to go to Jesus! 8 The other disciples then brought the boat to shore, dragging their catch of fish. They weren't far from land, only about a hundred meters. 9 And when they got to shore, they noticed a charcoal fire with some roasted fish and bread. 10 Then Jesus said, "Bring some of the fish you just caught."

11 So Peter waded into the water and helped pull the net to shore. It was full of many large fish, exactly one hundred and fifty-three, but even with so many fish, the net was not torn.

My Notes...

12 "Come, let's have some breakfast," Jesus said to them.

And not one of the disciples needed to ask who it was, because every one of them knew it was
the Lord. 13 Then Jesus came close to them and served them the bread and the fish. 14 This was
the third time Jesus appeared to his disciples after his resurrection.

Jesus Restores Peter

15 After they had breakfast, Jesus said to Peter, "Simon, son of John, do you burn with love for me more than these?"

Peter answered, "Yes, Lord! You know that I have great affection for you!"

"Then take care of my lambs," Jesus said.

16 Jesus repeated his question the second time, "Simon, son of John, do you burn with love for me?"

Peter answered, "Yes, my Lord! You know that I have great affection for you!"

"Then take care of my sheep," Jesus said.

17 Then Jesus asked him again, "Peter, son of John, do you have great affection for me?"

Peter was saddened by being asked the third time and said, "My Lord, you know everything. You know that I burn with love for you!"

Jesus replied, "Then feed my lambs! 18 Peter, listen, when you were younger you made your
own choices and you went where you pleased. But one day when you are old, others will tie
you up and escort you where you would not choose to go—and you will spread out your arms."
19 (Jesus said this to Peter as a prophecy of what kind of death he would die, for the glory of
God.) And then he said, "Peter, follow me!"

20 Then Peter turned and saw that the disciple whom Jesus loved was following them. (This
was the disciple who sat close to Jesus at the Last Supper and had asked him, "Lord, who is
the one that will betray you?") 21 So when Peter saw him, he asked Jesus, "What's going to
happen to him?"

22 Jesus replied, "If I decide to let him live until I return, what concern is that of yours? You must still keep on following me!"

23 So the rumor started to circulate among the believers that this disciple wasn't going to die. But Jesus never said that, he only said, "If I let him live until I return, what concern is that of yours?"

My Notes...

Conclusion

[24] I, John, am that disciple who has written these things to testify of the truth,
and we know that what I've documented is accurate.
[25] Jesus did countless things that I haven't included here.
And if every one of his works were written down *and described one by one*,
I suppose that the world itself wouldn't have enough room
to contain the books that would have to be written!

My Notes...

Reflections at the Table

Christ Jesus came into the world to save sinners—and I was the greatest of them all. But God had mercy on me so that Christ Jesus could use me as an example to show everyone how patient He is with even the worst sinners, so that others will realize that they, too, can have everlasting life (1 Timothy 1:15–16 TLB).

Paul explains the purpose of Christ's mercy: "to show how patient He is with even the worst sinners." Paul had an impressive list of sins from his past, and he had persecuted Christians even to the point of death. After his conversion, however, Paul became a driving force for the spread of Christianity.

As you come to the table, reflect on the truth of who you are as God's daughter. Furthermore, when you pull up your chair to dine with the living God know that He forgives your past. Our plates are laid clean before the first course. His death on the cross redeemed everything.

My prayer is that as you work through these reflection questions, they help you not only lay your burdens down and rest but allow you to reflect and grow on who you already are and who you are becoming...a holy and beautiful daughter of the Most High.

What does your heart connect most to at the table?

Practice the power of confession. Write a list of all the things you would like to confess at the table of Christ.

Look back at your life. How has something that was dead been resurrected?

Describe how your own faith is represented at the table of those you love.

What is a difficulty you are facing that you would like to leave at the table?

Write out your own story of what God has done in your life.

How has God glorified you through a struggle?

What is God's purpose for your life? How is it different than the one that you created for yourself?

How can you reframe a current struggle into a promise?

In what ways has God shown you, His goodness? How could you share that at a table with others?

In every part of your life, are you seeking the way of God?

What spiritual battle do you feel you are losing right now? How can you bring it to the table of Christ?

How can you let Jesus guide you fully into a holy and beautiful life?

Think of a person that needs to know Jesus. How can you use your story to introduce them to who Christ is?

What do you really think faith is?

Do you find it hard to release worry and fear? How can being a forever guest at the table of Christ allow you to release it?

How do you handle weakness? Suffering? How has a loss made God more real to you?

How does the book of John challenge you and your own sin?

What does grace mean to you?

How have the holy Scriptures been a voice of God to you?

What gifts do you bring to the table?

How has the body of Christ nurtured you? Sustained you?

How does the life you are currently leading reflect the beauty that can be found?

What do you think of when you think of the Cross? The Eucharist?

What is the table a place for? For you?

What burdens do you bring to the table?

What gifts do you bring?

What desires do you have?

Are you a good listener at the table?

How do you pray and reflect on what God is doing in your life?

Are you in unity at the table?

What does reconciliation mean to you?

How does competition spoil a good meal?

Do you pray at the table?

What do you ask for? Give thanks for?

Are you distracted with what your true identity is?

Describe a time you felt joy at a table. What was the event? The circumstances? Who was there?

Jesus welcomes all. He invites us to feast and enjoy the love of the Father. Are you responding to His invitation?

We are all lost, then we are found.
This is the story of the Gospel of Jesus Christ.
This is the story of God.

Reconciliation, peace, and restoration is an open invitation to all.
This is how the Father responds to all who come to His table.
Enjoy the feast.

Amen

the holy beautiful team

Jennifer C Howard RDH, MCM

Author & Founder of the Holy Beautiful Ministry for Women

Jennifer Howard was born in Singapore and has been a health professional for the last twenty-five years. She has been married to her husband Erik for twenty-three years, and they have three children, Jackson, Katie, and Keaton.

Sharing Christ with others is a true passion of hers, as is encouraging others to live out their purpose in him. She considers herself a free spirit and has a heart for all people. She loves to lead others in forming an authentic Christian community.

Jennifer had the deep honor and privilege of being the Directress of the Junior Daughters of the King Ministry in Marshall, Texas, for ten years, leading young girls and women into a closer relationship with Jesus through prayer, service, and evangelism. Jennifer has an Associate's degree in Applied Science, a Bachelor's in Interdisciplinary Studies, and her Master's degree in Christian Ministry and Discipleship from Liberty University. She is also a 500-hour Master Certified Holy Yoga instructor with the international ministry of Holy Yoga with additional training in leadership and touch. Jennifer founded the Holy Beautiful Ministry for women four years ago in an effort to bring the Word of God to women all over the world. She strives to bring health to women in body, mind, and spirit.

Jennifer sees herself as a connector, bringing women together to foster authentic Christian relationships. Her dream is to make our world a more holy beautiful place for everyone.

After living in Texas for over twenty years, Jennifer is now currently calling the beautiful and scenic area of Nellysford, Virginia, home. She is passionate about antiques, gardening, cooking, and travel.

Kristine Cotterman

Kristine was born and raised in St. Paul, Minnesota. She has been happily married to her husband Rick for 30+ years. They have 3 grown children, Alex, Andy (Cody), and Tiffany (Mike), in their 30's and 2 very young grandsons, Simon and Adrian.

Kris & Rick enjoy spending time with family and friends. They love adventure dining–discovering unique restaurants and trying new flavors from around the world. They also love traveling and going back to Jamaica, where they went on their honeymoon, whenever possible. Their bucket list includes Europe and the Mediterranean.

Kris loves the outdoors and grew up camping with friends and relatives. She and Rick recently bought a camper and set it up on a site that has been transformed into their island escape in the woods of Northern Minnesota. They love having all their kids and grandkids up.

Kris is a graphic designer, web designer/programmer, and a book publisher. She started Exodus Design Studio in 1998 after giving her life to Jesus Christ. She went to college, finally, and got her Associate Degree in Graphic Design Technology. Kris and Rick work together to serve clients around the world, on every continent except Antarctica. They also volunteer when ever possible to design and coordinate over the top themed events for weddings, fundraising galas, and dances. There is nothing they can't do together.

The best description of them is on her Facebook page which says, "Rick & I = insanely creative + eclectic, mixed with a tantalizing "je ne sais quoi!" Est Mar 5, 1988"

Her best advice to women of all ages, "You can do it, that dream you've had since you were a little girl. It must be your gifting or you wouldn't think about it so much. Hone it, then own it. You were born with a purpose!"

"*But you are God's chosen treasure...set apart as God's devoted ones. He called you out of darkness to experience His marvelous light, and now He claims you as His very own. He did this so that you would broadcast His glorious wonders throughout the world* (1 Peter 2:9 TPT)."

Caroline Atuzarirwe

Caroline Atuzarirwe was born in a family of 12 in Mbarara, a small town in South Western Uganda. She has two children Ryan and Ruby. She is lecturing in the Faculty of Marketing and Hospitality Management at Makerere University Business School (12 years now). She did her BA (Literature and French) and MSc. in Tourism and Hospitality Management at Makerere University. She is doing several trainings and continues to carry out research in the tourism industry.

Reaching out to nations is her passion. She believes in the power of the Holy Spirit and the spoken Word of God. When she received the transformational touch of the Holy Spirit, she experienced the presence of God in her life, and shares some of these experiences in her writing. Her passion is to use the Word of God to cause a total turnaround in the lives of the readers as she writes for Holy Beautiful

Caroline has hosted a Bible study cell based fellowship in her home which later outgrew her home due to increase in attendance. She has carried out outreaches with the Bible study group. She has taught in Children's church at Watoto Church Downtown when it was still Kampala Pentecostal Church (KPC). She continues to join the Watoto Church Downtown community for prayers and continues to share the Word of God on her face book account and face book page Beauty for Ashes. She loves reading, travelling, chess, golf, swimming, learning new languages and meeting new people.

Bethany L. Douglas

Bethany is a thirty-something lover of Jesus, coffee, camping, reading, and writing. She married her best friend Gabe 18 years ago, and they currently reside within the Missouri Ozarks. They have 3 biological children—Jesse, Jonah, and Anna, who was born with Down Syndrome—as well as foster kids who God loans them from time to time. In a past season, Bethany was a full-time flight nurse, but she now writes and speaks full-time. She also serves every summer as medical director at Camp Barnabas, a Christian camp for mentally and physically disabled people.

You'll find very quickly that her writing is real and raw. Though she claims no perfections, she is honest in her desire to encourage, refine, challenge, and make people think. She founded LIFT! Ministries in 2015 which challenges the Body of Christ to Live Intentionally Fearlessly and Truthfully. Bethany has authored *Helicopter Mom*, a quirky but impactful and scripturally sound book written primarily for moms who struggle with fear for their kids.

Through her trials and tribulations, she strives to make those seasons count, by imparting what God taught her through them to others. She seeks to glorify God through the good, bad, and the ugly this life has to offer.

Shari Finkler

Shari spent 30 years as an English teacher, teaching high school, community college, and university level. She holds a B.A. in English Education, a M.A. in English Education, and an Ed.D. in Teacher Leadership. After retiring from public school teaching, she joined the faculty at a local Christian school. She is delighted to be able to teach Shakespeare and pray with students as a regular part of her day.

In addition to her weekly contribution to Holy Beautiful, she writes a follow-up devotional for her pastor's sermon called "Take It with You." She teaches an adult Sunday school class, sings in the choir, assists with the youth choir, and teaches weekly Holy Yoga classes. She is 595-hour Master Holy Yoga instructor with additional training in leadership and trauma-sensitive yoga.

Shari is married to Andrew, a retired Army nurse and ordained minister who works as a pastoral counselor and chaplain. They have one son, Walker, a Boy Scout and competitive bagpiper. Her passion is glorifying God through her writing, teaching, speaking, and encouraging others in her work.

Karen Guthrie

Karen Guthrie and her husband of 47 years live in rural Missouri, and she loves the peace of their life together. She finds that her children and her grandchildren are truly her heart's delight.

She describes herself as a Daughter of the King, wife, mother, grandmother, sister, aunt, and friend. She is Body, Mind, and Spirit; God's creation, unique in the universe."

Sheila Millinder

Sheila Millinder lives in Dubois, Pennsylvania, with her husband of Michael and they attend the TriCounty Church. She is a mother of two boys and three stepdaughters, a grandmother to four of the most amazing boys and two granddaughters who are so precious. She cherishes her family and sees them as her first ministry. She values friendships and holds them dear. Sheila loves adventure, traveling, discovering new things, and being in nature. Being surrounded by water is her inspiration. Sheila is an avid reader of Christian-authored books, where she looks for inspiration to grow and share with others. She finds writing is a gift which she uses to serve others. Her passions are the church and community, leadership, and discipleship. She has a deep cry in her heart for women's ministry.

It has been her passion to lead others to discover their identity, develop their gifts, and deploy them for the work of the ministry.

She has worked with Love God Greatly, an international ministry. as the administrator of the online ministry and served in many different areas. In addition, she facilitates Bible studies online, and locally in her home where she strives to challenge others' growth, spirituality, and personal development. She writes weekly content for Holy Beautiful, hoping to encourage others with her words of inspiration and sound biblical truth.

Sheila is a John Maxwell Certified coach, teacher, and speaker. She can offer you workshops, seminars, keynote speaking, and coaching. Her desire is to aid your personal and professional growth, through study and practical application of John's proven leadership methods.

Sheila loves the Lord and has powerful testimonies of His goodness. It is her heart's desire to see others experience God's love in a powerful and life-transforming way. She has a strong desire to raise up leaders and celebrate their process of discovery as they take the steps necessary for their personal journey.

Sheila believes there is power in our own personal journey. She shares real-life experiences of trials and triumphs to inspire others to live fully alive and awake in every moment of their lives.

Her favorite quote is: "Owning our story and loving ourselves through that process is the bravest thing we will ever do." Brene´ Brown

Adriana Morales

Adriana Morales was born in Venezuela, is fluent in Spanish, and is the youngest of her family. Adriana relocated to the United States at a young age and lived in Florida for 26 years. She visits her family and friends in Miami often and delights herself with Cuban meals.

Adriana lives with her husband in Tennessee, has adjusted to southern living traditions, cares for a feline crew of 3, and works full-time in a leadership role with the state.

Adriana enjoys adult coloring, Bible journaling, piano playing, blogging, and considers herself as an avid reader who has served faithfully in numerous "book launch" teams over the years. She enjoys waking up at sunrise to read her Bible, pray, journal creatively, and lead an online Bible study for women.

For over a decade, she has delighted in serving faithfully in discipleship communities. Her motto is "Truth in action." Adriana is passionate about fulfilling the Great Commission.

Professionally, Adriana has been in the mental health field for over 26 years and has faithfully served children, adolescents, and their families, as well as adults with intellectual disabilities (ID) and Autism Spectrum Disorder (ASD). She worked as a Licensed Mental Health Counselor in Florida, and both as a Board-Certified Behavior Analyst and a Licensed Clinical Psychologist in Tennessee.

Faith Morgan

Faith knows a little bit about grace, and that it is best used on messy people. Growing up as a child in foster care being passed from home to home, she had believed the lie that she was doomed to spend the rest of her life with a one-way ticket on the orphan train. That is until her journey was interrupted, and the train was derailed after she discovered a story in the Bible about a little 12-year-old girl who Jesus raised back up from the dead Talitha koum!" (which means "Little girl, I say to you, get up!")

Her new journey would lead her to enlist in the U.S. Air Force as a military police officer where she traveled the world. She met her first husband while in Germany and together they were blessed with three beautiful babies. In a turn of unforeseeable events, she found herself thrust into a new role as a young single mom living out of a motel room in Georgia. She decided this was not how her story was going to end. She took a leap of faith and ended up in Montana. She worked in a thrift store while she enrolled in the Montana State University School of Nursing.

She had big dreams to be a nurse in the mission field, but God had other plans, and in 2013 she married a good Montana boy, and they laid their roots down in Hamilton, Montana. She had the joy of watching God redeem her messy and broken past and was blessed with an addition to their beautiful blended family, a son named Noah, who is the spitting image of her as a child.

Today she spends her time surrounded by God's beauty. She has learned that it's never too late to make a fresh start. She is a southern bell at heart and loves to read and journal. She feels right at home with the messy broken, hurting people, deemed misfits of this world.

Her favorite book in the Bible is Jeremiah, for it was in that book she found her life verse. "For I know the plans I have for you," declares the LORD, "plans to prosper you and not to harm you, plans to give you hope and a future." Her motto is "a little bit of Faith and a whole lot of JESUS!"

Jamie Taylor

Jamie is an outgoing introvert with a passion for encouraging others in their walk with Jesus.

She finds great fulfillment working alongside her husband in full-time ministry at Grace Bible Church in Nampa, ID.

She is the mother of four children, who bring her great joy while keeping her on her knees.

Jamie is a creative who loves music, photography, studying, and writing. She has loved to write for as long as she has known how to do it. Jamie believes there is nothing quite like the written word to inspire, encourage, and motivate an audience. Her greatest joy is to help people find healing in their most broken seasons.

Sheila Taylor

Sheila is a writer of stories as well as a holder of hands, babies, and hot cups of coffee.

She and her husband of 26 years, Duane, have built their home and family in Idaho. She has three grown children — Ashley, Alex, and Nichole.

Because of God's healing grace in their marriage, Duane and Sheila feel passionate about serving and walking beside other married couples. Together they lead classes within their church, and they serve as local volunteers for Family Life Weekend to Remember.

Sheila works part-time as an office administrator for a birth center and full-time as a keeper of home and family.

Jesus has redeemed her life from the deep pits of fear and despair, and through her words and her life, she desires to say, "Come and see what God has done!"

"'Behold, I stand at the door and knock. If anyone hears My voice and opens the door, I will come in to him and eat with him, and he with Me'"(Revelation 3:20).

Melisa A. Custer

Melisa, 42, is a single mom, government employee, and a retired veteran from the USAF. Melisa was born in San Antonio, TX. She was raised in, nearby, Universal City, TX and lived there until she joined the Air Force in 1995. She joined Holy Beautiful, as a weekly contributor, in 2018. She has traveled the world and has experienced many cultures, in her life, but is most content at home, with her family, and attending her local church. She lives with her four sons (ages 9-22) and her mother in Yorktown, VA.

Naomi Krstinic

Naomi is passionate about family, ministry, and writing. She is a wife of 38 years to Igor, mother of three, grandmother of five, with one furbaby rescue. She has been a missionary to Croatia and previously was Hospital Outreach Coordinator through her church. She also manages and designs her online website which reaches worldwide. Naomi holds a 2 year degree in Biblical Ministries and has been a Pastor with God's Living Words Ministries for four years. She actively teaches online Bible studies and continues to hunger in growth.

In her early years she knew what it meant to lose everything and experienced God's saving power. Though she has experienced great loss, she has come to know God in a deep and personal way which even today is reflected through her writing. She signs all of her writing, " I write for Him" because first and foremost it is for Him that she writes.

She has a deep desire to reach out to those who are hurting with God's Love. She believes it's important to remind others that they are loved, valued, and appreciated, by God and by her. She continues to be passionate about her writing and finds great joy in writing for Holy Beautiful and is thrilled to be a part of this wonderful team of anointed women.

"Go and enjoy choice food and sweet drinks,
and send some to those who have nothing prepared.
This day is holy to our Lord.
Do not grieve, for the joy of the Lord
is your strength."

(Nehemiah 8:10)